*YOU ARE
REVIVAL

Heb. 12 : 1 - 3

*

Heb. 19:1-3

YOU ARE REVIVAL

HEAVENLY
REALITIES
MANIFESTING
ON EARTH

MATTHEW L. SKAMSER

DESTINY IMAGE® PUBLISHERS, INC.

P.O. Box 310, Shippensburg, PA 17257-0310

"Speaking to the Purposes of God for This Generation and for the Generations to Come."

This book and all other Destiny Image, Revival Press, MercyPlace, Fresh Bread, Destiny Image Fiction, and Treasure House books are available at Christian bookstores and distributors worldwide.

For a U.S. bookstore nearest you, call 1-800-722-6774.

For more information on foreign distributors, call 717-532-3040.

Reach us on the Internet: www.destinyimage.com.

ISBN 13 TP: 978-0-7684-3622-8

ISBN 13 HC: 978-0-7684-3623-5

ISBN 13 LP: 978-0-7684-3624-2

ISBN 13 Ebook: 978-0-7684-9046-6

For Worldwide Distribution, Printed in the U.S.A.

1 2 3 4 5 6 / 14 13 12 11

DEDICATION

A *huge* thank you goes out to *all* of my friends, family, spiritual Fathers, and the great staff at Destiny Image for making publishing this book a reality. You know who you are.

As my only reasonable response to His Greatness and worthiness, I dedicate this book first and foremost to God (The Father, The Spirit, and The Son). If the pages of this book don't point to Him, it should have never been written. He blows my mind every day. How He could turn a sinner like me around, and keep me turned, is only a testament to His amazing love. It is my privilege to call myself a "Christ follower," and it is my honor to be friends with the person named, Holy Spirit. He truly wrote this book through me. *Thank you so much, Lord. I long to know you more, now and throughout eternity!*

Without the love, kindness, support and grace of my beautiful wife, Elizabeth, enduring my many sleepless nights of prayer and writing, this book would not have been possible. I am eternally grateful and forever in love. Babe, you complete me!

This book is also dedicated to my future natural children, spiritual children, and all those who call themselves *Revivalists*. Consumed with a passion for God's ways, unmoving in our quest for a movement. To those who desire to live with a reckless abandon for a life of doing the will of God, you are my family—*you are revival!*

The book *You Are Revival* is a flashpoint summons among a dark, desperation nation, and it calls for the ultimate catalyst known to humanity to bring a spiritual and moral revolution. Many times, revival is set forth like the stirring of the waters at the Pool of Bethesda (see John 5:1-18), where people are conditioned to sit back in passivity, as if God doesn't utilize human instrumentality. Matt has put together a treatise that brings both a holy respect for revival and an individual responsibility to cooperate with the Spirit of God in our day to be a part of the greatest ingathering and season of restoration that the world has ever seen. Get ready to be incited and ignited with a divine draft notice that will cause you to take your place in history as a world shaker and history maker; get ready to witness the underground revivalists move from the background to the forefront.

SEAN SMITH
Author, *Prophetic Evangelism*
seansmithministries.org
PointBlank International

Matt and Elizabeth are a young couple that have an incredible passion for the Kingdom of God; indeed, I believe the Lord has raised them up to impact and influence a generation of "world changers." Their gift to impart God's Word, their hunger for the supernatural, and their commitment to disciple a generation in signs and wonders are just a few of the characteristics that set them apart. I'm so very thankful the Lord allowed our lives to cross paths!

PASTOR ZANE ANDERSON, senior pastor
Victory Worship Center
www.vwcaz.org

You Are Revival is *The Purpose Driven Life* for all who have a passion for revival. It is a crucial, practical manual enabling the Lord to apply His eye salve so that the reader can see Him and His ways more clearly.

DR. DEAN C. LANDIS, vice chancellor
Ministry Relations
Phoenix University of Theology

Understanding the history of revivals in the light of Scripture is *key* to understanding God's heart for true revival. *You Are Revival* is a Biblical blueprint that teaches these essential truths.

TOMAS J. LARES
National Day of Prayer Task Force
Florida state Coordinator

I believe *You Are Revival* will shake the nations into a deeper revelation of what true revival looks like! Matt Skamser has great passion to see Christ magnified in the earth by being a walking manifestation of revival himself! This book will only...change your life!

BERNADETTE ALVARADO
Worship Leader
Out of the Fire Prophetic Worship Ministry

Matt has a unique calling and an amazing and unquenchable hunger for more of God and for revival, in his own life and for our nation. Matt lives revival and brings it with him everywhere he goes. He is truly a man of God, an inspiration to all who know him. And now with the release of his new book, he will be an inspiration to those who have never had the honor.

AIMEE DOBBINS, executive director
BreakDown International
www.breakdownunited.com

Matthew means "gift of YHWH"! And so he is! Matthew is a Kingdom man, passionate and wild about life in the Spirit. Matthew himself is an experience—you have to meet him! He believes God! He's a guy who gives away everything for the sake of the Kingdom going forward! And he is already touching lives internationally, ours included! And he lives in the joy of it all! We are blessed to know him! And in return, we speak blessing on him!

TIM AND KARYN MANN
AG Missionaries, Austria

Matt is a burning one for Jesus. His heart is tender toward God's presence. As a prophetic voice in southern Arizona and beyond, Matt's vision to uncover wells of revival will impact nations.

PASTOR PAUL SHORT
Unseen Ministries
www.unseenministries.com

I've known Matt for years, and he's a new generation revivalist! You go, man, God has your back! We look forward to working more closely in the future!

DARCI DUBE
Kingdom Harvest Ministries International
www.khmi.org

I have come to know Matt as a principled man of God. He's a guy that I like being around. He is a unique person who engenders smiles and practices grace, is dedicated to Kingdom living *now,* and steps out in faith consistently. I can't wait to see what is in store for us through his new book, *You Are Revival,* and the blessings God has for us as a result.

JOHN TABOR, executive director
The Crisis Pregnancy Centers

Rarely have I known a man with such passion and zeal for God's Kingdom and glory as Matt Skamser, who, like Paul, "will spend and be spent," that the Gospel of Christ Jesus will have its full effect for God's glory! Matt lives out the selflessness of Jesus and demonstrates Christ's authority with Spirit and power. His love for God, people, and righteousness is evident to all who know him for from the abundance of his heart his mouth pours forth rivers of living water. What a privilege for me to know and commend to you such a beautiful co-laborer in Christ as my brother Matt Skamser.

TODD PERROUD
revivalist/author
www.toddperroud.com

Matt and Elizabeth are dedicated to seeing revival come to Tucson. Their desire to hear and follow the Holy Spirit's leading is what drives them in all that they do. They are important to the Kingdom, and I am thankful to have a relationship with them and their ministry.

PASTOR E. ANTHONY LOPEZ
Mission View Assembly
Tucson, Arizona

Matt Skamser has been a great person to look to for leadership and creative wisdom on several ministry projects we've worked on together in our community. He enjoys challenge while having a vision for forward movement that really sets him apart from others. Watching him develop his ministry throughout the years has been a privilege, and now seeing him step into this new level of progress proves the Lord is doing a *mighty work through him*! Blessings to you, Matt, and all you do; may it continue to glorify our Father in Heaven!

SUZETTE HOWE
Pima County Coordinator
National Day of Prayer
Business owner, Praise Promotions

Contents

There is no doubt that we are living in some of the most pivotal and powerful times in all of history. There is such a deep sense everywhere that God is not only up to something, but God is, in fact, at work moving mightily in these days. There is a passage out of Luke's Gospel that, to me, summarizes this season that we have entered into. Jesus has just recently raised a young man from the dead, and the response of the people was amazement and wonder. They say one to another, *"God is back, looking to the needs of His people"* (Luke 7:16 MSG). God is, indeed, back, and He is raising up a generation of men and women who are possessed with a passion to see His Kingdom advanced—to demonstrate that we have a God, not of the past, but of today, who still works the miraculous.

Matt and Elizabeth Skamser are a part of that generation. They are a generation of *Revivalists*—a new breed of believers who are not satisfied with just a theology about God, but one that demonstrates He is alive and actively at work in our day. They are possessed with a deep belief and passion that God is looking for those who will believe Him and are willing to step out in faith to see Him transform lives, cities, and yes, even nations! They are "carriers" of Kingdom life and power.

You hold in your hand a book that will not only give you a clear and renewed perspective that God is at work, but also will provide for you tools that will help you join in the advancement of God's

Kingdom. Not theories and ideas, but tested principles and concepts that when employed with faith, God shows up and manifests His power.

As a pastor with 37+ years of ministry, my heart is thrilled to see young couples like Matt and Elizabeth and a whole lot more like them who are beginning to pray as Isaiah cried, "Open the heavens, Lord, and come down." And, indeed, God has opened the heavens and is coming down in unprecedented ways. I encourage you to take this book, read it, study it, meditate on it, let it get inside your spirit; and then, by faith, step out and begin to see God use *you* as a Kingdom advancer. This is our hour. Let's seize it and take hold of it with all of our hearts. You will be blessed by the experience that God has given this young couple and you will be enriched by the truths that the Lord has used him to help uncover. There's no doubt, this is our hour and I don't plan on missing it!

Introduction

A Revivalist Is Born

...He was seen by me also, as by one born out of
due time (1 Corinthians 15:8 NKJV).

We must learn to not just pray for revival in
*the world but to **be** revival for the world!*

As you pick up this book to see what it's all about, I am under no delusion that you will know who I am. My name is not a household Christian name nor may it ever be—and that's OK. The beauty of this book is that it comes from the perspective of someone most likely just like you. Someone who is pretty ordinary. Someone who has been radically rescued and transformed by Jesus and has lived an amazing journey of seeing God intervene in peoples' lives through everyday encounters and at times reluctant obedience to God's Word and at other times, faith-filled obedience to God's Word. I am not perfect, not always super spiritual, and not a superhero by any means, but I know who is—and His Spirit happens to live inside me. This book isn't so much about me; it's about who I know and what He wants to say to you.

This book is not for everyone. However, it is for people who want to know if there's more to Christianity than just going to church on

Sunday, people who need to know if the stuff in the Bible can really still happen today, and people who aren't satisfied with powerless Christianity. These are what I call *revivalists*. Revivalists are people who are consumed with knowing the love of Jesus more and who are compelled by God's Spirit to be different, set apart, and holy. These are the spiritual forerunners of the Christian faith and the shapers of the future spiritual identity of the Church as we know it. These are people who want to see reformation in the church and revival in their homes, communities, provinces, and nations. This revival is a Spiritual Awakening that must first start in the hearts of those people wanting more from God and from life. People probably a lot like you and me.

In Christianity there appears to be two camps that don't necessarily agree when it comes to topics such as revival. In one camp you have what I call *repentance preachers* that don't necessarily demonstrate the works of God's Kingdom but stress God's holiness and desire to see people repent and turn to Him. On the other hand, you have the *signs and wonders revivalists,* those who desire to see the miracles of Jesus manifest on earth for all to see that God's Kingdom is real. Both groups of people have their pluses and minuses and both can get into error if they lean too far one way or another. You could say, I am stuck somewhere in the middle of these two camps. Even my age at the time of writing this book is somewhere in the middle, 30—not young enough to be considered a youth, yet not old enough to be considered a peer in wisdom and experience of my fathers in the faith. However, I can understand both sides and communicate as a bridge effectively between them. I believe in signs and wonders, but I also believe in discernment. I value repentance, but also value listening to the Holy Spirit and doing what He says over what I think are good ideas. You can call me a new breed of revivalist. In many ways, I represent the sound of a generation. One of thousands of voices that God is raising up from around the world. With no official title, church, or ministry credentials, you may think I am not qualified to write a book with the caliber of touching the world and reviving the Church. I would have to agree with you, yet more than agreeing with that assessment, I agree with the Holy Spirit when He says otherwise. That's the story of my life, especially over the last handful of years. I simply try to hear God, believe and do what He says, often finding myself in situations where the supernatural is needed to invade a natural situation or circumstance. I find myself in situations where I'm speaking to large groups of people, small groups of people, and mostly to God, alone. I've had "regular" jobs and been in ministry the entire time, never considering my life in Christ to be a career, simply a lifestyle. Loving God is my passion. Through that love, He burdens me for other passions, like His desire to see a great awakening of spirituality and an outpouring of His Spirit to hit North America and around the world! Such things consume me; I love Jesus because of all that He has done for me and I want revival desperately. It is a burning passion of my heart!

THE VERY BEGINNING

The reality that the supernatural could be commonplace on earth became real to me at a very young age. Like many young "church kids," I was born on the altar, so-to-speak. My parents actively served in our church and attending regular worship services was a Sunday norm. Most of my very first memories are all related to church or birthday parties with my church friends. I apparently had a particular fondness of sleeping under pews and flirting with little blonde girls. My family had our standard dysfunctions, yet overall was pretty normal. When I was about four years old, we welcomed my beautiful little sister into the family. My only sibling, my sister, Michelle, was born with some complications. After she started growing before she was a year old, her legs and feet began to face outward, almost turning completely backward. I faintly remember her screams and cries as my parents forced her legs into shoes that were fitting for her yet had a metal bar connecting them. They were a specially made brace to try and correct her legs and force them to stay straight. This was an obvious struggle for both little Michelle and my parents.

Then came a revival service at our church, a very large and well-known Spirit-filled church in Tucson, that I now, over 25 years later, continue to attend. There was a guest minister that night. He must have truly believed in the power of God and God's never-changing desire to heal all those who are burdened and broken. My parents took my sister up to the front of the church to be prayed for, and the rest is history. Heaven came down, and God's grace and love touched her little legs and straightened them out right on the spot! This was truly a revival service to remember...at least for the Skamser family! Revival is not just about miracles, but something glorious must have seared into my spirit the day I observed the emotions of my parents when my sister was completely healed. All I remember from that day on is that they were able to throw away her brace and she never had a problem since, actively participating in many different sports growing up.

As a boy, I regularly attended Royal Rangers (a Christian Boy Scout-type group) and was a pretty spiritual kid. I was baptized at seven and remember having a couple angelic encounters at a young age. As I sat in "big-people church" (that's all us kids had back then after Sunday school) and listened to the pastor preach, I remember strong desires to get up and ask questions of what I was learning afterward. I remember once asking the pastor what he meant when he described the Apostle Paul as someone who "hated who he loved, then loved who he hated." The pastor kindly explained that this was because Paul first persecuted the church, then became the church's biggest advocate. Once after a Sunday school class, I asked my teacher about the Trinity, as I didn't quite understand this concept. "How could God be One being, yet three people all at the same time?" I asked. She had trouble explaining. I joke now that I understood the Trinity better when I was seven than I do now! I was always curious about God.

My high school years were pretty lackluster spiritually. I got very good grades in school and a full scholarship to Northern Arizona University in Flagstaff, Arizona, but wasn't too focused on God. I would have my "church camp" moments where God really touched my life, I would be slain in the spirit (fall down under the power of God), and feel God's presence powerfully upon me, but I never really followed through with living a sold-out to God lifestyle. Later I look back and realize that I was legitimately scared, deep down, to give my whole life to the Lord. I somehow knew I had such a calling on my life that if I did commit fully to the Lord, my life would no longer be my own. I would surely have to move out of the country to be a missionary or something. Little did I know at the time that a life of full surrender to God is the only way to really find purpose, and being a bond slave to Christ is the only true freedom. Everything else is a myth, an illusion of freedom that leads to bondage. I was caught in these bondages as an older teenager. Bondages to sin, to comfort, to confusion. I remember the period of time in my life as a sophomore in college when I made a conscious choice to completely turn my back on God. What little strength of the Spirit at work in my life was now completely quenched. I rejected Him, and paid a terrible price, spiritually. For four years I was totally lost—an average guy on the outside but hardened by sin and life on the inside.

In all of my anger and confusion, in an ex-girlfriend's apartment in Phoenix in November 2002, I had finally had enough. When I finally realized my life was not going too well in my own hands, in a split second I realized whose hands they should be in. Then in another instant, I realized God was there waiting for me all along. When I acknowledged Him in my heart, I broke! Sovereignly, in an apartment on a random weekend afternoon, God lifted away all the darkness of sin and baggage from my life and I felt like a million bucks! A *huge* burden of sin and death was lifted! I wept and wept in repentance and thankfulness for probably an hour. My life would never be the same!

THE VISITATION

About three months went by since my new conversion, and I had been hanging out with a fire-filled family of sold-out for God believers that spent almost every night worshiping God. Their adult children and sometimes church friends would also come by to join in. They were the only people I could find (OK, God put us together) that were as hungry or more hungry for God than I was! We were inseparable for a season. People from church would often invite us to pray for their sick family members in hospitals and invite us to their home for fellow-ship and worship meetings.

Then came February 9, 2003, I remember it like it was yesterday. God showed up, and all nine of us who were there would never be the same. As hard as this is to explain, after a time of extended prayer, intercession, and fasting that carried over from the night before, God literally manifested in that house for us all to see. He did this by "taking over" and inhabiting one of the girls present—actually, two of the girls at different times. You could loosely interpret what we experienced as the prophetic gift, but it was much more than that. God literally ministered to us all for something like five hours without leaving. Not that He isn't always with us, but in this particular case, He was really talking to us conversationally for hours through the *total* submission by two of the women in the group. God intimately communicated with each individual in the house, ministering to the depths of the heart of each person present that day.

For some reason, God saved me for last when He ministered personally to me. When He finally got around to me, He asked me, "Matt, what do you want?" I was too scared to answer. The entire house was so filled with His presence that there was a holy fear and honor. I could hardly lift my head, and when I did my face was stained with tears.

God asked me again, "What do you want?" This was the billion-dollar question. It was Solomon's question when God asked Him what He wanted (see 1 Kings 3:5) and He answered, *"Give your servant a discerning heart to govern your people and to distinguish between right and wrong"* (1 Kings 3:9). I suppose, like Solomon, I could have answered just about anything but there was just one thing on my mind. The only answer that came to my mind is something that didn't take much thought. It was the one thing that was burning in my heart since I committed my life to God. I answered, "Revival in Tucson!" Tucson was the city I lived in at the time. I didn't know my left foot from my right, spiritually speaking, yet this word *revival* consumed me. I wanted to know everything I could about this mysterious person named Holy Spirit and about these supernatural gifts I kept reading about in the New Testament. I also worshiped and prayed to Jesus for sometimes hours a day, yet I was still also consumed with this powerful and mysterious word, *revival*. God told me many other things, like that I would one day be a pastor/preacher, and He gave me a gift that day. It was a golden globe that spun so clearly in a vision. He told me to stretch out my hands to receive it in faith. It was the promise of a worldwide ministry. I knew I was supposed to one day take Revival fire around the world.

THE BATTLEFIELD

Like many new believers, I was consumed with God. When I wasn't praying to Him, I was talking about Him. I almost couldn't believe how real and awesome He is and that He is available to everyone on earth to get to know. I prayed to God for forgiveness for squandering so many years of my life not in pursuit of the knowledge of Him and of living out relevant Christianity. But God accelerated my growth greatly during this time and hasn't stopped. Other than reading the Word as often as possible, I was fortunate enough to get my hands on two books in the beginning of this journey that really helped me, *The Fourth Dimension,* by Dr. Yonggi Cho, and *Good Morning, Holy Spirit,* by Benny Hinn. Through these books, I learned right away that hanging out with God, hearing Him, and doing what He says is the absolute key to being a successful Christian.

As some time went by, God had me serve youth ministries and even start a young adult ministry at this same church in Tucson, seeing some confess Christ and many filled with the Spirit and touched by God's anointing. It became one of the largest and most influential young adult ministries in the city and state. We really lived out a culture of revival, oftentimes throughout the week gathering to worship God, pray, and to fellowship. One of my all-time favorite moments in this season is when I had the privilege of seeing my best friend give his life to the Lord as God had me prophesy to Him at a weekly men's Bible study meeting that I led. That same night, God had me baptize him in my pool in the backyard! It was early March, and the water was still very cold. God supernaturally made each of us not even feel the water as soon as we stepped in; it was amazing! My friend shook under the power of God for over an hour after he dried off!

For over three years, I led a weekly men's Bible study that should have at first been called a "man Bible study" because the first night, I was the only guy there! I just said to myself, "I don't care if anyone shows up, I'm going to praise God and read the Bible all by myself." The study grew to upwards of 40 guys at one point but averaged about 10 to 12, which is a pretty manageable number. Years later, I started a "Revival/Evangelism" school on Saturday mornings that averaged about four or five people a weekend. In some ways, it felt like a disappointment because I wanted to see a bigger turnout, but God never judges things the way we do, as through external appearances or by numbers.

The highlight of this time, for me, was when we went weekly for a few weeks to the local VA hospital and prayed for the men and women there suffering from various serious conditions. We had an open door because my uncle was recovering there from getting hit by a truck—any little excuse or permission to pray for people is all I need! Some people there had cancer, some had missing limbs, many were in wheelchairs. We just went for it, and God owned that place! His presence was so strong. Even when these guys wouldn't get an observable miracle, you could still see that God had touched their lives, and some were even in tears. While approaching people for prayer, you may get rejected quite a bit, but oftentimes even the people with the hardest hearts soften up when you demonstrate the love of Christ. People desire other people to care for them, whether they admit it or not, and are very appreciative when we're done praying.

During the early years, I would go out late at night on the weekends just to street evangelize outside of the bars and nightclubs, sometimes alone, something I realized later wasn't smart. Almost every weekend for a year I would go out. I was physically attacked once by a demon-possessed man that I rebuked and he had to leave, and had many other threats by simply asking people if they knew Jesus. Nothing special. No formulas, no effective methods. It shocked me to see how violent some people's reactions could be regarding this person named Jesus. Just saying His name definitely makes our enemy angry!

I also learned during this time to try and see the person behind the demons when I would encounter demon-possession and oppression. There are real people underneath those violent, angry, or perverted facades, oftentimes people who have been hurt greatly by religious people. Once I pulled over at a bus stop after church to confront a demonized man who had a strong spirit of sexual perversion that was harassing every woman who walked by him. When I showed up, he mocked me and kept saying, "Jesus is Lord, Jesus is Lord," in a growling sarcastic tone. This really confused me, because a day or so earlier I read in the Bible that to test the spirits, you need to ask them if Jesus is Lord! The forces of satan somehow knew I read that and were messing with me! He then proceeded to tell me he was going to kill me, a threat that I laughed at, knowing the power of satan's kingdom cannot compare to God's. Most of the demon-possessed people I have encountered used intimidation to try to stir up fear in my heart. Sometimes it worked, but most of the time a spirit of boldness would rise up within me to challenge any threat from the devil. It upset me that the demons were so bold. They would never have dared treat Jesus that way! What I realized through this is that they have gone unchallenged by "Christians" for so long that they have grown in much confidence. I desire to help raise up a generation that will reverse this trend!

I learned, too, that if we just open our eyes a little wider around our communities we will see great need...not just feeding the poor, but setting the captives free. These encounters taught me another *huge* lesson—I had to be prayed up and in right relationship with God at all times or the enemy would just walk all over me! There's no room for compromise on the battlefield! I have been approached by a prostitute and cursed by witches on two occasions. Once all my hair even started to fall out! The prostitute was easy enough to resist, but the curses had to be broken off by the powerful prayers of spiritual leaders that God put in my life with more anointing and authority than myself. I have seen gold dust manifest in revival meetings and prayer meetings, children confessing Jesus as their Savior for the first time in revival meetings, and even one lady had migraines and brain tumors totally disappear, verified by medical experts! I've seen men get out of wheelchairs and walk for the first time in years and a variety of other supernatural manifestations. These moments are priceless and worth every minute of struggle, effort, time, and money that it sometimes takes to get here (money in regards to radically sowing into true revival when I see it and paying for much of my own ministerial expenses).

May God receive all the glory through every victory over the enemy and every testimony! Each and every one of these things blows my mind and points to the fact that there is a spiritual realm we live in that can and often does break into the natural realm if we let it. My stories are too numerous to include in this book, but I try to use personal examples throughout where applicable. This book is not meant to be an autobiography, but rather, a guide to living a life of personal revival in partnership with the Holy Spirit. The more of us who start to understand how to live this kind of a life, the more God's heavenly realities can truly become a reality to people we affect on a daily basis and then revival will truly spread throughout the world.

THE JOURNEY

For years I was at church every time the doors were opened. When they weren't, I would try to open them! I was at the ground floor of a grassroots prayer effort at the church to start a 24/7 prayer ministry. I also helped setup two 50-inch plasma televisions to stream the International House of Prayer (IHOP) "live" prayer and worship into our prayer center. I absolutely love what IHOP is doing and what effect the "live" prayer and worship Web streams had on my life and continue to have. For nearly four years I held the late Friday night shift, from midnight to 2 A.M. I was a graveyard shift prayer warrior! If God taught me anything in all those early years, it was about prayer. Prayer was more than requests, it was hanging out with Him. Prayer was more than setting aside the time to talk to God, it was completely surrendering the time to the Holy Spirit and then seeing what He wanted to do. I learned a lot about God in these treasured times. The prophetic gift also began to develop in me at this time, and what I go on to explain in a later chapter is that the prophetic is really just an extension of your relationship with Christ.

On a couple occasions I have left my high-paying tech jobs to serve God full time for a season, even though I'm always serving Him full time even in the workplace. God has given me prophetic dreams for co-workers that have led to ministry and prayer opportunities right during the middle of the workday. I also never fail to share my testimony with all of my co-workers and any new contract that I may fly out to. To not share what God is doing in my life is holding back a piece of myself. When I hold back, shrink back, and hide from who I am, I'm never happy. I've learned to just fully be who I am. Some people will like me and some people won't.

My first few sermons, or few dozen sermons, were so rough on the listeners, God's sheep, because of my no-nonsense prophetic approach to speaking the truth without holding back, that I'm not too surprised that I wasn't given more preaching opplortunities in the early days. I was only allowed to preach one sermon to the youth at my own church in Tucson after the pastors found out I preached against sexual immorality one Wednesday night and a teenage girl complained to her parents. I guess they thought it was too real. A couple of young people were actually troubled and in tears afterward, and I prayed with them and asked them what was wrong. They said it was because they didn't know that sin actually condemned you to hell. It shocked me that in a mainstream Charismatic church like ours, some young people had gone their whole lives without even knowing they needed to repent of sin and stop sinning.

Such experiences shaped even my present-day mindsets regarding what I call *Churchianity*. This is going through positive religious motions yet leaving people trapped in sin and spiritual bondage. Many churches fall into this trap—not on purpose but by default if they're not pressing into God's Kingdom and preaching the whole Gospel.

Before a group of Christians can enter into any state of spiritual awakening, they must first be set free. Oftentimes, the bodies of believers that I have observed hardly get past this point, especially in the larger, "more positive, more people," churches. I think there is a *huge* place for the positive messages of the pastors of such churches, and some of the pastors do preach very relevant and biblical messages without holding back, but I believe there is great value in the teaching and preaching of the whole Word of God, God's love and His judgment.

I don't glorify sin, but I hate it with a passion and hate to see the consequences of death it brings on God's people. Sometimes the Church is infected by liberal viewpoints and efforts to conform too much to postmodernism and other ideas to attract and retain people that they lose focus on why we have Church in the first place. God never intended Church to be about programs, buildings, or more people. Church is about a fellowship of believers celebrating their freedoms in Christ together, regardless of their ethnicity, spiritual background, limitations, or locations.

There have been many times where I was angry at God. Times when I thought I heard His voice but a situation or circumstance turned out completely different. These times always confused me, yet God was always there through it all. There were plenty of times where I felt alone in my quest for revival, in my quest for living out what I perceive as "normal" Christianity. It seemed like I was the only one doing this at the time. I know I wasn't but certainly nowadays there are hundreds and thousands of such sold-out Christians in most cities that I observe! It blesses me beyond measure to see this movement rising up! In many ways, this book is for them. It's a lot of stuff I wish I knew when this journey began for me at the end of 2002. There just wasn't a book quite like this out there that I could find, or a guide, other than the Holy Word of God. The Bible, and the Holy Spirit teaching me through experience, have taught me most everything I know. Religiously consuming sermons and books from anointed men and women of God and hanging out with spiritual people with varying perspectives have taught me much as well.

There have always been spiritual mothers and fathers that God has brought into my life, sometimes for only a season at a time. There are also those big brothers in the faith that are living out radical revival ministries that I can observe and glean from. All of these teaching mechanisms are God-orchestrated in the life of every true disciple. All of our stories are different, and not one of our lives should look too much like anyone else but Jesus. He is the only one who you should try to imitate and should be all of our number one Teacher.

For every frustrating experience battling my own carnality and emotions getting in the way of God, I've had many more glorious encounters with the living, active, clear and powerful Word of God in my life and the person, Holy Spirit, who brings the Scriptures to life. The greatest of such experiences for me was at the time when I was dating my wife for about eight months. Being frustrated with not knowing for sure if I was supposed to marry her and the problems that obviously caused for that first half a year, I finally had enough and wrestled with God until I got my answer.

After worshiping God with abandon in a hotel room in Maryland (I was consulting for a company out there), I desperately sought God for His final Word on the matter. This is not something I could take lightly, nor should anyone. After praying with tears and passion, God spoke to my heart to open the Word of God. I did, directly to First John, chapter 4. This chapter held the answer to my question, as God profoundly ministered to me from His Word. I had struggled with completely surrendering to love for many years for whatever reason— likely some internalized issue because my own parents split up after twenty-plus years of marriage. The Scripture found in verse 12 says, *"No one has ever seen God, but if we love one another, God lives in us and His love is made complete in us."* This had a wonderful meaning to my heart that day, far beyond what words can explain. So much so, that I engraved this Scripture on my wife's engagement ring. 1 John 4:18 went on to say that *"perfect love drives out fear."* It was God's perfect love on this day and many others that poured out on me and prepared me for this next step in life. We have been on a journey of revival together ever since.

THE JOURNEY CONTINUES THROUGH YOU!

Throughout this book I'm going to explain what revival is and isn't, birthed from years of studying revival, learning the hard way from the Holy Spirit, prophetic ministry, street evangelism, marketplace ministry, and just simply living my life daily "sold out" for God. I have prayed for revival for many years, led healing tent revival meetings, and even had a revival radio program for a year and a half where I exhorted, taught, prophesied, and had callers call in for prayer. I have also traveled the nation to pray for our country at almost every "Call" national prayer event. I was made the liaison for "The Call" for the Tucson area, and attended various "outpourings" around the nation. The Call is a large prayer ministry led by a man named Lou Engle. I have organized citywide prayer events in Tucson for four years for the National Day of Prayer youth rally, participated in outreaches and prayer events in northern Mexico and interceded for every city in the United States and abroad that God sends me to on business or ministry trips. Regardless of the city or country that we reside in, there are always prayers to be prayed and people to reach with the love of Jesus Christ and the message of the Gospel.

This whole Christian walk comes down to our love and obedience to God. Love on Him, do what He says in His Word, and He'll do the rest. This journey is very unpredictable but extremely exciting. In many ways, it's about the ups and downs of life and sticking with God and depending on Him through it all. It's not so much about spiritual victories and being a supernatural superstar; it is simply about being yourself. It's about failing and trying and failing again. In God's Kingdom, the place of your greatest failures can often become the testimony of your greatest success! I pray with everything in me that the words of this book encourage you on your journey. *I pray* this book empowers you to walk in the freedom and power of revival while seeing an expansion of God's Kingdom influence throughout the world. It is designed to break us free from hindering religious mindsets and capturing time-less biblical principles that if we act on can leave a spiritual inheritance for our children and their children.

These pages are intended to capture and communicate a depth of Christian spiritual experience that can be experienced by all. Prepare to have your faith revived, your spirit filled, and your destiny made clearer. The world needs Jesus. The world needs revival. The world needs you.

PART I

REVELATIONS
OF REVIVAL

Chapter 1

CAN YOU HEAR THE SOUND?

Will You not revive us again, that Your people may rejoice in You? (Psalm 85:6)

Lord, have mercy on my soul and send revival to America!

We are the song of the Lord, to bring glory to God; we are played by the Holy Spirit through the musical notes of our souls.

It sounds like a rushing mighty wind—the sound that represents Heaven invading earth with a fury, the sound of God's glory meeting the Church's cry, the sound of His sound meeting ours.

Before I get into the sound I'm hearing today, let's take a step back to observe when it all began, 2,000 years ago on the famous day of Pentecost.

When the Day of Pentecost had fully come, they were all with one accord in one place. And suddenly there came a sound from heaven, as of a rushing mighty wind, and it filled the whole house where they were sitting. Then there appeared to them divided tongues, as of fire, and one sat upon each of them. And they were all filled with the Holy

Spirit and began to speak with other tongues, as the Spirit
gave them utterance (Acts 2:1-4 NKJV).

Imagine how that time must have been. I'm sure they felt anxious
fear and excitement over the possibilities of persecution on the one
hand, yet thrilled in the glorious revelation of the Christ, the Messiah,
on the other. Just days and weeks earlier, it had all changed. Their
lives were forever turned upside down by the sacrifice on Calvary's
hill. Just days and weeks earlier, they had denied the man, abandoned
Him in His time of greatest need. Yet the pain was healed by His
forgiveness and grace. He came back just to give them (and us) a few
more words of instruction and encouragement. Then He ascended
into the heavens like a Cirque De Soleil act with only the word of His
soon return and promise of power from on high.

What next? they surely thought. *Who's with us and who's against us?*
What more could happen? I'm sure anything seemed possible in their
minds after the craziness they'd experienced over the last few weeks.

They turned to fellowship and prayer—a desperate heart's cry of a
prayer that I'm sure wailed out from that upper room day after day and
night after night with no end in sight. They ate, they slept, they took
shifts—anything to not break unity, anything to not break obedience
lest they miss His latest promise. After all, they knew that He is a man
of His word. He did rise again like He said. He is the Messiah!

Then it came ten days later. That's when it all changed for them, 120
of them. That's when they found the key. That's when *He* arrived. Not
Jesus—better (see John 16:7). He's better only because He can be at all
places at all times. Omnipresent, yet on earth; all God, yet all Spirit; one
with the triune Godhead—the person named Holy Spirit had arrived.
He single-handedly, overnight, instantaneously turned Christ-denying
simpletons (in the case of Peter and those disciples who had abandoned
Jesus when He went to the cross) into fire-filled, tongue talking world-
changers with seemingly no fear!

The world has never been the same. Once the melee calmed down,
a first-fruits harvest of 3,000 people was added to their numbers that

day. Who could resist this new, mighty force? He is the power to prick hearts, change minds, and draw all people to Christ. He is our ultimate weapon, our atom bomb, our top mentor and giver of wisdom and strategy. What a gift! And it all happened because they tarried in prayer, obedience, and unity—that and divine timing, of course.

DIVINE TIMING AGAIN

Is divine timing once again upon us like a thief in the night? Are we waiting on God for something, or is He waiting on us? Maybe there's something we still need to get, still need to understand. Are our lives fully in alignment with His biblical instruction?

What would the disciples do if they were here today and they heard that familiar sound rumbling in the distance? What would they tell us? How would we prepare? There's no Holy Spirit number two coming, yet many have yet to be introduced to Him in the first place. Revival begins with that introduction. The sound manifested on the day of Pentecost represents the awareness of God's Kingdom reality breaking into our present, natural world. It is a spiritual Kingdom, and that is a spiritual event. Thus, we need the Spirit to reveal spiritual things.

The sound was a reward for their obedience. It was a sound of heavenly partnership, of power, of glory. It was God and humanity in unity—with one plan because of one man, Jesus. The sound represents that God has come. But it also represents the beginning of our responsibility to steward the results of His coming. Jesus restored relationship between us and God, thus initiating the ability for us to live as sons and daughters of God on earth. Knowing this aspect of our identity is one of the first steps to living a life of revival.

When God wants to do something spectacular, He does so in His power so that no human can get the credit. Too often we get in His way. We are in the midst of a season of supernatural surprises and mysteries of His Kingdom unveiled and revealed. Is this God doing a new thing, or are we simply on the verge of experiencing a sound like that of that glorious day? Does God really change, or do people just misplace the memories of their heritage? Did He really go anywhere, or did we? These questions are important to ask when we consider why the Church of today oftentimes does not even compare to the biblical standard of Christianity that is laid out for us in the New Testament.

The sound is like a train approaching through the subway, like a jet at takeoff. I can hear it. It's growing stronger. Will you dare tune in your spiritual ear to hear that same sound? Maybe you've heard it already.

Now it's time to prepare. The time is short. The cries of a remnant generation are being rewarded. The Spirit and the Bride say come! Revival is here!

God's call to arms is one of preparation and stewardship. He is preparing us to understand *His will* and *His anointing* so that we may shine as *His glorious Church*.

It's time that we start digesting the meat of our faith and understand the timeless principles of the Kingdom of God. It's time we set aside our religious differences and denominations and embrace the fact that the only theological absolute truth is that the person of Jesus is perfect theology. Most other differences are simply because we all see dimly (see 1 Cor. 13:12).

It's about Christ; it always has been. Yet we live in a world that's lost and dying in need of a Savior. Our hourglass of evangelism is running out of sand. God has equipped us with bazookas in the Spirit, yet we're fighting the enemy with squirt guns. It's time we understand the things of the Spirit, partner with the person of the Holy Spirit, and start living lives of radical faith, a life of normal Christianity!

DEFINING *REVIVAL*

The term *revival* isn't in the Bible. It didn't need to be. Yet simple observation will show that the purity and power of the Gospel (Good News), as it was intended in the Word and lived out by our forefathers in the faith, is far from our modern Christian agendas, especially in the Western culture.

If Jesus came in a vision today to a prophet like John when he was on the island of Patmos and wrote the Book of Revelation, I believe He would give our churches similar rebukes or maybe even worse (see Rev. 2 and 3). It's time we get back to our first love. That's where all ministry, true spiritual power, and authority are derived from. He is our source, our limitless well of refreshing.

Revival is about a location. It's wherever you are because that's where He is. This will be explained in more detail in subsequent chapters. We have the person of the Holy Spirit with us always, which is something that not even the greatest prophets of old had! As the Bible says, *"...Among those born of women there has not risen anyone greater than John the Baptist; yet he who is least in the kingdom of heaven is greater than he"* (Matt 11:11). The fact that the God who created the Universe, the Alpha and Omega, deposited a part of Himself in us so He can be with us always is almost incomprehensible to the human mind—but important to at least try to understand.

JOIN THE JOURNEY

Will you lay down your preconceived ideas of who you think Jesus is and who you think you are for just long enough to reject human-made, human-led religion and embrace revival? Will you let yourself be turned inside out so that we together can turn the world upside down? The early Christians were described in this way. Will the world say of us the same thing? *"...These who have turned the world upside down have come here too..."* (Acts 17:6 NKJV).

Join me on this journey of learning, through the Holy Spirit, some fundamentals of Spirit-filled, Spirit-led faith that will first renew our minds in hopes of renewing our behaviors so we can truly be ready to embrace this season of God's grace.

He's looking for a few good men and women who are up for the challenge. Of all the years throughout history that He could have picked, God decided to release you to earth through your parents in this generation for such a time as this. You will be held accountable for all that you read. Life may never be more exciting, dangerous, or rewarding. Now can you hear the sound?

This book is intended to be like flint that you strike your stone upon to create fire. I pray that this book becomes a tool that helps light or stir your fire within and helps you come alive in Christ at an even greater level!

It is to be used as a reference also that you may be able to refer back to for years to come. It's a starter guide to living the lifestyle of a revivalist. A Revival 101 of sorts, it is an exciting picture of what is possible for believers today, and it has been birthed from years of true-life revival experience.

As you read, above all, remember to love Jesus before anything else. Next, remember that your knowledge and wisdom of revival gained from this book helps nobody. It's the application of that knowledge and the power of the message of Jesus that will be the true testimony of revival.

QUESTIONS

1. Have you never before fully committed your life to live for God as a follower of Jesus? If you are not 100 percent sure that, if you died tonight, you would spend eternity in Heaven, you need to say and believe the following words:

PRAYER (YOU TO GOD)

God, I want to give You my all. Please cleanse me and forgive me of all my sins and anything in my life that separates me from You. I receive the blood sacrifice of Jesus that He made on the cross so that I can be saved. I believe He is now the boss of my life. Fill me with Your Spirit and Your love. I'm ready for this journey.

_____

_____

_____

2. If you are already a believer, on a scale of 1 to 10, where would you rate your walk with the Lord (1 is the coldest and 10 is the hottest)? If you are anything less than a 10, please read this prayer and receive the words of it over your life.

PRAYER (ME TO GOD FOR YOU)

God, bless this new friend in Jesus to know You more and to learn what it is to live an exciting life of revival. Set my friend free, heal, and fill Your child with Your Spirit to a level never experienced before, in Jesus' precious name.

_____

_____

_____

Jesus is not an idol on a cross.

He's not a picture on a stained glass window.

He's not a theology.

He's not just a historical figure.

He's alive and well and living in me!

He knows you and wants to be known by you.

He loves you and gave His life for you so that you may have life and life more abundantly.

Will you let Him in? Will you cry out to Him for Him to wash away your sins, take away the anguish of your soul, and make all things new?

Jesus is real, and He is here.

Will you experience Him today for yourself?

Will you make a decision today to give your whole life to Him?

Chapter 2

HISTORIC REVIVAL

O LORD, I have heard Thy speech, and was afraid:
O LORD, revive Thy work in the midst of the years,
in the midst of the years make known; in wrath re-
member mercy (Habakkuk 3:2 KJV).

Revival is proclaiming and walking out the
revelation of the true Gospel, the new covenant.

If you're like me, you may find great pleasure in reading about the great "moves of God" in the past. Honoring the past often paves the way for future; this holds true throughout history, revival not withstanding.

First and foremost, there is God's move through His Church, by the power and leading of the Holy Spirit, in the Book of Acts. Later, also, after the Dark Ages, there was the Reformation, which continued on through many wonderful expressions over the last few centuries. Hearing how Methodism started, and even the Salvation Army—both birthed from wonderful moves of God—gives me goose bumps. Reading about Azusa Street, the Welsh revival, and many other subsequent revivals in India, China, and the Hebrides is just overwhelming to my spirit. My heart rejoices with each and every testimony of the works of God's grace for the salvation of humankind and even His hand moving in miracle-working power over people and regions. I dare not leave out the Great Awakenings of the eighteenth and nineteenth centuries. God has truly moved powerfully throughout history!

God also has used many men and women over the years to usher in, and in many cases simply ride the wave of, what He was doing through them in their respective generations. Let us not forget the exploits of David Brainerd, who ministered powerfully and sacrificially to the American Indians in the 1700s.

God worked through John Knox, the Scottish reformer; John Wesley, the founder of Methodism; and Jonathan Edwards, one of the earliest American revivalists who helped usher in the First Great Awakening. Let's not forget the great lawyer-turned-preacher, revivalist Charles Finney, or one of the first great American evangelists, D.L. Moody. Let us remember men of God who helped lead great revival outpourings, like Evan Roberts of the great Welsh revival of 1904. And then shortly after Roberts, there was William Seymour, who led arguably the most famous revival outpouring of all time in a warehouse that began on April 9, 1906, on Azusa Street in Los Angeles. We honor great people of faith over the past hundred years, like Smith Wigglesworth, Maria Woodsworth-Etter, R.A. Torrey, A.B. Simpson, and Charles Price, all the way through the tent revivalists of the 1950s, like William Branham, Oral Roberts, and A.A. Allen. These were people of God who helped shaped history. We owe them much credit as forefathers of Pentecostalism and revival. We honor their lives and their memory.

I have followed and learned from many modern-day revivalists like Randy Clark, Heidi Baker, Rodney Howard-Browne, and others. Modern-day revivals have swept through South America through the likes of Carlos Annacondia and Claudio Freidzon. Guatemala and many parts of Africa are experiencing supernatural favor and blessing. God is even moving powerfully in Pakistan and other Middle Eastern countries. There has been revival and an explosion of the growth of

Christianity in India and China since the early twentieth century that still continues today! The Gospel cannot be stopped and God's Spirit is being poured out on all flesh!

It would take years to write about all the heroes of revival throughout history and those living today, giving them credit for the faith that they lived. These include intercessors, preachers, missionaries, and just "average-Joe" Christians from all races and generations. Heaven is filled with the annals of their exploits. In many ways, this book is dedicated to those heroes of the faith whom we may never read about and never know of until the day we join our eternal family and pass from this life to the next.

> The Gospel cannot be stopped—God's Spirit is being poured out on all flesh!

DO YOU BELIEVE IN REVIVAL?

I believe there are five categories that people fit into when it comes to understanding biblical and present-day revival.

1. Unbelievers who don't know what it is and don't care.

2. Modern-day Pharisees who are so bound by religion that won't even consider a Spirit-led reformation of their religious systems and traditions.

3. Believers who don't understand and don't care about revival (Sunday morning-only Christians or "Chreasters"—Christians on Christmas and Easter).

4. Believers who love the idea of revival, study it, and even pray for it, but consider it something they will likely never see in their lifetimes because it is so rare.

5. Believers who are simply lovers of Jesus, who follow the Spirit, and who love anything to do with seeing the Kingdom manifest on earth. They are not too stuck on one viewpoint of anything theological or of the

Kingdom; they simply receive and follow the promises of God's Word.

Although we may not be able to communicate to the religious about the idea of revival (even Jesus, who was a walking revival, was rejected by religious authorities), I believe all other viewpoints can receive the revelation of and be touched by true revival in this life. When true revival breaks out in a believer's life, the people in the fifth category are usually the first to receive and walk in it. Many nonbelievers and Sunday-morning Christians can and will likely get touched by a newfound awareness of Heaven through the many fire-filled believers who are burning with the flame of revival. Despite these positive signs for many people, I'm fearfully aware that the believers in category four who love God and who love the idea of revival may be the second least likely group to truly embrace God's revival today.

> God will not hold back His holy hand—He will give you the good gift you ask for.

Many of the same people who believe we can pray desperate prayers until God blesses us with revival are the same people who believe that revival is a completely sovereign God-experience. They believe it can only happen if we have found enough favor with our Father in Heaven and happen to live at the right time and worship in the right place when God decides to grace a church and community with this wonderful Heaven-on-earth experience.

When you think that you can pray and God will hear you and answer your prayers, why would you also think that God would stay His holy hand and not give you any good gift that you would ask for?

This message is a contradictory one and not in alignment with God's heart and will. It lacks understanding of God's ways and His heart toward people. Not only that, but it shows a lack of knowledge regarding God's sovereign will. He desires to use His Church here on earth to usher in His Kingdom rule and authority in the midst of

His enemies until He brings all things to judgment and reconciliation under Himself.

Many are waiting around for revival to happen. Others are praying until they're blue in the face 12 hours a day. Both sets of people tend to agree that *revival is an overwhelming compelling force of supernatural proportions so obviously God that it literally leads to community-wide awareness of God and our own sin.* This awareness of God leads us to repentance because we are painfully aware that because of our sinful condition we cannot survive in His presence, a presence that now appears to be more real than ever. This repentance leads us to be reborn into the life of Christ as victorious Christians representing Heaven on earth.

WHAT'S THIS HAVE TO DO WITH ME?

Not many would argue that the previous description describes true historic revival. However, what we all must understand is that when God moves in a person, a city, or a community, it was someone's prayer somewhere that broke through the spiritually fallow ground of the person's heart or the sinful condition of the region. In the case of historic revival, it was often many people who got this revelation and who entered into God's wonderful intercession—leading to the blessing of revival.

> True revival is an outflowing as much as it is an outpouring.

This is one more reason why we are to understand the power of true intercession. God's Spirit draws His intercessors into deep places of sharing His burdens and praying down His will, sometimes long before we see what will manifest. We are praying for an outpouring and so is Jesus. The difference is that while we believe it is coming from Heaven, Jesus believes it comes from us! The Spirit that pours out now resides in us. True revival is an outflowing as much as it is an outpouring.

Revival is birthed through active partnership between believers and the Spirit of God. We have a personal responsibility when it comes to revival. Revival isn't a completely sovereign God-ordained experience in time anymore than your personal prayer time this morning was. God gives grace when we seek Him, but first He must be sought. *"My heart says of You, 'Seek His face!' Your face, LORD, I will seek"* (Ps. 27:8).

He has given people free will and His Spirit free reign. The key is reaching oneness in heart with God and His Spirit; only then can we begin to receive God's grace for true revival. The level of God's response in relation to His people's passionate pleas may be sovereign.

> God has given people free will and His Spirit free reign.

But one of the most fundamental points in understanding what revival is and your relationship to it is this: revival requires *your faith*, *your prayers*, and *your obedience* through a close relationship with God.

Revival has become something to talk about as a long ago historical event rather than as a *now* reality. Like many things of the Kingdom, once people try to figure it out, they make it too hard. We have made the very thought of revival a sacred thing, and we immediately assume that any revival we hear about cannot possibly be true revival like the revivals of old.

There was a time when people thought of the same thing regarding the baptism of the Spirit and speaking in tongues. In fact, only for a little over a hundred years (since the Azusa Street Revival) have many in the Church believed that this is a ready and attainable experience for all believers—or that it is of great importance to our spiritual lives! Could we now be making the same dire mistake when we think about revival, subtly believing that this is unattainable and thinking, *we'll never see it, so why pursue it?* In this time, literally over 100 million believers have been baptized in the Spirit in a little over 100 years![1] I believe this worldwide revival outpouring will have an equally dramatic affect on the next few generations of believers!

Do you truly believe that God has set aside only certain times in history and only certain locations on the map where He will manifest

His presence and Kingdom?! If so, you are gravely unaware of God's heart. He desires revival more than we do! He desires to pour out His Spirit upon all flesh (see Joel 2:28). He desires that none should perish (see 2 Pet. 3:9). When will we understand?

Historic revivals did not occur because God pre-ordained revival for just that particular time in history; they occurred because people tapped into God's eternal, never-changing will.

CAN I REALLY SEE REVIVAL FOR MYSELF?

We receive salvation by believing in faith. We receive the baptism of the Spirit by faith. It should not surprise us, then, that we also receive revival *by faith.* It is time we debunk the myths of revival and press in to God's Kingdom. If revival is such an unattainable and mystical experience in your mind, you likely will never see it. Even if it landed on your head and wiggled around like a worm, you wouldn't know it. Everything of the Kingdom must be received in faith like a child (see Mark 10:15; Luke 18:17).

> Historic revivals occurred because people tapped into God's eternal, never-changing will.

The first step to entering into revival is to receive it in our hearts. We must rebuke and repent of powerless religion and receive God's revelations about Jesus and His Kingdom. Then we let the transforming effects of God's Spirit and presence in our lives to burst through our hearts, giving a refreshing flood of God's love to the world around us. *When we start living with this level of a radical, burning love, full of faith and fire, overflowing with the Spirit of God, people will surely believe that revival **is** possible and that it **is** God's will.* It's really not as hard as you may think.

Is revival sovereign? You bet. But God has sovereignly chosen to use His Church to usher in His will on earth. He has also sovereignly given us free will. Revival starts with our Spirit-led intercession and ends with our courageous acts of faith.

How many potential revival moves throughout history were lost because people didn't respond adequately to what God wanted to say and do? God-forbid that this be said of our generation. Not on my watch!

How many potential revivals were lost because people didn't respond to what God wanted to say and do?

Remember, when God wants to move, He moves through people—through people's prayers and people's efforts. Of course, we must not misunderstand this by thinking that we can control the supernatural aspect of what God does. But we must also grasp that when He wants to do something—sovereign as it may seem—God implores His people by divinely leading those willing to listen to Him. You must be willing and ready if you want revival in your life and in your community!

QUESTIONS

1. What are some characteristics that most people associate with historical revival? Is there any reason why these things couldn't happen today?

_____

_____

_____

_____

_____

_____

_____

_____

2. Do you believe it is God's will to move as powerfully or more powerfully today than He has in the past? Why or why not?

_____

_____

_____

_____

_____

_____

_____

_____

3. Do you believe that revival is possible for you to experience now? Why or why not?

_____

_____

_____
_____
_____
_____
_____
_____
_____
_____
_____
_____

PRAYER (YOU TO GOD)

God we bless and honor all of the revival moves of the past, the revivalists of the past and present, and any and all unsung heroes of the faith whom only You know. We thank You for moving so wonderfully in their lives to bring Your blessings to the world around them. We thank You for using them to usher in Your will through their prayers and actions of faith. Lord, we believe that You are the same yesterday, today, and forever. We believe that You desire for none to perish and that Your Spirit be poured out on all flesh.

PRAYER (ME TO GOD, OVER YOU)

God we receive the burden of Your heart to see our generation come to know You. We will not be silent when we see the devil trying to ruin Your harvest. God let us cry out like the Moravians to win for You the ransom of Your suffering! God strengthen us, empower us, free us from any bondage that can hold us back. Open our hearts and minds to receive from Your revelation as we continue on this journey through the pages of this book.

Endnote

1. This is my estimate based on the fact that Pentecostalism claims to have over
    250 million adherents in 2007. See "Pentecostalism," *BBC Religions*, http://
    www.bbc.co.uk/religion/religions/christianity/subdivisions/pentecostal_1
    .shtml. Accessed July 16, 2010.

Revival is not about cheap prophetic parlor tricks or "fire tunnels."

Revival is not about large tent meetings, overtime offerings, or overexaggerated healings.

Revival is not about planned evangelism or ministry "outreaches."

Revival is not about advertising.

Revival is not about big-name preachers with big reputations.

Revival *is* about those who will to have no reputation for Christ's sake.

Revival is about an unquenchable fire, not the fire of hell but something more dangerous, the fire of God's Spirit.

Revival is about being a "burning one" for Jesus.

Revival is when somebody sees you and they see God.

Revival is when you're so full of the Holy Spirit that everyone around you knows it and either wants what you have or wants to leave when you're around because you are far too convicting.

Revival is about the throne room of Heaven becoming a reality on earth. It starts with you, the temple where His Spirit dwells.

Revival is about letting the chastisement of our Father turn us inside out and willfully being convicted and repentant.

Revival is about hating sin more than death.

Revival is about letting God's fire refine our will and motives.

Revival is about wanting more of God at *any* price.

Revival has nothing to do with your religion or church denomination. It has everything to do with you losing your life for the sake of knowing Him and being a messenger for the greatest message the world has ever known.

Will revival cost you everything? Of course; that's why it's so rare.

Are you willing to die for revival? I am.

Chapter 3

THE PROMISED LAND

And from the days of John the Baptist until now
the kingdom of heaven suffers violence, and the vio-
lent take it by force (Matthew 11:12 NKJV).

Are you willing to fight for God's best?

Thousands of years ago the Israelites of the Bible were captured
and forced into captivity and slavery by the ungodly Egyptian government led by Pharaoh. Ironically, God sent a Hebrew man,
adopted by the Egyptian royal family, to free the Hebrews from
this captivity. Ten plagues were unleashed on Egypt due to the
prayers and authority of this man, Moses, in partnership with the
divine agenda of God that finally convinced Pharaoh to release
these prisoners. As the story goes, the Israelites fled from Egypt
and pursued the land of promise, promised to them by their
redeemer and Lord God Almighty. This land was the land flowing
with milk and honey (see Exod. 3:8), a land of great abundance.
This land was going to be fertile and would provide for them a
refuge from nomadic desert living and finally a permanent dwelling place to call their own. However, before the people would be

ready for the promise God first had to get them out of Egypt and Egypt out of them. He didn't want them to be slaves and they, themselves, were crying out for freedom from captivity. God freed them indeed, although they would find out that it would be a long trek in the desert before they could get out of a "slavery mentality." God doesn't like mixing blessing and poverty. He doesn't want His children to carry baggage and bondage when He desires them to live free and blessed.

> Before the people would be ready for the promise, God first had to get them out of Egypt and Egypt out of them.

FINDING THE PROMISED LAND

Sin and salvation don't mix well. As we read in Exodus, this was quite the journey and quite the process. Paul further comments on the sins of the Israelites while they were in the desert, warning us to not fall prey to the same things. Unfortunately many of these are sins that modern-day Christians are sometimes very familiar with. The following exhortation by Paul explains some of the lessons that we should learn from the Israelites:

> *Now these things became our examples, to the intent that we should not **lust** after evil things as they also lusted. And do not become **idolaters** as were some of them. As it is written, "The people sat down to eat and drink, and rose up to play." Nor let us commit **sexual immorality**, as some of them did, and in one day twenty-three thousand fell; nor let us **tempt Christ**, as some of them also tempted, and were destroyed by serpents; nor **complain**, as some of them also complained, and were destroyed by the destroyer. Now all these things happened to them as examples, and they were written for our admonition, upon whom the ends of the ages have come* (1 Corinthians 10:6-11 NKJV).

> Sin and salvation don't mix well.

Freedom and trials both test our hearts. God gave His people freedom, and they took advantage of it to become bound by lust and immorality. God allowed the people to patiently endure the trials of their journey, and they complained. God's people had such a difficult time giving up the idea of being comfortable in their slavery and free to worship other powerless idols that the first generation rescued from Egypt never entered into the Promised Land of God (see Num. 14:29-30). Revival is God's Promised Land for today's believers; it is representative of freedom, but not without its costs.

> Revival is God's Promised Land.

The story of the Israelites escaping Egypt and being stuck in the desert for many years is a sad commentary on the modern-day Church. Like the Israelites, the modern-day Western Church is very much stuck in a desert of indecision. We carry burdens of sin and sacrifice God's best for what is familiar and comfortable. We are free yet don't know how to press forward to the greater things God has promised. We grumble, complain, worship other gods, don't appreciate the presence and direction that God gives us, and still struggle with godless, worldly, and religious mindsets.

Pharaoh represents the spirit of religion, a spirit of bondage and comfortable Christianity. The Jews were still Jews, but slaves. Christians may still be believers, but never really live as free people, never leaving the comforts of bondage and servanthood to religion in order to embrace their rescuer, Jesus! Moses was an Old Testament type of Jesus, who led the Israelites out from that bondage. Jesus also wants to lead us out from our cemented mindsets that can keep us back from the freedom of revival living! Religion tries to get to God the same way over and over. The definition of insanity is doing something over and over the same way, but expecting different results. By this definition it's pretty easy to determine that man-made religion is insane.

> Jesus wants to lead us out from our cemented mindsets that keep us from the freedom of revival living!

God says that true religion is taking care of the widows and the orphans and staying unspotted from the world (see James 1:27).

This is God explaining that He does not care about what you say to Him or how much you sacrifice for Him. He is saying through this passage that He wants people to prove their love to Him by loving what He loves and hating what He hates. We prove this shared passion through our actions. When we love God by taking care of those who can't take care of themselves, we are truly living out our faith. When we keep ourselves unspotted from the world, we are honoring God with our lives, loving ourselves enough to not get ensnared in sins and distractions, and loving Him enough to not have any worldly idols, something He hates. This is true religion, which comes from God's Spirit and is quite a contrast to the spirit of religion.

My wife and I regularly serve the poor and needy. Not always because we are trying to, but because God has placed people with need before our paths. This gives us an opportunity to be Jesus for them and the Bible also says that they are Jesus to us (see Matt. 25:31-46).

On three separate occasions, my wife and I have housed the homeless until we could help them get on their feet or get them to where they were going. It takes faith to open up your home like this and bear the responsibility for somebody's well being, but I figure, it is the least we can do to give back to Jesus.

We have also been avid supporters of the Crisis Pregnancy Center for years. I believe the single-mother is the modern-day widow, and these women need as much support from the Church as they can get.

We are big supporters of a ministry in Tucson called Hope of Glory, which feeds the poor twice weekly and has a grand vision to build a "Hope Center" to house the poor and needy. I'm not one of those guys who thinks that feeding the poor is all we need to do to gain favor with God, but I do know the principle that when we meet a physical need, people will often open themselves up to allow you to minister to their spiritual needs.

I'd prefer to break off the spirit behind a person's problems than to just support them through benevolence ministry, but both have their time and place. If we don't minister the Gospel of Jesus to them, we are only putting a bandage on their cancer. No matter how bad a person's life may seem, their worst problem, by far, is sin! As long as we keep that perspective, love people, and serve them as if they were Jesus, God's love working through us can draw them in to God's Kingdom.

THE SPIRIT OF RELIGION

But woe to you, scribes and Pharisees, hypocrites! For you shut up the kingdom of heaven against men; for you neither go in yourselves, nor do you allow those who are entering to go in (Matthew 23:13 NKJV).

The spirit of religion is a spirit whose power is based on fear and control. People manipulated by this spirit fear what they do not understand, fear that they may be wrong in a certain area, and fear the unknown. These people set up mental blocks in their minds that shut out any and all other mindsets from entering and challenging their mental comfort zones. Their hearts and minds are protected in an ungodly way by a wall of religion. They believe that their way is the right way and their way is the only way. It is very sinister, unbiblical, and the exact opposite of God's intention. Rather, God says His ways are not our ways and His thoughts not our thoughts (see Isa. 55:8-9). He also says that the natural person cannot comprehend the things of God (see 1 Cor. 2:14). So how can we think we have it all figured out?

> The spirit of religion is a spirit whose power is based on fear and control.

The Spirit of revival, the Holy Spirit, keeps us with an ever-learning mind and an ever-loving heart. He keeps us believing all things are possible, and He keeps opening spiritual doors of revelation, leading us to more Kingdom mysteries and possibilities.

We must know that the battle against religion is not a personal battle against individuals manipulated by this spirit any more than a demonized man threatening your life presents a personal attack against you. These are spiritual things that must be dealt with in that perspective. We certainly must not just lay down for any spiritual attack, but must take authority in the Spirit and know when to fight and when to walk away.

Never fight religion with religion; this just causes you to come into agreement with the spirit, thus giving it strength! Although there may be times for holy rebukes, usually you will simply need to let the spirit roll right over you. You take your lumps, you take your stone wounds, and *let the blood of that experience propel God's Spirit into that situation so that the Lord can now work on your behalf.*

A lot of people in the world think that because you go to church you are religious, but don't let anyone assume that you're religious. Tell them that you're spiritual. Not worldly spiritual, but Holy Spirit spiritual. If they don't want to talk about religion, say neither do you. Then promptly introduce them to the least religious of all people to ever live, Jesus Christ.

If you want to truly be a revivalist, you must not become religious in one theological concept or Kingdom truth. Remember that we see through Kingdom glasses dimly (see 1 Cor. 13:12) and that we are still fallible humans.

> Remember that God may have a greater truth to unveil.

No matter how close you come to understanding a truth, you must know that God may have a greater truth to unveil on top of that one. His Kingdom mysteries are like onions. He peels off each layer of understanding and introduces us constantly to different aspects of His heart and character. You will never know everything about God or His Word. He is infinitely fabulous and wants the deepest depths of who He is to be known by His beloveds, but in order to discover those truths we must be humble enough to admit how little we truly understand.

RELIGION=BONDAGE; REVIVAL=FREEDOM

Worldly freedom makes you a bondservant to sin; Holy Spirit freedom makes you a bondservant to Jesus Christ—freedom *into* righteousness, not away from it. Revival is something we as the Church hear about and long to attain, but we have so much baggage from our old lives holding us back. If we would just get over ourselves and have a little teamwork, we could enter into the Promised Land of revival!

Moses sent 12 scouts to check out the land. Only two came back and encouraged the people that, despite the giants occupying that territory, the land could and *should* be taken because God was with them (see Num. 13:25-33).

A modern-day scout could be anyone from a typical Western church who's curious about what God has promised His believers.

Caleb and Joshua, however, are not like typical curious believers. They are much more like prophetic forerunners who speak the words of the Lord in any given situation despite how it may look in the natural. Caleb and Joshua knew who their God was so they knew they would be victorious if they went in to take the land. In my ministry ventures, I've seen that only about 15 to 20 percent of the Western Church is composed of Bible-preaching churches that believe we can live in victory and revival despite spiritual opposition ("giants in the land"). Of all the churches I have worked with or attempted to work with for citywide ministry (around 100 total), in the context of revival and prayer events, from my observation, only between two and ten are doing anything to enter into the Promised Land of revival for our lives, churches, and communities and do anything proactive to see it come to pass. Caleb and Joshua represent those two.

Did the negative attitude of the other scouts, the people's lack of trust in God, and the Israelites' continued idolatry stop them from seeing the Promised Land? Yes, at first, as we read here in Numbers:

Not one of them will ever see the land I promised on oath to their ancestors. No one who has treated Me with contempt will ever see it. But because my servant Caleb has a different spirit and follows me wholeheartedly, I will bring him into the land he went to, and his descendants will inherit it....Not one of you will enter the land I swore with uplifted hand to make your home, except Caleb son of Jephunneh and Joshua son of Nun. As for your children that you said would be taken as plunder, I will bring them in to enjoy the land you have rejected. But as for you, your bodies will fall in this wilderness. Your children will be shepherds here for forty years, suffering for your unfaithfulness, until the last of your bodies lies in the wilderness. For forty years—one year for each of the forty days you explored the land— you will suffer for your sins and know what it is like to have me against you. I, the Lord, have spoken, and I will surely do these things to this whole wicked community, which has banded together against me. They will meet their end in this desert; here they will die (Numbers 14:23-24,30-35).

> The generation who are not overly churched and full of faith and trust God are the ones who will lead today's Church into the Promised Land of revival!

Even though God originally promised Moses that he would see the Promised Land, Moses tragically upset God and never made it in. He and the other older Israelites who were in the desert for 40 years never made it in. In this case, the older generation of doubters was punished and missed out on God's best for their lives. However, the next generation, not familiar with Egypt-living, entered the Promised Land victoriously. The generation of people who are not overly churched, who are full of faith and trust in who God says He is, and who are born into freedom with no memory of religious bondage are the ones who will lead today's Church into the Promised Land of revival. However, this generation must spend time with the older Moses generation to gain wisdom and knowledge of the Lord's ways.

It is a great honor to be associated with the Phoenix University of Theology. Originally founded by Dr. Richard Drake, and others, God gave Dr. Drake a vision that the University would include officers and generals in God's army. God told him He would send him the best of the best to implement Apostolic curriculum that would shape nations. Men like Dr. Drake, Dr. Ed Delph, Dr. Dean Landis, and others have really poured into me at P.U.T events. I just love sitting under their teachings and learning from the wisdom of these spiritual fathers.

It would take me too long to talk about the influence that spiritual fathers like Pastor Zane Anderson, Rick Ibarra, Richard Noel, Pastor David Swift, Tim Mann, Jim Smith, Don Pirozok, Stan Moser, Darcy Dube, Sean Smith, Bob Griffin and others have had on my life. I thank God for crossing my path with theirs, if only for a season. I don't know where I'd be without them. Their influence fuels me to pour myself out for the subsequent generations to propagate and multiply God's Kingdom through building up people.

THE GENERATIONS TOGETHER

God's original intention is that the rod (authority) of the older generation gets paired with the sword (strength) of the younger so that both groups of people can enter in. Now we must drop our differences and limiting mindsets and work together to see this Elijah anointing really be fulfilled!

> *Look, I am sending you the prophet Elijah before the great and dreadful day of the LORD arrives.* **His preaching will turn the hearts of fathers to their children, and the hearts of children to their fathers.** *Otherwise I will come and strike the land with a curse* (Malachi 4:5-6 NLT).

God is raising up many leaders who are young enough to be the "older brother" to the youth, yet mature enough to walk in a level of respect, honor, and understanding of the Fathers that went before us. In that gaining of wisdom and revelation from the fathers in the faith, my age-group of leaders can now communicate to the youth God's intentions and communicate to them how not to make the same mistakes as the prior generations.

The Bible promises that in the last days (which began on the day of Pentecost), God will pour out His Spirit on *all* flesh, young and old!

> *And afterward, I will pour out My Spirit on all people.*
> *Your sons and daughters will prophesy, your **old men** will*
> *dream dreams, your **young men** will see visions. Even on*
> *My servants, both men and women, I will pour out My*
> *Spirit in those days. I will show wonders in the heavens*
> *and on the earth...*(Joel 2:28-30).

The Promised Land is a place where we as spiritual children can grow-up in our faith to spiritual maturity. We can live and fend for ourselves as truly free people—free to worship Jesus how we want and free to occupy and multiply!

REVIVAL REQUIRES A FIGHT

God destroyed the Israel's religious enemies (Pharaoh's army in the Red Sea), just as He did for all of humanity when Jesus died on Calvary and the veil of the Jewish temple that separated people from God was torn (see Matt. 27:51). God sets us free, but we must learn how to get across the desert and enter the Promised Land.

God always goes with us into battle when we face our giants, but we still must be willing to fight and obey. Not many churches engage in spiritual warfare to break themselves free from the bondages of sin or sinful thinking, let alone to take a city for Jesus! Many of us have giants in our own lives, things that cripple us spiritually. But nothing we have and nothing we have gone through or are going through can stand up to

> God sets us free, but we must learn how to get across the desert and enter the Promised Land.

a Christian praying in God's authority with the blood of Jesus and name of Jesus as our weapons! *Pray for yourself, pray for your friends, pray for your family, pray for your leaders, and pray for your enemies!*

At a "Call" event in Montgomery, Alabama, the Lord had me drop to my knees and intercede for a friend who had been struggling with a certain immoral lifestyle tied to his identity. This wasn't your standard quiet prayer, the Spirit of God wanted me, personally, to stand in the gap and repent on his behalf. I was embarrassed to do this at first but knew what had to be done. I argued with God that I didn't want to verbalize this request. When I questioned God, He asked me rhetorically if I'd rather go up on stage and repent in front of the entire crowd of thousands of people. I said, "OK, I get the point." With tears, love, and led by the Spirit of God, I cried out for God to forgive *me* of homosexuality. I personally cried out loudly, "God, I repent of homosexuality." That prayer broke off the influence of this spirit that was attacking my friend! Within days, this individual was back on the right track with God, and is still serving God to this day and engaged to be married! This was God teaching me true intercession and humility. Praise God for His wonder-working power to destroy the works of the enemy through our prayers and obedience!

On two occasions I have personally visited individuals in their homes who were suffering from drug and alcohol abuse. In both cases, I prayed as the Spirit led and broke off the power of the enemy from their lives to help set them free! One of those men is serving in ministry to this day! Demons of drugs, alcohol, and sexual promiscuity flee when confronted and prayed for in the power of God and name of Jesus!

No past, present, or future giant, like homosexuality, sickness, disease, depression, pornography, alcoholism or a religious spirit, can hinder God's revival from breaking out among His people—those who cry for freedom, who fight the giants of our culture, who fight for righteousness, who fight with a holy passion. *These people will not be denied!*

Once you break free, let your journey be as short as possible. The Israelites were stuck in the desert between Egypt and Canaan for 40 years. The crazy thing is, this journey should have only taken them 11 days (see Deut. 1:2). They went around and around in circles, never truly free from bondage mindsets and the urge to slip into idolatry. Let us learn our lesson once and for all through this timeless story—stop spinning in circles like the Israelites and make a beeline for revival Kingdom-living.

When I was seeking the baptism of the Holy Spirit, I fasted one week (per God's direction), but I didn't receive it until day 11! God had to break away any doubt and any fleshly or mental bondage in me before He could empower me! When He did, I then began my endless pursuit of revival in my life and in every place I go. The baptism (the empowerment) of the Spirit was just the beginning. I have had to fight spiritually for every soul whom I have affected and every piece of ground in this world that we are taking back for Jesus' name. I'm still fighting!

PAUL'S EXAMPLE

The apostle Paul fought arguably longer and harder for the sake of the Gospel than any documented saint in history. I'm sure there have been tens of thousands since him who lived with this sort of abandon, but his story has been recorded for us in Scripture. Let your heart catch Paul's spirit as you read of his passion. He was talking not just about himself, but also of the other apostles and warriors for the Gospel:

> *We put no stumbling block in anyone's path, so that our ministry will not be discredited. Rather, as servants of God we commend ourselves in every way: in great endurance; in troubles, hardships and distresses; in beatings, imprison-ments and riots; in hard work, sleepless nights and hunger; in purity, understanding, patience and kindness; in the Holy Spirit and in sincere love; in truthful speech and in the power of God; with weapons of righteousness in the right hand and in the left; through glory and dishonor, bad report*

and good report; genuine, yet regarded as impostors; known, yet regarded as unknown; dying, and yet we live on; beaten, and yet not killed; sorrowful, yet always rejoicing; poor, yet making many rich; having nothing, and yet possessing everything (2 Corinthians 6:3-10).

This is such an amazing example from Paul's life that we should learn from and model. When Paul was nearing death, writing his last documented letter, he had the amazing testimony of being able to say that he did everything he could for the Lord Jesus during his lifetime. *"I have fought the good fight, I have finished the race, I have kept the faith"* (2 Tim. 4:7 NKJV).

This is one of my primary dreams (and a dream of many others)—to achieve in my lifetime whatever God has set before me to do in my generation. This is the fulfillment of destiny. King David is another Bible personality who had many great things said about him: *"...for after David had done the will of God in his own generation, he died and was buried with his ancestors..."* (Acts 13:36 NLT).

Let us walk in freedom from the religious captivity that God has broken us from. Let us press forward in things of revival, learning from the wisdom and experience of our Fathers in the faith. And let us all pray that God will lead us, like David, to complete His will for our lives in our generation!

QUESTIONS

1. How can the Church break free from any religious con-
    fines that keep us from experiencing true revival?

    _____

    _____

    _____

    _____

    _____

2. Have you seen the spirit of religion at work in your life
    or in your church?

    _____

    _____

    _____

    _____

    _____

3. What is God revealing to you right now regarding your
    role in helping to see His purposes advanced in this gen-
    eration? What could be stopping you from this? Is it
    possibly a spirit of religion, apathy, or doubt?

    _____

    _____

    _____

    _____

_____

_____

PRAYER (YOU TO GOD)

God, I pray that You would speak destiny into my life. Break me free of an Egypt mindset in Jesus' name. I pray that You would continue to help me hear You so that You can align me with Your Word and so that I can begin to discover more of Your will for my life.

PRAYER (ME TO GOD, FOR YOU)

Now let God fill you with His passionate warrior spirit as I pray this prayer!

In Jesus' name I release a militant anointing to this reader to fight from bended knee and prevail over any darkness in his or her life, in the lives of loved ones, and in the community where this warrior lives! Receive my prayer over your life. I believe there is an impartation, and I know for a fact that God's anointing is able to be captured by any form of media, including the pages of this book. Receive freedom from religion, break free from ungodly religious leaders, receive God's provision and blessing, and follow His presence straight to the Promised Land of revival in your life! God, empower this warrior in Jesus' name to live in victory, despite difficulties and any giants that might have to be faced.

I have no bow of burning gold

To shoot my arrows of desire;

And yet, O God, I crave a life

That will transmit Thy holy Fire.

I shall not cease from mentor strife,

Nor shall my pen sleep in my hand,

Till I have seen God's holy men

Arise and shake our needy land.

—LEONARD RAVENHILL[1]

Chapter 4

Why Revival Really Tarries

*After two days He will revive us; on the third day
He will restore us, that we may live in His presence.
Let us acknowledge the LORD; let us press on to acknowledge Him. As surely as the sun rises, He will appear; He will come to us like the winter rains, like the
spring rains that water the earth* (Hosea 6:2-3).

You are God sought, blood bought, and Holy Spirit taught!

To understand why revival apparently tarries, we need to understand a couple fundamental truths about God's character. Furthermore, we need to understand what revival is and what it isn't.

Some define *revival* as a time where many people get saved and touched by the power of God in such a way that true repentance and transformation occurs in people's lives and their community. I believe we use the word *revival* to describe something mysterious, miraculous, and possible as a high mark for those who are really hungry for more of God to reach toward. We define revival as historically documented

> *Revival* describes something mysterious, miraculous, and possible as a high mark for those hungry for more of God.

71

occurrences of Heaven breaking into earth. Just the fact that we define revival means that we make it attainable. We use it as a measuring rod to represent the greatest expressions of God manifested on earth, and we believe He can and will show us similar manifestations again. Unfortunately, many people believe in revival about as much as they believe in Big Foot, and they think of it as being equally elusive.

I will go into more detail about the definition of revival in relation to the Kingdom in the next chapter. However, for now I think we need to understand a few things about God's heart and will regarding revival before we can move on.

1. He wants revival to happen even more than we do.

2. He's a good Father, which means that He does *not* just give us anything we ask for without conditions, but we can trust that He does give us what is good for us.

3. God has sovereignly assigned His Church to usher in His will, and He's given us all the tools necessary and empowered us with His Spirit to do so.

ENABLING VERSUS EMPOWERING

When God works powerfully through an imperfect Church, all principalities, powers, and people in Heaven and on earth can see His wisdom at work (see Eph. 3:10-11). He's not going to sovereignly do everything for us; that would not give Him much glory at all. He's not going to make us Christians even more spoiled and selfish by enabling us! *Enabling* is a psychological term that essentially means taking somebody's responsibility away from them by making things too easy for them, thus not allowing them to grow to maturity.

The best things of the Kingdom must be fervently sought after. God says that we must first draw near to Him before He draws near to us (see James 4:8). This is not true for salvation; in the salvation experience, *He finds us.* But it is true for the promise of His presence. We need to stop treating our relationship with God as surface level and superficial and dig deeper into the Word, pray and fast more, seek His intimacy, and desire His greatest gifts. All Christians have been graced with the same possibilities, but only a few really attain even a fraction of what is possible in His Kingdom.

If you have been praying for revival, or anything for that matter, you need to understand the truths about prayer.

The only time God doesn't answer prayer is for three reasons:

1. He's already answered it! How often do we pray for things we already have!

2. It will hurt us because we're not ready to handle the answer.

3. It's just not in accordance with His will.

Obviously, revival is in accordance with God's will. The only things in question, then, are whether it will hurt us to experience God's outpouring and whether we already have the answer to our prayers living inside of us. We'll talk more about stewarding revival in Chapter 6, "Revival Is a Gift, His Name Is Jesus," which answers the question of whether we're ready to handle revival. What we'll focus on now is the question of whether God has already answered your prayers for revival and why, if this is true, you are not experiencing or seeing it.

MORE TO DO WITH YOU THAN YOU THOUGHT

Next to Wesley Duewel, one of the fathers of the faith with the greatest passion for revival that I have ever read or read about, has to be Leonard Ravenhill. He wrote multiple books on revival and preached more fervently on prayer and intercession, revival, and the Church's need to change than anyone I have ever heard. He was a man on fire

> We need to stop treating our relationship with God as surface level and superficial and dig deeper into the Word, pray and fast more, seek His intimacy, and desire His greatest gifts.

for God, to say the least. He burned with a holy passion. He was burdened to the point of breaking for what He saw as the Church's need to "wake up" and be once again moved by historic revival, like in the days of old.[2]

Leonard Ravenhill, in all his passion, to my knowledge never saw revival, according to his definition, in his lifetime. Was God playing a mean practical joke on a man who was far more in love with Him than almost anyone I have ever seen or read about? Of course not! Although Leonard Ravenhill wanted corporate and national revival so badly, it is an undeniable truth that he, himself, was in a state of personal revival for most, if not all of his adult life, whether he really thought of revival this way or not.

Leonard Ravenhill was revival. His passion for corporate revival was that he wanted to see others in the state that he was in. He wanted to see more people take God, and the need for God to move in their lives, churches, and cities as seriously as he did. If they had, I have no doubt that corporate revival and citywide transformation would have occurred!

Ravenhill may have died thinking that he had never really experienced a true revival like that of his friend, Duncan Campbell, in the Hebrides, but I say that he experienced revival as much or more than any person who has ever lived. Corporate revival is simply many people like Ravenhill getting together and pressing in together for more of God and for His will to be made manifest.

JACOB'S GENERATION

Through my personal experiences with various "outpourings" and my study of historic revival, I have concluded that revival is not impossible to attain. *Nobody can own revival, but anybody who believes in Jesus can **see** revival and **be** revival.* Simply put, revival is believers on fire for God who refuse to let go of God until they are blessed, just like Jacob (see Gen. 32:22-30). I've never wrestled with the Lord and not felt blessed afterward.

Who may ascend into the hill of the LORD? *Or who may stand in His holy place? He who has clean hands and a pure heart, who has not lifted up his soul to an idol, nor sworn deceitfully.* **He shall receive blessing from the** LORD, *and righteousness from the God of his salvation.* **This is Jacob, the generation of those who seek Him, who seek Your face.** *Selah* (Psalm 24:3-6 NKJV).

This Jacob's generation, talked about in this Psalm, is a current reality. I believe we are in the midst of a Jacob's generation awakening and outpouring, the likes which have never been seen! It's an awakening of our souls and spirits that started just over a hundred years ago. And through revelation to the lay people and the proper positioning of the fivefold ministry leaders, who equip the Church to usher in God's Kingdom, I believe we will see a continued progression of this Kingdom awareness throughout subsequent generations.

> I believe we are in the midst of a Jacob's generation awakening and outpouring, the likes which have never been seen!

REVIVALIST ESCHATOLOGY

It has been reported that revivalists Jonathan Edwards and Charles Finney held the revivalist postmillennial eschatological view. *Eschatology* is the theology of "last things" or the *end times,* a common Christian phrase representing the return of Jesus and the end of the world as we know it. This view teaches that we are able to usher in God's Kingdom now with an ever-increasing Kingdom influence (not a literal thousand-year reign) until the Lord's return. The problem with this theology is that—after many years of revival, so much so that half of America was born again—evil began to once again become prevalent in society. The spiritual revolution that these men helped to ignite in two different centuries lost steam, and continuing the revival became more difficult. Due to their end-time theology, they thought that the revival would continue until the Lord returned to earth. When this wasn't happening, the people got very discouraged and stopped fighting passionately for revival and its continued increase throughout the generations.[3]

Participants in the great Azusa Street Revival that began in 1906 and many mainstream Pentecostal denominations since adhere to the eschatological view of premillennial dispensationalism. This is the expectation that the Lord will return to rapture the Church before any great tribulation, and before Jesus' millennial reign on earth. The participants in this revival believed in the Lord's imminent return so much so that they knew they were to speedily send out missionaries around the world to help reap the harvest of the nations before the Lord's return.[4]

Not that we are to not eagerly expect the return of the Lord, but the Bible clearly says in the parable of the Minas, in relation to God's Kingdom on earth, that we are to "do business until the Lord's return" (see Luke 19:13). We can set our eyes on Jesus and on Heaven without being preoccupied with premil. dispensationalism, or any other views that can distract from God's present will on earth. If we are hoping for the Lord's return and He tarries, we can fall into the trap of hope deferred. The Bible says that hope deferred makes the heart grow sick (see Prov. 13:12). When we are not preoccupied with the hope of future events rather than with experiencing Jesus now, and ushering in God's will on earth, such discouragements will not distract or deter us from seeking God's best in our generation and the next.

> End-time dramas, beasts, constant guessing games, and fantasies sell a lot of books, but they don't save a lot of souls.

Let us learn from the past so that we don't inadvertently kill the next move of God by our discouragement. *We must have the right attitude about revival and embrace the fact that it's not all about us!* We may not be the last generation before the Lord returns and we need to accept that so we can positively pour into the next generation of spiritual leaders imparting to them a long-term perspective to seeing God's Kingdom plans fill the earth today as well as 50 years from now. End-time dramas, beasts, constant guessing games, and fantasies sell a lot of books, but they don't save a lot of souls. Over the years some have twisted and manipulated prophetic Scriptures to fit them conveniently within the context of dates in time most relevant to themselves and their generation. Many people will certainly try to convince others that, although the Book of Revelation was written two thousand years ago, it definitely must apply to 2012. Other leaders have done that same thing throughout history. The year 2000, the year 1988, 1967, and 1844, were all dates that leaders in the body of Christ definitively declared that the Lord is returning. Such interpretations are not profitable and can greatly distract from God's plans and purposes, not to mention, make us look like fools to the world. The Bible clearly states, *"But about that day or hour no one knows, not even the angels in heaven, nor the Son, but only the Father"* (Mark 13:32).

It is vanity to think that the world revolves around us today even in historical biblical context. Preoccupation with things we cannot control paralyzes us from the works of ministry. Sometimes it seems like more people are looking for the antichrist than for Christ. We need to set our eyes on Jesus alone and let all of the end of the world drama happen whenever God wants it to. We need to do His business and His will on earth *now* while we still can. Much of what we worry about is a waste of time, at best, and extremely selfish, at worst. *God has a plan for this present generation. Who is willing to embrace His heart and His will and be His hands and feet?* Who will reject false mindsets or distracting theological mysteries and follow Jesus?

LOCATION THEOLOGY

Another big reason why revival tarries is that Christianity has historically relegated revival to locations, as if God honors buildings over people. God is no longer in the Jewish temple! He destroyed the temple in A.D. 70 as a sign that He no longer honors that structure as the abode of His presence (see Matt. 24:1-2). He has now written the law on our hearts and has given us His Holy Spirit to reign in and through our mortal bodies (see Heb. 8:10; Rom. 8:11). He is here with us right now, and He always will be! David was so keenly aware of the presence of God with Him that He knew God would always be wherever he was. *"If I ascend into heaven, You are there; if I make my bed in hell, behold, You are there"* (Ps. 139:8 NKJV).

Paul also preached that no created thing and no change in location can possibly separate us from the love of God. Hallelujah!

> *For I am persuaded that neither death nor life, nor angels nor principalities nor powers, nor things present nor things to come, nor height nor depth, nor any other created thing, shall be able to separate us from the love of God which is in Christ Jesus our Lord* (Romans 8:38-39 NKJV).

God is always with you. A location only feels like it houses the presence of God because there are saints who leave an aroma of Heaven in that place (see 2 Cor. 2:15). God is no respecter of places or people. We desperately need to get away from the false "location theology" and know that we are temples of the Holy Spirit whom God resides in always.

Is God's presence stronger in Israel where Jesus walked? What if God's people worshipped Him in a bar and the bartenders held a party in the church? Where do you think God's presence would appear stronger? Think about it...does it matter where you're at when you pray? Does it matter where you're at when you worship? One of the many profound points in the parable of the woman at the well is to explain to us that *it doesn't matter what location God is worshiped from; true worshipers can worship God anywhere* (see John 4:23).

So what about those times we've read about, heard about, or experienced where the atmosphere is extremely thick with God's glory, where repentance was necessary, and where God's Spirit poured out on entire regions? Many people falsely think that He pours out revival from some fountain in Heaven and that, if our prayers are sincere enough, He will turn the faucet on over our location. But God doesn't pour out of Heaven—He pours out of us! We are fountains of God. It is imperative that we understand this concept in order to understand true revival.

In religious services, we often say that God is there when our spiritual senses are heightened—others are pressing in and pouring out with us, and we start to feel His manifest presence. However, that doesn't mean that those spiritual realities didn't exist prior to our sensing of them or that they couldn't be experienced from anywhere. No, it just means that we are more aware of God's presence in our lives at that particular moment. *When more revivalists get together, worshiping and interacting with Him, God's presence always feels more magnified.* We can give the same level of praise and worship to Him in parks, schools, churches, stores,

> True revival will break out in businesses, cities, and homes worldwide!

malls, you name it! We can pray and release Heaven anywhere! It's not until we wake up and realize the precious gift of Heaven that we carry—the Holy Spirit—that true revival will break out in businesses, cities, and homes worldwide!

My wife and I have seen this firsthand in so many different venues. God's given me prophetic dreams for people at work that opened up prayer opportunities during the middle of the work day; I've seen people get healed and accept Jesus as their Savior at the shopping mall and on the beach. God sent my wife and I to Tucson after living out of state for half a year to rent and set up a large tent for healing revival meetings. God showed up so powerfully in those meetings with signs and wonders in nature, people accepting the Lord for the first time, and many healings and miracles. We had over 50 nights of revival meetings (not all in succession) under the tent, open air, and even in hotel conference rooms. It gives me fond memories to look back at that season of our lives, but I know that was just the first fruits, just the beginning of what I believe in my heart God wants to do in our city, in America, and beyond! We're believing for stadiums! Even now, as we are "laying low" during this season, almost every time people come over to our home it turns into some kind of prayer-revival meeting! We just can't help it, God is so good!

JESUS NOW

If you want to truly embrace this move of God, your hope should not be in Jesus' return, but in experiencing Jesus now. Your hope should not be in some cataclysmic end-time event culminating or preceded by the rapture; it should be in the desire to see the next generation of believers carry on with a passion for revival and revelation and experience of God's Kingdom on earth greater than you ever had!

"A good man leaves an inheritance for his children's children..." (Prov. 13:22). We need to be good men and women who have our hearts and sights set on leaving a spiritual legacy for future generations that far supersedes our experiences. We must propel forward the generation that will supplant us by letting the ceilings of our revelations and experiences be their floor.

What good is revival if it isn't passed on and spread? If we want to see revival happen in this nation, we must have a dedication to continue to spread the fire until it catches. God doesn't want revival just so you can have some giant spiritual portal that sucks in tons of people to one geographic location. He wants revival to spark a holy fire in you so that you can go out and carry His Kingdom refreshments to all who hunger and thirst—so you can come alive and carry His revival wherever He sends you!

In the great Welsh revival of the early 1900s, many young people touched by the revival went out and started their own "missions." Missions were similar to churches, but not so religious in nature and more outreach focused. They began to pop up everywhere, especially in the most destitute areas with the hardest to reach people.[5] This is just like God's heart, and it is a great barometer for whether a revival outpouring is real. If people carry the revival with them to their families and workplaces and it lights in them a divine spark to want to see the world introduced to our awesome God and Savior, then this is truly a move of God.

For a year and a half I would declare on my Revival radio program in Tucson that God said revival is here. I made prophetic declarations, as the Lord led, and spoke life over the city. Almost immediately after the program ended, I started to see the fruit of what God had me do in that season and it continues to increase to this day. At multiple churches throughout the city, we are seeing young adults and older adults, alike, living out their faith like never before. Almost every day I hear of a new story of young people praying for other young people to be healed at their high schools, serious cases of sickness and disease being healed during "Healing Rooms" meetings at various churches, more unity in churches throughout the city, and more pockets of believers from around the city getting together through combined prayer and worship meetings. Such things were almost nowhere to be found five years or so earlier. I am but one voice of many, but we are starting to see the roots of true revival sparking the hearts of God's saints throughout the entire Southwest region causing a fire that continues to grow.

> A move of God is really a move of His people being led by His Spirit.

A move of God is really a move of His people being led by His Spirit. God imparts gifts, empowered by the Spirit, and powered by prayer so that you can bring revival to the world around you! *Let the reality of God's Heaven on earth be your goal.*

GETTING OVER OURSELVES AND MORE INTO JESUS

Once we taste of something so wonderful and great—like Ravenhill had and many of you have—our lives become dedicated to seeing others introduced to this same experience. It is the experience of knowing our Lord Jesus, *really* knowing Him. It is knowing Him so much that everyday we wake up and think about how little we know Him and can't wait to spend fresh time with Him to get to know Him more! I know that doesn't make sense, but being in love doesn't often make sense. Thank God that His mercies are new every morning (see Lam. 3:22-23).

God wants us to quit searching for some unattainable ideal or some experience that was only possible in the days of old; instead, He wants us to know that we *are* revival. *Today. Now.* You, too, can embrace every spiritual aspect of this truth if only you will fully surrender to God's will. It doesn't matter what you've done or who you are. This gift, like the gift of the Holy Spirit on the day of Pentecost, is for all (see Acts 2:39).

QUESTIONS

1. Do you consider yourself a revivalist? Why or why not?

_____

_____

_____

_____

_____

_____

_____

2. Have you been guilty of any false theology that may not allow you to see the revival that God wants to bring to your life and to this nation?

_____

_____

_____

_____

_____

_____

3. What can you do now to experience Jesus more?

_____

_____

_____

_____

_____

_____

_____

_____

PRAYER (YOU TO GOD)

God, thank You for who You are and for wanting to equip me to empower future generations. Help me to understand Your ways and to get to know Jesus afresh every morning. You are my one desire. The one thing I live for is pleasing You. You are holy and awesome. Amen.

PRAYER (ME TO GOD, OVER YOU)

God, impart a fresh hunger for revival in this precious saint reading this book. Bless and fill this saint to overflowing. Break off any end-time apathy (Heaven's waiting room mentality), and release this warrior to the world to be a burning one for You, no matter how young or young-at-heart they are. Impart to Your child a deep revelation that You are with us always, no matter where we go, and that Your servant can release Heaven anywhere through Your prayers and our obedience. For Your glory, and in Jesus' name, amen.

Endnotes

1. See Leonard Ravenhill, *Why Revival Tarries* (Minneapolis, MN: Bethany Press International, 1959).
2. To search through some of Ravenhill's interviews and teachings, go to http://sermonindex.net.
3. Steven R. Pointer, "American Postmillennialism: Seeing the Glory," *Christian History* 61 (January 1999), http://www.christianitytoday.com/ch/1999/issue61/61h028.html (accessed July 17, 2010).

4. Gary B. McGee, "From Azusa Street to the Ends of the Earth" *Christian History* (April 1, 2006), http://www.christianitytoday.com/ch/2006/issue90/2.46.html.

5. Norman Grubb, *Rees Howells: Intercessor* (Fort Washington, PA: CLC Publications, 1997).

To express it simply, the Kingdom is where the King is. So, early in the gospels, the news is announced: *"The kingdom of God is near you"* (Luke 10:9). The Kingdom was near because the King was near. And yet, though near, the Kingdom was not a locality, not a province to be entered. —JAMES LONG

The Kingdom is to be in the midst of your enemies. And he who will not suffer this does not want to be of the Kingdom of Christ; he wants to be among friends, to sit among roses and lilies, not with the bad people but the devout people. O you blasphemers and betrayers of Christ! If Christ had done what you are doing who would ever have been spared? —MARTIN LUTHER

Give me one hundred preachers who fear nothing but sin and desire nothing but God, and I care not a straw whether they be clergymen or laymen, such alone will shake the gates of Hell and set up the kingdom of Heaven upon Earth. —JOHN WESLEY[1]

Chapter 5

KINGDOM 101

*This **gospel of the kingdom** shall be preached
in the whole world as a testimony to all the nations* (Matthew 24:14 NASB).

*Repent therefore and be converted, that your sins may
be blotted out, so that times of refreshing may come
from the presence of the Lord* (Acts 3:19 NKJV).

*Our hunger for revival is really just a strong desire
to see God's Kingdom manifest on earth.*

Revival is just a word. It's been overused, misused, exaggerated, and
abused. It's been used to describe the annual week where the guest
preacher comes to speak at our church or used to describe anytime
supernatural things begin to manifest in any religious meeting.

The American Heritage Dictionary defines *revival* in this
context as:

1. A time of reawakened interest in religion.

2. A meeting or series of meetings for the purpose of re-
   awakening religious faith, often characterized by im-
   passioned preaching and public testimony.[2]

Today, revival may include preaching and testimonies, but it is a lot more than just that. To me *true* revival really represents God's Kingdom awareness and Kingdom manifestations on earth at anytime, not just in an organized meeting.

> Revival might include preaching and testimonies, but is a lot more than just that!

In the Gospels, Jesus said the Kingdom was *near, upon,* or *within.* Both John the Baptist and Jesus preached to the people about the nearness of God's Kingdom:

In those days John the Baptist came, preaching in the Desert of Judea and saying, "Repent, for the kingdom of heaven is near." (Matthew 3:1-2).

After Jesus' baptism He also went out preaching the same message

From that time on Jesus began to preach, "Repent, for the kingdom of heaven has come near" (Matthew 4:17).

The good news for the Jews was that this spiritual Kingdom was at hand; their Messiah had finally come to establish His Kingdom! This is good news for all of us!

Later in the Gospel of Luke, Jesus says the following,

But if I cast out demons by the finger of God, surely the kingdom of God has come upon you (Luke 11:20 NKJV).

Jesus' ministry before the cross was to administer His Kingdom on the earth to destroy the works of satan (Acts 10:38). When He cast out a demon, He proved that the time of His Kingdom on earth had come. The Kingdom came *upon* the people because they were now held accountable to receive the fact that their Savior and His Kingdom had come.

The final pivotal point about the Kingdom that we all must understand is that this Kingdom lies *within* us who believe.

Once, on being asked by the Pharisees when the kingdom of God would come, Jesus replied, ""The coming of the kingdom

*of God is not something that can be observed, nor will people say, 'Here it is,' or 'There it is,' because the kingdom of God is **in your midst**"* (Luke 17:20-21).

If they believed in Jesus, the Kingdom of God could be established *within* and rivers of living water would flow out of their hearts (see John 7:38). If you do not believe in Jesus, the Kingdom it is not within you; it is only around you through others who already believe in Jesus. We will continue to discuss this critical point throughout the book and in subsequent paragraphs below to help bring some understanding on the matter. First, let's see what Jesus taught and lived.

GOSPEL OF THE KINGDOM

The good news isn't simply that Jesus saves us so we can avoid hell. That's undoubtedly good, but that shouldn't compel me to accept Him as Lord. *If I accept Jesus as Lord based on the Gospel of salvation only, it is a Gospel of humanism because I'm accepting His sacrifice just to save my butt from the flames!* It has become about what's in it for me. The Gospel we typically preach is the beginning, but it's incomplete. Jesus made the way. He opened the door. The full Gospel isn't just to talk about that door, but to explain what's behind the door. That's truly good news! What's behind the door is God's Kingdom.

> The full Gospel isn't just to talk about that door, but to explain what's behind the door.

Have you ever wondered about the fact that Jesus never preached the Gospel as we know it today? It's true; look it up. Our Gospel message today is certainly good news—that Jesus died for our sins and that today is the day of salvation if we receive His atoning work in faith. But that was not the Gospel that Jesus declared for His disciples to preach. The Gospel of Jesus *was the Gospel of the Kingdom.* The first thing Jesus proclaimed when He began His ministry was that people should repent because the Kingdom of God was near! *"From that time on Jesus began to preach, 'Repent, for the kingdom of heaven has come near'"* (Matt. 4:17).

What did He mean by that? Why repent? Was the Gospel of the Kingdom a foreign topic back then, or did the people know exactly what He was talking about? I would guess that few really understood all of what Jesus talked about and proclaimed. However, that is the majority of the reason why John the Baptist preceded the ministry of Jesus; his message was also about the Kingdom. He readied the people. He helped make a way for our Lord:

> *During the high-priesthood of Annas and Caiaphas, the word of God came to John son of Zechariah in the wildreness. He went into all the country around the Jordan, preaching a baptism of repentance for the forgiveness of sins. As is written in the book of the words of Isaiah the prophet: "A voice of one calling in the desert, 'Prepare the way for the Lord, make straight paths for Him'"* (Luke 3:2-4).

People had to turn from religious thinking about who God was and who the Messiah would be and embrace the present reality of the person of Jesus and the Kingdom of God. The two are inseparable.

What, then, is the message of the Kingdom? It's really quite simple. Where God's will is happening, His heavenly rule enters the picture that supersedes our present natural reality. The rule of this higher governmental authority of Heaven can now be observable on earth. This is the Kingdom of faith, hope, and love. This is the government of God's will, empowered by the love of Jesus, enforced by the saints on earth. It is freedom in the Holy Spirit; freedom from death, disease, sickness, or heartache. It's how things are in Heaven being lived out on earth through the Ambassadors of God's Kingdom, us (see 2 Cor. 5:20).

> What we call revival is what Jesus calls God's will.

Kingdom (King-dom) means, "King's Domain" and "King's Dominion." Jesus prayed, *"Thy kingdom come, Thy will be done on earth as it is in heaven"* (Matt. 6:10 KJV). What we call revival is what Jesus calls God's will.

Jesus prayed that God's Kingdom would manifest on earth as it is in Heaven. Jesus is the King of God's Kingdom. The new reality is that wherever He is, this truth can be observed. This includes wherever His Spirit is. Thus, the ministry of Jesus was to usher in God's Kingdom. He didn't have to do strive to make this happen; it simply *was* because He *is*. Furthermore, the power of the Kingdom, the Holy Spirit, was living inside of Him, providing Him with the supernatural spark and insight from God's throne. *This same Spirit that raised Christ from the dead now lives in us* (see Rom. 8:11) *and now assists us to also usher in God's spiritual Kingdom on earth!*

REPENT

You purge all sin from your life and release it to God by confessing it and changing your actions to not go back to it (see 1 John 1:9).

A revivalist is someone who has repented and lives in a state of continuous repentance. To repent you must simply love God more than your sins and give them all to Him, no matter how large or small, shameful or silly.

> To repent you must simply love God more than your sins and give them all to Him.

If you cover up sin, it cannot receive the blood of Jesus. It is the reverse of repentance; it is retention! Do not let any stone of sin be left unturned in your heart, and do not hold on to any sin, no matter how familiar or petty you think it is. Open your heart to God, ask Him to show you your sins, and give every bad thing you've ever done to Him so that He can take it away and cleanse you with the powerful blood of Jesus. The message of repentance that Jesus preached is much the same message of revival that we preach today. Our understanding of the Kingdom is essential to us preaching the full Gospel of Jesus Christ and the Gospel that He, Himself, preached.

INTERNAL LEAVEN OF THE KINGDOM

Curiously, Jesus describes the Kingdom with an adjective of a baking ingredient. Even more curious than that, I believe God is revealing that this is one of the keys to spreading this revival move around the nations!

> *And again He said, "To what shall I liken the kingdom of God? It is like leaven, which a woman took and hid in three measures of meal till it was all leavened"* (Luke 13:20-21 NKJV).

Leaven is technically defined as "a substance, as yeast or baking powder, that causes fermentation and expansion of dough or batter; an element that produces an altering or transforming influence; to add leaven to (dough or batter) and cause to rise; to permeate with an altering or transforming element."[4]

Leaven causes fermentation. *Fermentation is defined* as the following: "the act or process of fermenting; agitation; excitement."[5]

In summary, *leaven is an altering and transforming expansion caused by an agitating and exciting influence.* How true is this of the Kingdom! The Kingdom causes an agitation of our flesh and is an exciting influence in our lives. That's why being a Kingdom person, being a revivalist, is never boring! True Christianity is the most exciting experience in the world! However, we must be aware that the devil tries to counterfeit everything good from God. Jesus warned His disciples to guard themselves from the leaven of the Pharisees (religious leaders), which can be equally zealous against the true things of the Kingdom (see Matt. 16:6).

> True Christianity is the most exciting experience in the world!

God wants to reach the lost all over this world with the message of what was accomplished through Jesus—which is available to us today. This includes first salvation from our sins, so we can spend eternity with Him, and second the ability to live out heavenly realities on earth.

One frustrating aspect to this can be that in so many parts of the Western world people's hearts are very hard, and it's not so easy to spread the message of the Gospel all the time. However, I believe that God is releasing a harvest strategy based on leaven! What He has spoken to my heart is that as we live life on purpose each day, whether at work, home, church, or the health club, we simply must continue to talk about the great things that God is doing in our lives. As we do, it releases a little bit of leaven into the soft parts of the hearts of our listeners! We don't have to see every single person around us give their lives to the Lord every day. However, we can release God's Kingdom leaven and let that influence work inside of them to grow and expand until one day they will not be able to resist God's loving heart's pull of grace, and finally they will repent and surrender their lives to Him! Share your heart for God, share the testimonies of the great things He has done in your life, and let His Kingdom influence work in the hearts of those with a listening ear.

Before I began formally preaching, I would just share testimonies of what God is doing and has done in my life. I've done this at an outdoor plaza in downtown Nogales, Mexico, with a Spanish interpreter, and I have also shared my testimony with thousands of high school students at assemblies that promoted abstinence before marriage and making positive choices in life. The great thing about your testimony is, nobody can argue against it. They can accuse you of lying, I suppose, but a testimony is fact, history, truth, it cannot be denied. Your testimony will always give God the glory if you share with the purpose of pointing to what Jesus has done for you, not anything you could have accomplished yourself, apart from His wonderful grace.

As an additional strategy, God has specifically, prophetically revealed to me that He is bringing the revival in the classes before the revival of the masses. I believe there is going to be a great wave of teaching across the Body of Christ, as which has begun already through expressions of revival, like that from Bethel Church in Redding, California, that will help prepare God's people to receive and walk in revival for themselves. Sometimes God has to rewire His Church before He can revive us. If we have any theology, unbelief, or naivety that is hindering our minds from comprehending what God is doing and what He wants to do, those mindsets need to be removed and reformed before we can be restored and revived.

As we hear and embrace Kingdom revelation, we can receive the fruit of it for ourselves. That's why people can't receive salvation of their souls until they *hear* that Jesus died for their sins and that they can spend eternal life with Him. Likewise people don't receive healing for their bodies until they *hear* that Jesus was beaten and killed to pay the price for their sicknesses, diseases, and pain (see Isa. 53:5). Once any revelation of the Kingdom is received in our hearts with faith, we can embrace the promise! The same goes for any promise in God's Word. This is even more reason why we should read and receive the Word of the Lord with faith, knowing that it is a living and active influence in our present lives, not just a historical narrative. The best description of God's Word as such is found in Hebrews:

> The more His Kingdom expands inside us, the more we will see His Kingdom expand around us.

> *For the word of God is alive and active. Sharper than any double-edged sword, it penetrates even to dividing soul and spirit, joints and marrow; it judges the thoughts and attitudes of the heart. Nothing in all creation is hidden from God's sight. Everything is uncovered and laid bare before the eyes of Him to whom we must give account* (Hebrews 4:12-13).

The Word will always have the power to pierce hearts, transform lives, and teach us God's Kingdom will!

KINGDOM EXPANSION

Where there is Kingdom leaven, the Kingdom is expanding. This expansion first is in our hearts and minds. Once we open our hearts and minds to receive more Kingdom, the Kingdom influence in our lives will expand outward as well. The more His Kingdom expands inside us, the more we will see His Kingdom expand around us. The more we Christians understand this, the more we can truly influence and change the world! Evil and radical, violent faiths around the world are always growing.

The Kingdom of God also grows. I'm not of the assumption that the Kingdom of God will overtake all until there's some sort of Christian-only, Christian-ruled utopian world. What I am implying, however, is that the internal leaven of God's Kingdom can expand your faith to continue to believe for more. Through this internal expansion, God's Kingdom expands outwardly as well, not just through church growth or mass evangelistic efforts.

There will always be Christian people in this nation with Christian ideals, but we must remember that there is a supernatural, spiritual Kingdom of God that supersedes all natural law and authority. It is from this realm that we can make a difference and have every right to!

The leaven of God's Kingdom releases into the hearts of people so it can grow and expand their lives into greater revelation of Jesus and all things of His spiritual Kingdom—divine health, peace, righteousness, justice, God's presence, and every other heavenly reality. This has little to do with the physical or numerical spread of more Christians; it has everything to do with Christians receiving more of God.

> The more we release the Kingdom through our words and actions the easier it will be to preach the Gospel and the more irresistible God will appear.

Naturally, the more we release the Kingdom through our words and actions the easier it will be to preach the Gospel and the more irresistible God will appear.

Because of this, we will likely see many new people becoming Christians as we live our lives as Kingdom men and women of God.

KINGDOM PEOPLE

Whether there are 20 Christians in the land or 200 million, the positive impact of their lives is determined by their revelation of the Kingdom.

The 20 with a full revelation of God's Kingdom authority can arguably make more of a difference in a nation through their prayers and influence (not natural influence, but spiritual) than 200 million who do not carry a revelation of God's spiritual Kingdom. These 200 million will always be waiting for a born-again president to solve their problems rather than praying and ushering in the answers to those problems regardless of their natural circumstances or positions!

It's been said that the Queen of England feared the prayers of John Knox, the great Scottish Reformer, more than anything else.[6] What modern-day Jezebel fears your prayers?! Is hell afraid that you're alive?

Revival is an internal expansion of the revelation of God's Kingdom.

The more you let God rewire your mind to truly believe this and receive the Kingdom of Heaven by your faith in Christ, the more you can experience this within you and throughout your daily life. Let God change any restrictive thinking so that you can know and walk in God's perfect will for your life.

> *Don't copy the behavior and customs of this world, but let God transform you into a new person by changing the way you think.* ***Then you will learn to know God's will for you****, which is good and pleasing and perfect* (Romans 12:2 NLT).

QUESTIONS

1. Did this chapter reveal to you any new revelation regarding God's Kingdom and revival? If so, what? Let it sink in, search out these teachings in prayer and in the Word, and let God confirm in your Spirit that you are on the right track to becoming revival.

_____

_____

_____

_____

_____

2. Are you receiving and acting on revelation from Heaven? What can you do to understand more about God's Kingdom?

_____

_____

_____

_____

_____

3. How can you activate the Kingdom so that it shows up in and through your life?

_____

_____

_____

_____

_____

_____

PRAYER (YOU TO GOD)

God, thank You for changing me, shaping me, and helping me become a Kingdom-Christian. Let Your Spirit lead me more into your truths about Your Kingdom. I repent of any sin or anything else that would hold me back from Your best. Thank You for Your grace on my life.

PRAYER (ME TO GOD, FOR YOU)

God bless this Kingdom-warrior in Jesus' name! Touch this warrior with Your power and rip open his or her mind to receive more of Your Kingdom revelation. God change the world through this person's life. Let Your servant be a carrier of Your glory—one who prays with Your perspective and walks in the realities of Your Kingdom for the remaining time on earth. Thank You, Father.

Endnotes

1.   James Long, quoted at http://www.pietyhilldesign.com/gcq/quotepages/godskingdom.html. Martin Luther, quoted at http://www.pietyhilldesign.com/gcq/quotepages/sinners.html. John Wesley, quoted at http://www.pietyhilldesign.com/gcq/quotepages/preaching.html.

2.   *The American Heritage® Dictionary of the English Language,* Fourth Edition copyright ©2000 by Houghton Mifflin Company. Updated in 2009. Published by Houghton Mifflin Company. (n.d.) www.thefreedictionary.com, last accessed, September 8, 2010. s.v. revival.

3.   *The American Heritage® Dictionary of the English Language*, 4th edition Copyright © 2010 by Houghton Mifflin Harcourt Publishing Company. Published by Houghton Mifflin Harcourt Publishing Company. All rights

reserved. Accessed via www.yourdictionary.com, September 8, 2010. s.v. repent, verb, second definition.

4. *American Psychological Association (APA) Dictionary.com, Unabridged.* Retrieved September 08, 2010, from Dictionary.com website: http:// dictionary.reference.com/browse/leaven leaven. (n.d.). s.v. leaven.

5. *Ibid.,* s.v. fermentation.

6. Roberts Liardon, *God's Generals II: The Roaring Reformers* (Pittsburgh, PA: Whitaker House, 2003).

The Next Great Awakening

I see you in the valley
Transferring death for life
I see an army coming
They all bear your light
I am not bound to reason
I live in violent love
This world can not define me
My heart's set above
For me to live it Christ
For me to die is gain
I am not shrinking back
I'll never be the same
Four walls can not contain me
I know I've been possessed
I know that God is love
And there's no failing love
So I am fearless
Come, love is overtaking me now...[1]

Chapter 6

Revival Is a Gift; His Name Is Jesus

...You who make mention of the LORD, do
not keep silent (Isaiah 62:6 NKJV).

And the church is His body; it is made full and
complete by Christ, who fills all things every-
where with Himself (Ephesians 1:23 NLT).

We're required to understand the teachings of Jesus before
we can learn about the mysteries of the Kingdom.

On a tiring daytime commute across country, Jesus prophetically took a glorious detour through Samaria. Normally this was a no-no for Jews—comingling with the Samaritans (mixed-breed descendants of Jewish ancestors)—but Jesus once again followed His heart and the leading of the Spirit, not some limiting tradition. God had a divine appointment for Him.

The story of the woman at the well is profound in its many truths. Jesus used prophetic evangelism (I'll explain what this is later in the book) to show her and her whole community that He is the Christ, the first time He openly revealed His identity in public! He taught them and showed them many things about Himself, but one of the greatest statements He made was one of the first things He told the woman after He asked her for a drink.

> *...She said to Jesus, "You are a Jew, and I am a Samaritan woman. Why are You asking me for a drink?"...Jesus replied, "If you only knew the gift God has for you and who you are speaking to, you would ask Me, and I would give you living water"* (John 4:9-10 NLT).

This may be one of the most touching and powerful statements in His entire ministry, given the circumstances. He described this living water as water that, when you drink it, would lead to eternal life. Like He had done so many times, He took something in the natural that could be understood by the common person and related a spiritual truth from this. The truth is related to eternal life that comes by faith in Jesus alone.

"If you only knew the gift...." Jesus was referring to Himself. He is this gift. Do you know that He is right here waiting for you to acknowledge Him? He is God's gift to you, predestined before the beginning of the world to be the sacrifice for all mankind (see Rev. 13:8). Furthermore, an atmosphere filled with the manifest presence of Jesus is what many equate with revival, which leads me to proclaim that Jesus is revival! Let's try to understand what this means and how to live in this reality.

OPEN YOUR PRESENT

Is there anything you can receive from God that wasn't already given before you were even a twinkle in your parents' eyes? Jesus is the Lamb who was slain before the foundations of the earth (see Rev. 13:8). God has known us for all eternity and has already provided for us with every good thing in advance, according to His will.

God knew us before we were born. *"Before I formed you in the womb I knew you, before you were born I set you apart; I appointed you as a prophet to the nations"* (Jer. 1:5). If God knew Jeremiah, He also knew you. God lives in eternal timelessness. He sees the beginning of things and the end of all at the same time! He sees absolute greatness and perfection in you because that's exactly what you will eventually be in Heaven—and it's what you can be now.

He also has predestined us according to His great plan:

> *In Him also we have obtained an inheritance, being predestined according to the purpose of Him who works all things according to the counsel of His will* (Ephesians 1:11 NKJV).

As I was praying deeply for a certain gift of the Spirit, a gift from Heaven that I desperately wanted to attain or at least learn how to move in, God showed me a vision. It was a Christmas tree with lots of gifts under the tree, some of them unopened. I believe that God got so frustrated with my request that He showed me in the dream that He had already given me the gift that I was praying about. The silly thing was that I was refusing to grab and open some of the gifts because I was acting unworthy. I was refusing and acting like the gift wasn't mine or like that certain gift was for someone else. However, it clearly had my name written right on it! God was apparently not too happy with my prideful humility. I woke up with the sick feeling that I had been praying for something that God had already given me and I just needed to take these steps:

1. Receive it.

2. Open it up.

3. Activate it.

4. Learn how to use it.

When we pray for specific spiritual gifts that we desire, we must realize that God gave us that desire. If it's a God desire, then it is meant to be. We must realize that if it is meant to be and it is from God, then our timeless God has already given it to us. The problem is not on His end; it's on ours. We must simply receive it in faith and make sure to thank Him for it. And we must ask His Holy Spirit to show

us how to use it in such a way that we do not abuse it and that God
gets the glory from it.

Revival is also much like this. Revival, like salvation through Jesus,
is a gift because He *is* the gift! We don't earn either through experience
or education. We simply receive them in faith because of who Jesus is
and what He already did for us! When we acknowledge that Jesus is
alive, we can then begin to personally get to know Him. This is the
essence of our Christian faith. The more we ask to know Him, the
more real He becomes to us—so real that we can sense His very presence strongly with us wherever we go.

STEWARD THE GIFT

When we meet together to worship God and join in one accord in
our prayers and praises to the Lord, our goal should be to touch Heaven
so that Heaven touches us. In this environment, we
can start to sense and experience supernatural things
because of the portal from earth to Heaven that is
opened to receive more of the presence and person of
God. The thing about the gift of Jesus' manifest presence in revival is that it requires a certain amount of
responsibility and stewardship, like any special blessing.

> Revival, like
> salvation
> through
> Jesus, is a
> gift because
> He *is* the
> gift!

Revivalists have a burning hunger and passion to
experience God's presence. This burning passion is
what we call being "on fire for God." A revival meeting
is sure to have been instigated and facilitated by those burning with this
fire. If our personal revival fires are going to combine into one extremely
large bonfire—which is sure to gain some attention, good and bad—
it will require wisdom in knowing how to steward, lead, and maintain
that "fire." This is similar to God's mandate to His priests of the Old
Testament Jewish temple structure, who were commanded to keep the
fires on God's altar burning: *"The fire must be kept burning on the altar
continuously; it must not go out"* (Lev. 6:13).

As God's New Testament priests (see Rev. 1:6), *we must also keep
the fires of revival in our lives burning continuously.* The more we do

this as individuals, the more the fire will catch and we will see the community revival we are after. We will see a revival that shuts down bars, and nightclubs, a revival that transforms communities, saves whole families at a time, and truly brings blessing upon the land. It is a concentration of the consecrated ones. It also is Heaven's brightly lit-up billboard to the world. We must do our part to let our lights shine: *"Arise, shine, for your light has come, and the glory of the LORD rises upon you"* (Isa. 60:1).

In Tucson a few years ago, some women intercessors began to meet and pray on an empty land lot on a street called Miracle Mile. Miracle Mile has been known as a pretty bad area of town. It was known for rundown hotels, a strip club, and prostitution. This street wasn't always known for this. Its name actually came from the large miracle healing tent revival meetings that were held there by William Branham over 40 years earlier! This is a prime example of revival breaking out but subsequent generations of saints not "keeping the ground" of the Kingdom in the city; instead the enemy made what started as something great into something bad. However, God always raises up a standard when the enemy comes in!

These ladies prayed and fasted over that area and years later took me to the very spot where they setup a rock altar in that place, the very same place we were planning on setting up our own modern-era healing tent meeting. This is right near the corner of Flowing Wells and Miracle Mile, a prophetic intersection indeed! Anyhow, as surely an answer to prayer, a brand new large police station was recently built on Miracle Mile right next to that lot, and now the Gospel Rescue Mission has come in and purchased a dilapidated hotel to turn it into a women and children's center. God's peace and justice, His Kingdom, is manifesting itself in that area of the city. The prayers and prophecies of God's saints are helping take back what the enemy tried to steal!

As we shine, God's whole Church will be like the city on a hill that Jesus talked about: *"You are the light of the world. A city that is set on a hill cannot be hidden"* (Matt. 5:14 NKJV).

People will come to see God's Church shine brightly out of curiosity, but they will leave changed. People will come with doubts, daring God to win their hearts, and He will. There will be attacks from the world and attacks from church people alike. Revival will bring the sword, the sword dividing freedom from bondage, religion from Kingdom, grace from works, selfless love from selfish love, and on and on. It will even divide family. Jesus said:

> *Do you suppose that I came to give peace on earth? I tell you, not at all, but rather division. For from now on five in one house will be divided: three against two, and two against three. Father will be divided against son and son against father, mother against daughter and daughter against mother, mother-in-law against her daughter-in-law and daughter-in-law against her mother-in-law* (Luke 12:51-53 NKJV).

Jesus warned us ahead of time that the world will hate us because it hated Him (see John 15:18). When Heaven breaks in, all of the forces of hell will try to push it out. This is even more reason why we must daily pray for continued consecration and wisdom to steward such a move. In addition, a great harvest of souls will start to come in. Revivalists in the marketplace, on the streets, and at the pulpits will be plucking fruit left and right (winning souls). Where God is lifted up, He will draw all people unto Himself (see John 12:32). We then must disciple and baptize them (see Matt. 28:18-19).

Revival is not a gift that God doesn't want to give. Instead, it always occurs wherever the Holy Spirit is allowed to work, wherever Jesus is truly welcome. Jesus said that where two or three are gathered, He will be there (see Matt. 18:20).

The greater revival manifesting from our own lives and in our communities, the greater level of power and the greater level of responsibility that comes with it; revival is a gift that isn't free. A kid's science kit or remote control car at Christmas comes with directions. So do God's gifts. The directions are found in His Word. For greater gifts, such as cars, our parents would surely not give us the keys if we didn't first learn how to drive or had the desire to learn how to drive. *Gifts from God are conditional, based on our diligence to learn about them.* If you don't want to open them, then you don't have to. If you don't want revival in your own life or in your city, that's your choice. It does take quite a bit of responsibility. However, since *Jesus is revival,* you should consider what you are really saying to Him if you reject greater revelations of the His fullness of love.

KEEP THE GROUND

You must have a large shield of faith to block the constant fiery darts and a security and rootedness in your relationship with God that is unshakable. Revival will bring the storm. The devil certainly doesn't want to see Heaven invading earth with a fury. He hates to lose ground, which is even more reason why we should be taking it!

Jesus said to Peter, *"And I also say to you that you are Peter, and on this rock I will build My church, and the gates of Hades shall not prevail against it"* (Matt. 16:18 NKJV). The gates of hell shall not prevail against the Church! The Bible says *shall not,* not *should not.* This is not a half-hearted declaration; it is a full-blown fact stated by Jesus that we should take literally!

Revival is God's way of ambushing the enemy, vanquishing His foes, and releasing His people to a whole new level of Kingdom revelation. It is His way of sending forth promises and miracles that have been bound up in the heavens due to His people's lack of prayer. It is His way of bestowing upon His people spiritual riches that are our inheritance here on earth as well as in Heaven.

> Revival is God's way of ambushing the enemy, vanquishing His foes, and releasing His people to a whole new level of Kingdom revelation.

Revival refreshes our souls, but burdens our hearts to press in to Him in times when we would have been doing other things. It brings an awareness of Him, which generates the only reasonable response—bowing facedown in repentance, tears, and worship.

The greatest gift, salvation through Jesus Christ, is free. However, if we want to see Heaven break into earth through our lives, it will cost us everything. Salvation is just the first step to experiencing this mysterious and powerful person name Jesus. Revival is the Spirit-led journey of power, love, and grace, which are extensions of His character. To reject revival is to reject Jesus.

> The greatest gift, salvation through Jesus Christ, is free.

QUESTIONS

1. Are you willing to receive more of Jesus and more of the revival that comes from Him alone?

_____

_____

_____

_____

2. Are you willing to pay the price of discipleship and take up your cross daily (see Luke 9:23) for the sake of the One who died on a cross for you?

_____

_____

_____

_____

3. Are you in personal revival? What can you do in your daily life to experience this passion for God's presence at a greater level?

———————————————————————

———————————————————————

———————————————————————

———————————————————————

PRAYER (YOU TO GOD)

God help me receive this wonderful gift of Heaven (the presence of Jesus) ferociously invading every aspect of my life. Please give me the wisdom to steward Your move and the grace to not offend Your precious Holy Spirit. Please help me to get out of Your way, yet at the same time not let You go. You are the worthy awesome God of Abraham, Isaac, and Jacob and now of all who call out to You. Your wisdom is eternal and Your love is unsearchable.

PRAYER (ME TO GOD, FOR YOU)

Blessings to You, God, as we let You continue to shape our understanding and strengthen our character. Impart Your wisdom and passion to Your servant so that Your servant would not get in the way of revival, but be instead a "burning one" who helps usher it in! We praise You, in Jesus name. Amen.

Endnote

1.   Jake Hamilton, "The Next Great Awakening," *Marked by Heaven* (Jesus Culture Music, produced by Banning Liebscher, 2009).

DEEP IN LOVE WITH YOU

Sitting at Your feet is where I want to be
I'm home when I am here with You
Ruined by Your grace, enamored by Your gaze
I can't resist the tenderness in You

I'm deep in love with You, Abba Father
I'm deep in love with You, Lord
My heart, it beats for You, precious Jesus
I'm deep in love with You Lord

Humbled and amazed that You would call my name
I never have to search again
There's a deep desire that's burning like a fire
To know You as my closest friend

Lord, my redeemer, Your blood runs through my veins
My love for You is deeper than it was yesterday
I enter through the curtain, parted by Your grace
Oh, You're the lover of my soul[1]

Chapter 7

ATTITUDES OF REVIVAL

But we all, with unveiled face, beholding as in a mirror the glory of the Lord, are being transformed into the same image from glory to glory, just as by the Spirit of the Lord (2 Corinthians 3:18 NKJV).

Revival is God's people responding to the burning of His Spirit within.

There are attitudes, some subtle, some not so subtle, that positively and negatively affect how we perceive and experience the things of God. This chapter will try to highlight both.

Often in life, consciously or unconsciously, we believe the world revolves around us. This is very childish, but it can carry over into adulthood. The scenario plays out in almost every aspect of life, even in church. If the worship music isn't the way we like, we don't give God our all that service. If the pastor doesn't seem to have a teaching that rubs us the right way, we'll let people know about it. God forbid if somebody takes your chair you usually sit in! Don't they know that it is an unwritten rule to not take the chair you've been warming all these years?

On a grander scale, the Church in America has often become self-focused, putting most of its attention on the needs of the local fellowship instead of the much greater needs of our fellow brother and sister churches around the world who are suffering persecution and hardship. It's not wrong to focus on the needs of the local fellowship; however, when we become too focused on ourselves, it perpetuates selfishness.

> It's not wrong to focus on the needs of the local fellowship; however, when we become too focused on ourselves, it perpetuates selfishness.

Sometimes we're more worried about whether our shoes match our belts and whether our church smiles are nice and polished up for the casual "God bless yous" at service than we are about truly important things around our community and the world.

Immature Christians are naturally narcissistic. But it's something we must grow out of. Such attitudes are extremely detrimental to you if you want to walk in Kingdom living. Most of you reading this book want to live a life filled with heavenly love. *Let us continue to encourage one another to grow in maturity and godliness so we can truly answer the call of God's revival in this generation.*

THE GOSPEL OF SELF

It is no secret that Christians around the world have been decoupled, segregated, and separated by petty theological differences. Much of this comes from the endless interpreting of the Bible around our experiences, or lack thereof, instead of letting the Bible shape our experiences. A prime example of this is cessation theology—the belief among many Christians that the gifts of the Spirit, especially the gift of tongues, are not for today.

When we read the Bible, we clearly see that Jesus and the early believers all walked in the supernatural power of God. And the Bible gives us no reason to believe the same would not be true for us today. Not believing in the gifts and power of God for today makes no sense at all to a generation of people being raised up to see God's power manifest firsthand on a regular basis. Those who still have a problem with this should not take my word for it but take the Bible for what it says and believe it as truth. Just because someone has not seen a miracle does not mean that God can't or won't do it, especially if the Word of God says such things are possible, probable, and are demonstrated as a part of normal Christianity by the early Church in the Book of Acts. We must beware of forming and molding Gospel interpretations to support our own ideas; our focus needs to simply be on learning more about Jesus, knowing that other Christians may not quite have the same revelation of Jesus as we do. Vibrant, living faith constantly demonstrates new aspects of God's character.

Even Philip, a *nonapostle* and former *table-waiter turned evangelist* (that is, he was chosen to help serve food to the widows; see Acts 6:1-5; 21:8), moved in the supernatural power of the Gospel in signs, wonders, and miracles because of being filled with the Spirit (see Acts 8:6). Where is the Holy Spirit now? He resides in those who have received the message of Jesus in faith; thus, we can all see miracles like Jesus and His early followers did. Do we have any waiters out there who want to move in signs and miracles? What about teachers or doctors or techies?

> Selfish attitudes are the exact opposite of how we must usher in the Kingdom.

People with these sorts of unbiblical theologies, based primarily on themselves (their personal experience) rather than on the person of Jesus Christ, are teaching what they've been taught. They've never truly stepped out in faith to embrace such promises of Scripture because that would shatter their comfortable, religious worlds. We must beware of forming and molding Gospel interpretations to support our own ideas; our focus needs to be on learning more about Jesus!

The greatest hindrance to the Kingdom is us. Selfish attitudes are the exact opposite of how we must usher in the Kingdom. We have to put aside what we want the Bible to say and start reading it and taking it at its word. Much of the Bible is historical, and most prophecies have been fulfilled, yet God's heart toward His people remains the same. The ministry of Jesus remains the same. The proper model in which God builds His Church remains the same. The work of the Holy Spirit remains the same.

We need to be open to learning from the Bible as a living and active instruction manual that emphasizes the works of the Godhead that are alive and well today. These works require our responses in action.

THE KINGDOM IS ABOUT LOVE

The opposite of love is not hate; love and hate can be two sides to the same coin. I've heard passion described as half hate and half love. *Revivalists are almost always passionate people.* Revivalists hate sin and anything that displeases God or grieves the Spirit, but they love Jesus with all their hearts!

The opposite of love is selfishness. Selfishness is the opposite of selflessness, which is one of the very definitions of love in the Bible (see 1 Cor. 13:5). As Kingdom people, we must stop selfishly interpreting the Scriptures to fit our present natural condition and, instead, get focused on Heaven. The Bible says that our treasure is where our hearts are (see Matt. 6:21). If your heart is always thinking about the situations and circumstances of this world and how they relate to you, if in your heart you think of your own self preservation and daily benefits and advancement in this life above all else, if in your heart the things of this world drown out the voice of God and the perspectives of Heaven, *then* you will have a really hard time receiving God's Kingdom.

If we want to be Kingdom people with Kingdom attitudes, Heaven must be our priority. The things of the Spirit must outweigh the things of our natural world in our minds and hearts. We must be floored with the love of God—so much so that our hearts rest in heavenly places with Him. We will want to spend our time praying just to enter into that place of heavenly rest.

We will want to know Him so much more everyday that everything in our lives will revolve around that desire. We won't want television, not because we think we're missing out or because we're piously just not wanting to be like the "secular" family down the road, but rather because we know it distracts us from His voice. Our carnal desires for things even so primal as food and sex cannot compare to our heart's yearning for the next spiritual encounter with our God, Creator, Savior, and friend! *Our heart's cry of "Abba, Father," will immediately turn our childishness in the natural to a childlikeness in the Spirit.* According to *Merriam-Webster's Dictionary,* when an adult maintains juvenile characteristics, it is defined as *neoteny.*[2] We definitely need more "neoteny faith" in Christianity!

The Kingdom may not always look like typical expressions of revival. We need to understand that the Kingdom is still all about love at its core, not necessarily healings, signs, and wonders. My wife and I traveled to Lakeland, Florida, to take part in the revival meetings now referred to as the Lakeland Outpouring, on two separate occasions. One day that we were there, we somehow met an awesome man of God and his mother. We will call him Peter for the purposes of publishing privacy. Peter is in a wheelchair with a major condition that keeps him skin and bones (extremely thin) and not able to walk. He also has some kind of blood disease that wouldn't allow some of his open wounds to heal.

Like any good revivalist, I prayed heaven down on Peter. The power of God was all over him as he attended night after night of the revival meetings. The first night we met them, we walked them to get a cab to go back to the hotel. I lifted Peter and put him in the cab. The next night and subsequent nights we picked them up at their hotel and I would wheel Peter around and lift him in and out of the wheelchair to get in and out of the car. We prayed with he and his mother almost every night, and even covered their hotel expenses. Faith was there. Prayer was there. Was revival really there? They seemed pretty revived in their spirits to me. However, Peter was never miraculously healed. Some may call that a failure or even false revival. I hate the fact that

Peter is still in a wheelchair, that he wasn't miraculously healed. I hate wheelchairs altogether.

But I look back now and see that the demonstration of the love of God's Kingdom was present the entire time. This, God has shown me, is something far more important than our limited definitions of "revival." We are still friends with Peter and his mother to this day, even though they live in another country.

Did Jesus come to earth to demonstrate the authority of God to prove He was from God or to destroy the works of the enemy? Both are true, but when I read about His mission on earth and His job description found in Isaiah, Chapter 60, what stands out to me is *love*. Kingdom works should always be motivated by love and things may not always turn out the way we hope, but God can still be in it.

GO ALL IN

One important attitude of the revival lifestyle is being willing to give everything. If you have to pray every evening, cut out all worldliness, separate from ungodly relationships, worship God every day and night, and so forth—that's OK because you're willing to do whatever it takes! Worldwide revival and awakening will only come through an army of believers with this kind of commitment! It may not look like massive crusades and conversions, although we are still believing for such things. It may simply be a bunch of everyday Christians like you and me who look back at our lives years later and realize how many people we really helped to be saved, set free, filled with the Holy Spirit and loved. Just think, one life changed can change a family tree forever! It is well known that the Patriarch Jacob had 12 sons, but within 400 years, their family became millions of people strong! Don't underestimate your impact by thinking short term.

When your focus is 100 percent on Christ and the things of Heaven, then and only then will your carnality melt away long enough for you to embrace the *truths of the Kingdom*. Such truths are that where Jesus is there is peace, there is no suffering. In Heaven there is no sin, sickness, or fear of death. The sicknesses and diseases of the devil do not and cannot exist there. Sorrow and pain are gone. Servanthood and true selfless love for others abound. When our hearts embrace these spiritual truths, then who we are in the natural can become a flesh vessel used for God's good purposes for the glory of His Son.

The world does not revolve around us. Neither does the Bible. We must fix our eyes on things above, like David, like Jesus, like Paul:

> *If then you were raised with Christ, seek those things which are above, where Christ is, sitting at the right hand of God. Set your mind on things above, not on things on the earth. For you died, and your life is hidden with Christ in God. When Christ who is our life appears, then you also will appear with Him in glory* (Colossians 3:1-4 NKJV).

When we are so overwhelmed with the realities of God's heavenly Kingdom, we will be ready to carry the revelation of those realities to the world we live in. Before we go any further on this journey called revival, you must have your priorities straight. You need to be all in for Jesus! Can we make that commitment to each other together? If so, we can partner with God to see lives changed and nations transformed one person at a time!

YOUR HEART

A revivalist's number-one ministry is loving God. The Bible says that where our treasures are is where our hearts (our attention and affections) will be.

> *Do not lay up for yourselves treasures on earth, where moth and rust destroy and where thieves break in and steal; but lay up for yourselves treasures in heaven, where neither moth nor rust destroys and where thieves do not break in and steal. For where your treasure is, there your heart will be also* (Matthew 6:19-21 NKJV).

A revivalist's number-one ministry is loving God.

Revivalists make it their number one commitment to love God above all else. If He is your treasure all of your heart's affections are centered on Him. It's very easy to tell who loves God just by listening to what they talk about. The Bible says that out of the overflow of the heart the mouth speaks (see Luke 6:45). Eleanor Roosevelt said, *"Great minds talk about ideas, average minds talk about events, and small minds talk about people."*[3] Please don't be a small-minded Christian. Revivalists speak about the great things of God and God's Kingdom because they are consumed by them. Any talk that does not glorify God should be completely avoided.

> Revivalists speak about the great things of God and God's Kingdom because they are consumed by them.

In the business of life, it is apparent that we spend our greatest resources on things that are closest to our hearts. *Our greatest resources are our time, energy, and money. Where do you spend most of your time, energy, and money?* Do you live to give and love to give? Do you find yourself at prayer meetings whenever possible and in service to others whenever the Lord leads, or are you preoccupied and caught up with the intangibles or unimportant distractions? To see true revival break forth from our hearts, God must challenge us all to the greatest level of commitment that we can possibly offer Him.

QUESTIONS

1. Have you ever consciously or subconsciously allowed the Scripture to be interpreted through your beliefs rather than letting the Scripture shape the way you believe?

_____

_____

_____

_____

_____

_____

2. Do you treasure God more than anything? Did you know that if you don't you are breaking the main commandment in the whole Bible?

_____

_____

_____

_____

_____

_____

3. Are you one who cannot stop talking about God and things of the Spirit? If so, this is a great sign. I want you

to sit back and meditate on what you do or don't talk about throughout the day. Are you always talking about work, about money, or maybe even gossiping? A revivalist is not concerned with such things.

_____

_____

_____

_____

_____

_____

_____

_____

PRAYER (YOU TO GOD)

Lord help us shake off the influence of the world and repent of our lack of showing our love for You in our time, energy, thoughts, and worship. God, please help us to fulfill the number one commandment in the Bible. We want to love You more than anything. Help us to know that this is more important than any relationship we may have, any selfish desire, and even any ministry that You would have us do. Without loving You, we are lost. Without Your love, everything we do is vain and powerless anyway. Help us, oh God!

PRAYER (ME TO GOD, FOR YOU)

God, ruin this precious saint (in a good way) with the passions of Your heart.

Endnotes

1. Michael W. Smith, Debbie Smith, Christa Black, "Deep in Love With You," *A New Hallelujah* (Nashville, TN: Reunion Records, 2008), track 8.

2. Webster's New World College Dictionary Copyright © 2010 by Wiley Publishing, Inc., Cleveland, Ohio. http://www.yourdictionary.com/neoteny, s.v. neoteny. Used by arrangement with John Wiley & Sons, Inc.

3. Eleanor Roosevelt, quoted at http://www.dictionaryquotes.com/ authorquotations/672/Eleanor_Roosevelt.php.

THE MARTYR SONG

They overcame by the blood of the Lamb
And by the words of their testimony
They loved not their lives even unto death
They loved not their lives even unto death

Raise up an army of laid down lovers
Raise up an army of laid down lovers

If we die with Him, we will live with Him
If we move with Him, we will rule with Him
If we lay down with the Lamb, we'll
roar with the Lion of Judah
We'll roar with the Lion of Judah[1]

Chapter 8

VIRTUES OF A REVIVALIST

*You were bought at a price; do not become
slaves of men* (1 Corinthians 7:23).

A revivalist lives life for an audience of one.

Nothing can kill the work of God in and through someone more than a people-pleasing spirit. It is the attitude most opposite to a successful, Spirit-filled person. One of the greatest virtues of revivalists and revivalists-in-training is that they do not care what people think. They value God's Word and direction over peoples' opinions.

When someone was filled with the Spirit throughout the Bible, they did what God said. Period. They rebuked the religious and acted on strange requests of faith without one hindering thought of what others around them would think. We must do the same today to really live a remarkable life of supernatural God-pleasing.

One example is Stephen, who delivered a powerful speech right before he became our first ever Spirit-filled martyr. May his spirit live on as he is honored by our remembrance. Read his rebuke of the religious leaders of his time in Acts 7:

"You stiff-necked people! Your hearts and ears are still uncircumcised. You are just like your ancestors: You always resist the Holy Spirit! Was there ever a prophet your ancestors did not persecute? They even killed those who predicted the coming of the Righteous One. And now you have betrayed and murdered Him—you who have received the law that was given through angels but have not obeyed it." When the members of the Sanhedrin heard this, they were furious and gnashed their teeth at him. But Stephen, full of the Holy Spirit, looked up to heaven and saw the glory of God, and Jesus standing at the right hand of God. "Look!" he said, "I see heaven open and the Son of Man standing at the right hand of God!" At this they covered their ears and, yelling out at the top of their voices, they all rushed at him, dragged him out of the city and began to stone him... (Acts 7:51-58).*

God doesn't need you to have any special gift or talent. But He does need you to not care about what others think. It is extremely difficult for many people because this people-pleasing spirit has permeated our Western culture and even our churches, manifesting as image without substance, fake-it-till-you-make-it, and other such nonsense. *The way to battle this spirit is simply to continue to be filled with the Holy Spirit.*

> God's opinion of you makes peoples' opinions of you irrelevant.

God's opinion of you makes peoples' opinions of you irrelevant. God-pleasing people have a strong relationship with the Father. They know Him personally and value that relationship above all others. However, those who care what others think are, in a way, limited from God's best because they have put other relationships above their relationship with God. These people are motivated by fear of others and vanity. The fear of the Lord is far from them. These people are idolatrous.

A GOD-FEARING PERSON IS A DEAD PERSON

The fear of the Lord will cause you to be dead to flesh and dead to self. When revival starts breaking out in your life, when you start winning with the Spirit, flowing in the Spirit, leading people to the Kingdom, and gaining crowds around you (people like to watch things burn)—religious and ignorant people will be sure to try and pull you down. Your shield is faith in Christ (see Eph. 6:16); that faith in Him and the assurance of salvation by the seal of His Spirit will be a refuge in times of trial. When you abide in God, the whole world can be against you and it won't matter. David understood this when he wrote, *"You prepare a table before me in the presence of my enemies. You anoint my head with oil; my cup overflows"* (Ps. 23:5).

Jesus often warned His disciples of rejection and persecution. He also told them that to be a disciple they must daily take up their cross. *"Then He said to them all, 'If anyone desires to come after Me, let him deny himself, and take up his cross daily, and follow Me'"* (Luke 9:23 NKJV).

We must violently reject the ways of the world so that we may partner with the Holy Spirit to help save the world. We must get militant about our love for God, reject people-pleasing temptations and the praises of people, and get ready for people to hate us. We must be comfortable with that and be ready for verbal and even physical beat downs from ignorant and hate-filled unbelievers.

The fear of the Lord is the beginning of wisdom (see Prov. 1:7). Fear the Lord enough to not fear people. You cannot live for both people and God. Choose today who will be your Master—who will be the one who influences how you live your life. *Don't be sold out to what others think; be mastered only by what Jesus says so that you can truly live the dynamic, Spirit-filled, Spirit-led life of a world-changer!*

UNPOPULAR POPULARITY

Jesus never promised that we'd be popular. He gained favor with God and people in His teenage and young adult years (see Luke 2:52). But the Bible never says He had any favor with people after that. Once He was filled with the Spirit, He only gained favor with God. He was a divisive figure, and the more we truly live like Him, the more we will be, too. Our culture tries to popularize Jesus as "buddy Christ," but it is a ploy from the enemy to water down the true message of His life. Make no mistake; although He laid down His life on His own accord, He wasn't killed for no reason. The religious zealots burned with hate and resentment against Him. This is the antichrist spirit that John warned us about (see 1 John 2:22, 4:3).

Before you read any more of this book, dedicate to yourself that you will be an enemy of man-made, powerless religion and know that it will be an enemy of yours. You have to be comfortable with that.

Revivalists have shunned self-preservation and the world and have embraced a love for Christ so deep and so rooted in who He is that no storm in the world can shake them.

If you're willing to embrace the fight and embrace the cross, then these pages will give you the tools you need to succeed. They will propel you forward in your life of radical faith and give you a hunger for more of God's Word. The Bible says, *"Your word is a lamp to my feet and a light to my path"* (Ps. 119:105). You won't find a ten-step program to things of the Spirit or any one formula for anything. But the person of Christ will be revealed, and God's will for your life will be clearly shown through His Scripture and the countless testimonies of our Lord and His many apostles, prophets, and disciples, past and present.

DON'T BE AFRAID TO TAKE A STAND

If we don't stand for something, we'll fall for anything. Before we can live lifestyles of revival, we must stand for God's unaltered living and active Word, and we must stand up for the Holy Spirit. We must guard Him with everything in us, refusing to allow Him to be grieved by us or by the world around us. He is the key to spiritual Kingdom advancement, the manifest presence of God, and the working of faith to see miracles. He is our partner and friend. We are His armor bearers and must be willing to fight alongside Him to see spiritual victory in our lives and the lives of those around us.

The first three Gospels are called the synoptic Gospels because they share many of the same testimonies and parables. However, there is a story about Jesus calling one disciple, who we know as Matthew, that doesn't quite match up in the three Gospels. Look at how Luke and Mark wrote about this compared to what Matthew, himself, said about how he was called by Jesus.

> *After these things He went out and saw a tax collector named Levi, sitting at the tax office. And He said to him, "Follow Me"* (Luke 5:27 NKJV).

Who's Levi? I thought this story was about Matthew. I don't remember a disciple named Levi. But Mark also refers to Levi:

> *As He passed by, He saw Levi the son of Alphaeus sitting at the tax office. And He said to him, "Follow Me." So he arose and followed Him* (Mark 2:14 NKJV).

Matthew, by contrast, in his parallel recording of this event, obviously and vehemently referred to himself by what Jesus called him. Matthew was a revivalist who refused to be who others called him. He chose to only believe what Jesus said about him! When others continued to refer to him as Levi, he wasn't having it:

> *As Jesus passed on from there, He saw a man named Matthew sitting at the tax office. And He said to him, "Follow Me." So he arose and followed Him* (Matthew 9:9 NKJV).

Matthew was a revivalist who refused to be who others called him.

Jesus called Levi to a new life, and somewhere along the line, He gave him a new name. This happened with Jacob when God renamed him Israel; it happened when Jesus renamed Simon as Peter and changed Saul's name to Paul. It is something that was not unprecedented by any means.

The example that we can learn from Matthew, however, is that we should not and must not identify ourselves with our old lives. We are new creations in Christ Jesus (see 2 Cor. 5:17). Other disciples possibly remembered him as and continued to look at Matthew as a sinner and a greedy, scheming tax collector. Maybe he made some mistakes and still acted like his old man once in a while, which helped to feed his companions' mindsets. However, he just refused to be that old man. *He knew who he was because he knew who **He** was.* He heard Jesus call him Matthew and a sense of eternal destiny rose within his spirit; surely Jesus had spoken to Matthew as God had created him to be. Jesus always sees us through God's eyes and not our own.

> Jesus always sees us through God's eyes and not our own.

DON'T CONFORM TO THE OLD

Jesus doesn't think of us like we do or like the world does. *We must conform our thoughts to the thoughts God has for us and conform our words to the words God says about us.*

> *Do not conform to the pattern of this world, but be transformed by the renewing of your mind. Then you will be able to test and approve what God's will is—His good, pleasing and perfect will* (Romans 12:2).

Only when we renew our minds to be transformed by what Jesus says will we truly believe we are the great people whom God sees. We can then live out the reputation that God has given us without thinking and caring about what others think and who they (and we) previously identified ourselves as, and we can live according to God's perfect will for our lives.

When it comes to God's invitation to be used as vessels of honor for His greater glory, God is much like those advertisements to join the Marines. Like the Marines, He doesn't accept applications, only commitments.[2]

> He doesn't accept applications, only commitments.

If you're ready to make this commitment in your heart to not care what others think and to once and for all dedicate your life to truly being sold out for God's will, then keep reading. But be forewarned that God will hold you accountable to live according to the truths you learn.

REJECTION

Revivalists get a strange pleasure from being rejected by the world. Look at Peter and John when they got a major beat down for Christ— the first documented beating of those standing up for Christ after He rose to Heaven. They were excited! And why shouldn't they be? They had stood for their faith and for someone they loved. Both are very honorable and very satisfying.

> *...and when they had called for the apostles and beaten them, they commanded that they should not speak in the name of Jesus, and let them go. So they departed from the presence of the council, rejoicing that they were counted worthy to suffer shame for His name* (Acts 5:40-41 NKJV).

Revivalists rebuke religion. John the Baptist, Jesus, and Stephen provide a few examples. When we are filled with the Spirit, it's just part of the job description. This wasn't in their own power or out of their own frustration; it was *from God* and *for a purpose*. If we know anything about God it is that He doesn't like sharing His glory with another spirit (see Exod. 34:14). He's a jealous God and wants us to be so full of Him that we'll let the Holy Spirit speak or do anything through us that He needs to.

Revivalists aren't
afraid of speaking
a hard word, but
they are afraid
of not speaking
the truth.

Revivalists aren't afraid of speaking a hard word, but they are afraid of not speaking the truth. It is because the Spirit inside of us is the Spirit of truth. If we embrace Him, He will fill us with all the virtues we need to truly be great Christians.

QUESTIONS

1. How have you seen a spirit of religion rise up against you in the past? How does this usually manifest, and through whom?

_____

_____

_____

_____

_____

_____

_____

_____

2. Can you identify leaders, people, churches, or denominations around you who have false, limited religious mindsets that do not accept obvious truths of God's word, like the baptism of the Holy Spirit or the gifts of the Spirit? What can you do to help them see the truth of the present power of the living and active Word of God?

_____

_____

_____

_____

_____

_____

_____

_____

_____

_____

3. Have you ever been paralyzed by fear of people or struggled with a lack of understanding regarding who you are in Christ? What can you do to help avoid such things in the future?

_____

_____

_____

_____

_____

_____

_____

_____

PRAYER (YOU TO GOD)

God, protect me and keep me from evil distractions and discouragements based on false assumptions about You. Help me to release a spirit of freedom to the world around me, not a spirit of bondage to people or religious traditions. God, You know my journey and I give it to You, honoring and trusting Your opinion of me and Your perfect plan for my life. Amen.

PRAYER (ME TO GOD, FOR YOU)

God, I impart to this reader a grace and strength to have thick skin regarding the discouragement and attacks of the enemy. I break this warrior free, in the mighty name of Jesus, from any spirit of religion or fear of people that would muzzle the mouth to keep Your Spirit's words of power and freedom from going forth! God, please anoint this saint with the faith to be a modern-day martyr for Your glory. Amen.

Endnotes

1. Rick Pino, "The Martyr Song," *Songs for an End Time Army* (Cedar Hill, TX: Fire Rain Music, 2009), track 1.
2. Marine slogan from a recruitment video, available at http://www.recruitparents.com/bootcamp/recruiters.asp. Accessed September 20, 2010.

Why I Think We Need Revival, Part 1

- Traditions have taken the place of Spirit-led services.

- The Church looks more like the world than the world looks like the Church.

- In our lives, the sins of families, churches, and communities are often left unaddressed, and the work of satan is left unchallenged.

- I believe we should look more like the powerful Church of the Bible, not the powerless church of America.

- Our hearts are not broken for the lost like they should be.

- Ministry has become too much of a business rather than a service.

- The potential of most believers, even though they serve an all-powerful God, is rarely achieved.

- Commandments like healing the sick, casting out demons, and raising the dead have become exceptions rather than the rule.

- For the most part, the Church is not being raised up into all maturity in the fullness of Christ, but is increasingly dependent on others for spiritual growth.

- Broken marriages and fatherless homes are as commonplace in the Church as in the world.

- Religion often prevails over Spirit-filled, Spirit-led lives and churches.

Chapter 9

Just Believe

*It is impossible to please God with-
out faith...* (Hebrews 11:6 NLT).

There's only one guaranteed way to move Heaven—it's faith!

Hearing about or seeing something new tends to open up a realm of possibility that was never there before. It registers the memory of that thing in our souls and creates an invisible trigger of faith inside us that now believes in what we have just seen or heard.

Reading books can change our lives because they create windows of belief where we can imagine things we've never seen before and, thus, be able to achieve them for ourselves. It would be complete luck to hit a target that we can't see. The same is true of the spiritual and natural life; we cannot succeed without seeing the goals we want to hit. This includes everything from landing a job to seeing a specific prayer answered.

Belief is also known as faith. Faith is fully believing that something you are now hoping for can and will come to pass. Jesus said, *"Anything is possible if a person believes"* (Mark 9:23 NLT). This seems like an abstract motivational statement, but take a minute to think about how this works exactly.

SEEING AND HEARING

What creates belief? Hearing and seeing create belief. We believe that if we see something done, then we can do it too. Look at the young adults who perform ridiculously amazing and dangerous tricks one after another in the X Games competitions. They simply see someone else do it and then know they can emulate it. Then they try something crazy and pull it off—which leads others to see and believe they too can do it. When we see someone do something, it gives us permission to do it ourselves.

This is how I learned many things in life. I had to see people pay off debt before I really believed and achieved debt-free living myself. I had to see a peer of mine dunk a basketball before I believed I could do it as well and then did it. The same went for tricks off of a diving board, starting a business, praying for the sick, you name it. It's just how people learn.

Faith goes one step further. Faith believes even when things can't be seen in the natural realm. *The key to unlocking faith is the ability to see things in the spirit realm.* Dreams are the language of the Spirit. God also often speaks in visions, pictures, and what is known as *"dark sayings"* (Num. 12:8 NASB). They are visuals of a spiritual reality, and they enable our internal belief systems to lock onto that reality, which enables us to receive it for ourselves.

I'm not suggesting we become crazy New Age people who say we can visualize everything from riches to the man or woman of our dreams and it will just appear like magic. That's witchcraft. Such tricks just use mental manipulation, not true faith that comes from God.

Witchcraft and many other worldly perversions steal from spiritual truths that God intended for good. The spirit realm is a real as this natural realm. If our spiritual eyes are tuned to see into this realm, more spiritual things will be possible on earth.

Furthermore, what we hear can lead to our openness to belief. This is why the Gospel is preached, so that many can hear it and believe.

How, then, can they call on the one they have not believed in? And how can they believe in the one of whom they have not heard? And how can they hear without someone preaching to them? And how can they preach unless they are sent? As it is written; "How beautiful are the feet of those who bring good news!" But not all the Israelites accepted the good news. For Isaiah says, "Lord, who has believed our message?" Consequently, faith comes from hearing the message, and the message is heard through the word about Christ (Romans 10:14-17).

TESTIMONIES

When we hear the Gospel and believe it to be true, it's like opening up an airport for Jesus to land His plane of promise in our hearts. This is how testimonies work. Testimonies are an extremely powerful tool of the Church because they open our faith to receive more of what God will do if we would only believe! *Through testimonies we release verbally what is possible.* All those with ears to hear can receive this new reality of what is possible since it actually happened through the testimony. If they receive that openness to believe in their hearts for whatever it is that they just heard, then God can deposit that same promise in them as well!

> When we hear the Gospel and believe it to be true, it's like opening up an airport for Jesus to land His plane of promise in our hearts.

It's amazing how this works. Testimonies reveal possibilities that open up doors for God's people to receive the miracle for themselves—everything from freedom from drugs to divine healing of cancer. The testimonies of what Jesus has done show what is in His character and will to do now. This testimony of Jesus is the spirit of prophesy (see Rev. 19:10).

Testimonies are a great weapon against the enemy. The devil tries to contradict, counterfeit, and discredit the things the Lord has said through His Word, past and present. When we talk about the great things of God by giving testimonies of what He has done in our lives, it's a slap in the face of the devil, and it throws a wrench in his strategy.

> *And they overcame him by the blood of the Lamb and by the word of their testimony, and they did not love their lives to the death* (Revelation 12:11 NKJV).

The testimony is the lifeblood of revival. Revival in many ways is the human expression of a deeper longing to see God's Kingdom manifest on earth. When we as revivalists are in any situation, from corporate revival meetings to a family reunion with relatives, the testimony is always still our best weapon to spark an interest in others to believe in the greatness of our God. I like testimonies so much because, unlike doctrinal debates, they cannot be argued against.

When we as revivalists are in any situation… the testimony is always still our best weapon to spark an interest in others to believe in the greatness of our God.

Testimonies, like a good story with old friends of an event from many years ago, never grow old. For eternity, the stories of God's interventions with humankind will live on and grow into living, vibrant, active representations of who God is and what He can do. The word of our testimony, if truly a spiritual intervention from God, will become part of His eternal Word and character that never passes away.

Take some time to write down three amazing things that God has done for you. You can use these as weapons to flaunt God's goodness, mercy, and grace to the world around you and to the principalities and powers that continue to try and hinder God's Word from going forth.

If you're having problems thinking of something, thank God for the fact that you haven't had a cold in a year or that you finally graduated from college. Let His Spirit quicken to your heart some great things that God has done in your life that He wants to use as a testimony.

These are words that will lead others to believe. The Gospel is about what Jesus did for us that we can now receive if we will believe in Him. However, *people need to see that when we believe the power of the Gospel is actually at work in our lives.* That's where the testimony comes in. It drives home the point of the Gospel by proving Jesus' grace in our lives as something true and something to be received by all who believe.

GREAT FAITH

Jesus so often rebuked His disciples for a lack of faith. When I was meditating on whether or not it is my faith or God's faith that heals and allows for great miracles, God showed me that faith is much like lightning. *It's not just my faith or God's faith that's needed to perform miracles; it's both*! Lightning originates from electrical charges in the ground. The ground beneath the storm invites the lightning strike from the clouds above through an invisible positive and negative charge that is met with a powerful burst of electrical charged light from the clouds above![1] This is just like our faith. When our hearts are opened by hearing the Word, the electrical charge of faith begins. Our openness to His Word offers a landing spot for Heaven. Faith starts when our open hearts are willing to believe, and they are then filled with a holy, divine faith from God to make the manifestation of a miracle take place. This goes for the miracle of salvation as well as a miracle of healing. Our faith, or lack thereof, can hinder the work of God, but our faith (openness to His Word) is also what is needed for God to deposit *His* gift of faith into the situation.

The greatest faith believes so much in who Jesus is that it knows *without a shadow of a doubt* that whatever He says *is true and **will** happen.* This is what the Centurion did (see Matt. 8:10). He knew of Jesus, knew of His authority, and believed in Him. When Jesus said that his servant was healed, he just knew it was true. Jesus told him that He had not seen greater faith in all of Israel! What an example for us! If we believe in Jesus and what He says in His word or speaks to our souls, we will just know that anything He says **has** *to come to* *pass*. His Word includes the fact that Jesus healed any and all who were oppressed by the devil (see Acts 10:38). It also includes His promise that we will do even greater things than He did (see John 14:12). It includes any and all promises, past, present, and future. We must believe in Him and what He has said because our faith pulls promises into the present!

Once, when traveling to a Mexican beach town with some Christian friends, we rented a small fishing charter boat to take us fishing. This was the only boat that would agree to take us out because the waters were so choppy. Needless to say, we should have stayed on the shore! Four of us went and three, myself included, got extremely sick. I must have been turning green as I was fighting back vomiting with everything in me. Two of the girls on the boat with us were already losing it over the side of the boat. I distinctly remember this as being the sickest I have ever felt in my life.

In desperation I just prayed and prayed as I turned greener. Then something supernatural happened. I told myself that right now I am seated in heavenly places in Christ Jesus, quoting Ephesians 2:6. Something clicked at that moment in my faith, and in an instant I realized that my spirit was in heavenly places and all of my physical sickness left! I got so excited that I began jumping around the boat praising God! I can remember the horrified looks on the girls' faces as they were still in misery thinking I had totally lost my mind.

To this day, anytime I get sick, I try to kick that thing out of my body as quickly as possible. These may seem like silly stories of faith, but trusting God to heal me from seemingly small things like back pain or the flu has helped build my faith to trust Him to heal things in other people, like MS and cancer! In faith I once commanded a man to walk who was in a wheelchair and he got out of his wheelchair instantly! I wish I could say I always have this kind of faith. I really don't. But I know that Christ in me is *the hope of glory* (Col. 1:27)—and not only for me but for anyone who God puts in my path that needs His interventions of grace.

Start believing for the impossible! You must think big before you can do big. God says that He is willing to do infinitely more than we can ever ask or imagine (see Eph. 3:20). The question now is, are you willing to believe Him for the impossible and take Him at His Word when He answers?

QUESTIONS

1. Is there anything out there that is seemingly impossible that you would like to ask God for now? Write it down below. Write down multiple things. Be as specific as possible. Now in the section below, right next to that there is a line with a date for you to fill in when God achieves this thing for you. Believe it, see it, and know that if it is in accordance with His will, it will happen. Even visualize the date in the box on the right. Set goals for the date and pray to God that He meets that exact goal. You know why God loves to meet specific prayer? The more specific the prayer is, the more glory God can receive when it is answered. There will be no question that this is God!

I am asking God for...	Date

2. Have you ever been powerfully touched by God in a revival meeting, a camp meeting, or some other outpouring? Did you feel like God gave you a calling, a gift, a prophetic word for your life or a burden for ministry during this experience? What was it? Have you laid this down or any other gifts? Could God once again be encouraging you to pick this up? Write these things down here, also, and give them once again to the Lord.

_____

_____

_____

_____

_____

_____

_____

_____

_____

_____

PRAYER (YOU TO GOD)

God, I receive Your faith to believe that the impossible is possible in and through my life. Help me understand Your Word and Your ways in such a way that I can receive every single promise of the Word, from divine health to seeing the dead raised! Thank you for everything! You are awesome and holy. Amen.

PRAYER (ME TO GOD, FOR YOU)

Father, please open the spiritual eyes of this brother or sister to see Your supernatural realms, and open spiritual ears so that Your servant may hear and understand Your rhema (living and active) Word in his or her life. Impart a great faith to believe for things greater than any man or woman in history has ever believed for! May this great impartation of faith transform this reader into a world changer and history maker! In Your name we pray. Amen.

Endnote

1. How lightning works is documented at http://science.howstuffworks.com/lightning.htm. My quick definition is not entirely scientifically accurate, but is only a paraphrase.

Why I Think We Need Revival, Part 2

- Revival living is the only way we'll experience Jesus' promise of life and life more abundantly on this earth (see John 10:10).

- Many professing Christians have never experienced the presence of God for themselves.

- A disease in the Church that needs to be healed is narcissism.

- Many in the Church do not know how to hear God.

- Many in the Church do not know how to see God working in their lives.

- There is a great lack of character in many so-called spiritual leaders.

- There is a great lack of discernment in the Body of Christ.

- We need to fall more in love with Jesus and show true love for others.

- The "bless me" mentality has taken preeminence over passionate preaching and true repentance.

- Self-dependence and money often takes the place of God-dependence and faith.

- Many have become more watered-down than fire-filled!

- Christianity in America has become more about ease and blessing than about sacrifice and doing the work of ministry.

- Some in the Church have become more about politics than God's Kingdom.

- The world all around us is dying in their sin and going to hell, and we often show very little concern.

- We need a fiery passion in God's people and preachers!

- Our partnership with the Holy Spirit is often greatly lacking.

Chapter 10

OPEN HEAVEN

*Oh that You would rend the heavens! That You
would come down...* (Isaiah 64:1 NKJV).

You carry Heaven to the extent of your revelation.

That God would rend the Heavens and show Himself in person
was the prayer of the great prophet of God, Isaiah. That prayer was
answered in the person of Jesus. God came down in human form; the
Word was made flesh (see John 1:14). Jesus, who was and is and is to
come, physically manifested on earth as the Son of God and Son of
Man, setting aside His divinity so that He could resist temptation,
offer Himself to be slain to cleanse the world of our sins, and reverse
the curse of sin and death brought on by Adam (see Rom. 5).

When we worship God, we no longer need Him to "Come
down." Ten days after Jesus rose to sit at the right hand of God,
He delivered the wonderful promise of His Holy Spirit, who is constantly with us. He violently rent the heavens that day and sent a
force that shook Jerusalem and the world (see Acts 2). The power of
Pentecost is that God's Spirit is now here with us! *When we pray or
sing for God to come down, He's probably up in Heaven shaking His
head saying to Himself, "I **did**, and I'm there right now!"*

We sing popular worship songs in church like "Rain down." It's nice, but not entirely biblical or accurate. I understand the point of wanting God to shower us with His love and grace, but what we must understand is that His Kingdom and the well of His Spirit, the river of God, runs inside of us. The Bible says that *"...out of his heart will flow rivers of living water"* (see John 7:38 NKJV).

Revelation talks about the New Jerusalem (God's Church) and the river from His throne (see Rev. 22:1). The throne of God that is established in Heaven is the same throne of God that is established in our hearts. This river doesn't come from some heavenly place on high, but rather from within, because that's where the Kingdom is (see Luke 17:21). *When we feel God rain down His love and grace on us, it's really more like catching the drops from a geyser that is bursting forth from within us. This is magnified by those around us if we are praising and worshipping Him in a corporate setting.* When we worship Him in Spirit and in truth, this well of love flows out from our spirits and refreshes our souls and those near us who are also open to receive.

> When we worship Him in Spirit and in truth, this well of love flows out from our spirits and refreshes our souls and those near us...

In Christian circles we often talk about something known as an "open Heaven." Although this phraseology can represent a few different things, the term typically represents a free and open environment full of faith where the Spirit of the Lord is free to move and dwell. Let's now dig a little deeper in this concept.

AFFECT YOUR ENVIRONMENT

Certainly it is discernible when the spiritual atmosphere of a church is religious and there is a blockage between God's heavenly will and this earthly realm. Furthermore, when I drive through certain cities or come into different areas of my own city, I can discern the spiritual forces at work in that area. Some are ground forces, such as the spirits behind demoniacs, witchcraft, tarot card readers, New Age activity, and various forms of immorality. Others are what feel more like spiritual blockages in the heavens, often due to the stronghold in that area from certain evil principalities or powers. Oftentimes we target these areas as areas of prayer, especially regionally, so that God can move powerfully in that area. This is OK if we are directed by the Lord and have spiritual authority given by the Lord to do so. However, my focus is not usually on the spiritual atmosphere of a place; rather, it is *knowing* and *walking* in the spiritual authority as a believer that God has already given me.

I cannot control what the spiritual environment of a location is before I get there, but I can control the spiritual environment of a location after I get there. *Revivalists affect the environment around them so that God can infect the environment.*

These men and women of God do not have to be subject to the spirits in any city or region; they are subject to a higher authority. This doesn't mean that revivalists won't have to pray breakthrough in a place until a heavy burden lifts; it just means that they have the authority to do so and that just their presence can turn even the darkest environment into a portal of God's glory.

Whenever you minister, it is wise to pray beforehand that God would soften and open the hearts of the people to receive. When you sense that an environment is especially tough to minister in, consider it the greatest opportunity for God to show His glory! Don't ever be intimidated by a church that seems dry and religious. *It is the dry wood that lights on fire the quickest and is in the most need of spiritual rain!*

Jesus, Himself, couldn't control when people had a lack of faith that hindered His Kingdom from manifesting. One time He kicked people out of a house before He performed a miracle; the other time He just lamented about it later.

While Jesus was still speaking, some people came from the house of Jairus, the synagogue leader. "Your daughter is dead," they said. "Why bother the teacher anymore?" Overhearing what they said, Jesus told him, "Don't be afraid;

just believe." He did not let anyone follow Him except Peter, James and John the brother of James. When they came to the home of the synagogue ruler, Jesus saw a commotion, with people crying and wailing loudly. He went in and said to them, "Why all this commotion and wailing? The child is not dead but asleep." But they laughed at Him. **After He put them all out, He took the child's father and mother and the disciples who were with Him, and went in where the child was.** *He took her by the hand and said to her, "Talitha koum!" (which means, "Little girl, I say to you, get up!"). Immediately the girl stood up and walked around (she was twelve years old). At this they were completely astonished* (Mark 5:35-42).

Jesus lamented about the lack of faith of the people of Nazareth:

Now it came to pass, when Jesus had finished these parables, that He departed from there. When He had come to His own country, He taught them in their synagogue, so that they were astonished and said, "Where did this Man get this wisdom and these mighty works? Is this not the carpenter's son? Is not His mother called Mary? And His brothers James, Joses, Simon, and Judas? And His sisters, are they not all with us? Where then did this Man get all these things?" So they were offended at Him. But Jesus said to them, "A prophet is not without honor except in his own country and in his own house." Now He did not do many mighty works there because of their unbelief (Matthew 13:53-58 NKJV).

It says that He did not do many mighty works due to the people's lack of faith in Nazareth. This should catch our attention; we would be extremely blessed to just see *some* miracles in many of our Western churches!

Never once did Jesus or His apostles (as far as Scripture records) ever pray for a region or location. Jesus simply commanded His disciples to go and do the work of the Kingdom. This is important for us to understand because, as believers with God's authority, we have been given an open Heaven that never closes! It's called walking in the Spirit!

JACOB'S LADDER

Jesus said something extremely profound to the first disciple He called in the Book of John, Nathaniel. He told Him one of the most intriguing Scriptures in the New Testament.

> *When Jesus saw Nathanael approaching, He said of him, "Here truly is an Israelite in whom there is no deceit." "How do you know me?" Nathanael asked. Jesus answered, "I saw you while you were still under the fig tree before Philip called you." Then Nathanael declared, "Rabbi, you are the Son of God; you are the king of Israel." Jesus said, "You believe because I told you I saw you under the fig tree. You shall see greater things than that." He then added, "Very truly I tell you, you will see 'heaven open, and the angels of God ascending and descending on' the Son of Man"* (John 1:47-51).

Nathaniel's spiritual eyes would be open to see angels ascending and descending upon the Son of Man! Jesus was the walking, talking place where God was. He was the human fulfillment of Jacob's ladder.

> *Then he [Jacob] dreamed, and behold, a ladder was set up on the earth, and its top reached to heaven; and there the angels of God were ascending and descending on it* (Genesis 28:12 NKJV).

Jesus, on earth as a sinless man, being filled with the Spirit and having unbroken communication with God, had a continual open Heaven where angels, God's messengers, could ascend and descend between Heaven and earth. Angels won't be discussed too much in this book, but it's important to note that they are still alive and well and partnering with humans all the time to usher in God's will. They carry His presence and act on His words. *"Are not all angels ministering spirits sent to serve those who will inherit salvation"* (Heb. 1:14).

When we release words of authority that come from Heaven (as we hear something from God, we declare it), we are releasing an angel to deliver the fulfillment of that declaration.

Jesus had an open Heaven 24/7. Better yet, He made sure to emphasize the fact that Nathaniel would see the angels ascending and descending upon the *Son of Man*. He didn't say Son of God. He

> Jesus put aside His divinity to show us what walking and ministering in the Spirit is really supposed to look like for us as we follow in His footsteps.

wanted us to know without a shadow of a doubt that He had an open Heaven as a human. Jesus put aside His divinity to show us what walking and ministering in the Spirit is really supposed to look like for us as we follow in His footsteps. Everything He did He did as a human. Yes He was sinless, but being sinless just means having an open relationship with God at all times. When we sin, we step out from under God's covering and will no longer flow in His Spirit until we respond to His love and repent. Jesus never had this problem so He had continual, unbroken communion with the Father. Make no mistake, Jesus was tempted in every way that we are, but He did not fall to one temptation (see Heb. 4:15).

The moral of the story is that we, like Jesus, are to be walking Kingdom people with all the resources of Heaven available to us because of us walking under a continual open Heaven. These resources are delivered by angels as we move in obedience with God.

We do not need to pray about or sing about an open Heaven as if it's something not yet attained; rather, we need to just know it's there.

Oftentimes we are the answer to our own prayers. Sometimes we, as prayer warrior revivalists, can get too caught up on the mountaintop with the glory, like Moses (see Exod. 34:28), and forget about the people in the valley who need God's Word in their lives. Revival is certainly about a balance between lifestyles full of *prayer* and the *works* of Kingdom ministry. The privilege of having an open Heaven over our lives requires both.

When you know that God is with you and that an open Heaven is available to you at anytime, you will start to access the resources of Heaven so that you will see the work of God's Kingdom manifest through your life.

QUESTIONS

1. Have you ever spent more time worrying and waiting than praying and doing the works God commands us and empowers us to do?

_____

_____

_____

_____

2. Have you ever found yourself praying for God to do something in the heavenlies to make it easier to minister? Do you sometimes find yourself praying for things to happen more than actually ushering in the things you're praying for?

_____

_____

_____

_____

_____

3. Did you know before today that you, as a believer, have an open Heaven with you wherever you go? What will you change in your life due to this revelation? What will you stop doing? And what will you start doing differently?

_____

_____

_____

_____

PRAYER (YOU TO GOD)

God, we honor You and long to understand Your ways. We know You are with us always and that You answer prayer.

God help us to understand the power of Your indwelling presence and the fact that we carry with us the very Spirit of the God of gods and King of kings. Your rule can be ushered in wherever we are, regardless of the spiritual condition in a location before we got there. Amen.

PRAYER (ME TO GOD, FOR YOU)

In Jesus' name I release faith and confidence in the heart of this reader to walk with an open Heaven over his or her life 24/7 and to learn to usher in Your heavenly realities on earth through obedience to You and Your Word. We thank You for the release of Your revelation and understanding in our lives so that we can learn to live in such a way that we can change the world.

PART II

THE HOLY SPIRIT
AND REVIVAL

Chapter 11

SPIRIT FILLED

Again He said, "Peace be with you. As the Father has sent Me, so I am sending you." Then He breathed on them and said, "Receive the Holy Spirit" (John 20:21-22 NLT).

I am capable of nothing spiritually significant without the infilling and power of the Holy Spirit at work in my life.

There are not too many things in life that give me more joy than seeing someone gloriously filled with the Holy Spirit for the first time. It is usually such a wonderful faith-filled pursuit. Some receive this experience at their water baptism, others pray for it for years and years before learning to just open up in faith and receive. Others, like me, have to go on an extended fast to break unbelief before they can receive.

Being filled with the Holy Spirit, also known as the empowerment of the baptism of the Holy Spirit, is absolutely essential for any revivalist. This is not a one-time occurrence, either.

This experience is different than when we surrender and open the doors of our hearts to receive the initial seal of our salvation, the precious Holy Spirit. The difference is between the *one-time infilling of God's Spirit to confirm the message of the Gospel* and the *ongoing experience of being filled by God's Spirit with the power of the Gospel*. When we truly give our lives over to the Lord, we allow the Holy Spirit to dwell in us to see our souls fulfill the justification, sanctification, and glorification that is promised in Scripture (see 1 Cor. 6:11; Rom. 8:30). The Holy Spirit lives in all those who believe in Jesus as the Christ (the Anointed One sent of God to take away the sins of the world). However, there is an additional empowerment I will now speak of.

Unfortunately, I believe that many Pentecostal churches in America and beyond have misplaced their roots as churches that once depended on this empowerment from the Holy Spirit and emphasized this as an essential pursuit for any of their church members

The success of the early church was undoubtedly because of one reason only: the Holy Spirit. Think about it. What changed between the time when Peter wimped out, to the point of denying Christ, because of a little girl questioning him (see Mark 14:66-68) and the time when he stood up in front of thousands of the same people who had killed His Lord and pleaded with them to save themselves from this corrupt generation (see Acts 2:40)? He received *the baptism of the Holy Spirit!*

This baptism was so important that God had John the Baptist prophesy it before Jesus even came into His ministry:

> *I indeed baptize you with water unto repentance, but He who is coming after me is mightier than I, whose sandals I am not worthy to carry. He will baptize you with the Holy Spirit and fire* (Matthew 3:11 NKJV).

The baptism was so important to Jesus that He taught and readied His disciples to embrace this promise. After Jesus rose from the grave, His main emphasis before He ascended was for them to tarry and wait for the promise from on high:

> *Behold, I send the Promise of My Father upon you; but tarry in the city of Jerusalem until you are endued with power from on high* (Luke 24:49 NKJV).

He knew this preceded their ability to be able to fulfill the Great Commission. In fact, the core purpose of the baptism is to endow us with power to be witnesses in the first place.

*But you will receive power when the Holy Spirit comes on you; and **you will be My witnesses** in Jerusalem, and in all Judea and Samaria, and to the ends of the earth* (Acts 1:8).

This was the last thing Jesus said to His disciples before He ascended. Usually, the last thing somebody says is something we should pay the most attention to, something they really want us to understand.

Revival is what's in between passionate prayer and effective evangelism. Yet the spiritual source of power in any Kingdom endeavor comes from the Holy Spirit and the Holy Spirit alone. The power of the Holy Spirit is an absolute essential to effective evangelism. The Bible and history have proven this to be true.

The promise of the Holy Spirit ushered in an era that is continuing to this day. Peter said that the baptism represents the pouring out of God's Spirit on all flesh (see Acts 2:14-21), which was demonstrated throughout the era of the early Church, and I'm sure experienced by pockets of believers throughout the Dark Ages and since the Reformation era. However, although there were powerful revival moves in past centuries, such as the First and Second Great Awakenings, which can be studied historically, none of these "moves of God" had apparently emphasized the baptism of the Spirit like the revival movement that began in America somewhere around the turn of the twentieth century!

TO ALL WHO BELIEVE

The key to the promise of the outpouring of God's Holy Spirit is the fact that it was not just for those people on that day in Jerusalem. While preaching under the anointing (power and leading of God), Peter said that the promise was for all those there and all those who are afar off, to *all* who would believe! *"The promise is for you and your children and for all who are far off—for all whom the Lord our God will call"* (Acts 2:39).

This promise was especially evident when God initially began to allow the Gospel message to be preached to the Gentiles (non-Jews) and the Spirit fell on them as Peter spoke.

"He commanded us to preach to the people and to testify that He is the one whom God appointed as judge of the living and the dead. All the prophets testify about Him that everyone who believes in Him receives forgiveness of sins through His name." While Peter was still speaking these words, the Holy Spirit came on all who heard the message. The circumcised believers who had come with Peter were astonished that the gift of the Holy Spirit had been poured out even on the Gentiles. For they heard them speaking in tongues and praising God (Acts 10:42-46).

This baptism was such an essential in the building of the Church that when the apostles heard that a group of people had not yet received the gift of the Holy Spirit, they went to the people to pray for them and impart this gift.

When the apostles in Jerusalem heard that Samaria had accepted the word of God, they sent Peter and John to Samaria. When they arrived, they prayed for the new believers there that they might receive the Holy Spirit, because the Holy Spirit had not yet come on any of them; they had simply been baptized in the name of the Lord Jesus. Then Peter and John placed their hands on them, and they received the Holy Spirit. (Acts 8:14-17).

For lack of a better analogy, when a minister or fellow anointed brother or sister in Christ lays hands on you to pray for you to receive this gift of the Spirit, it is much like jump-starting a car. Your faith in this area is new and fresh, and for your spiritual car to start this first time, it's often good to get an extra burst of power from a person who lays hands on you. Spiritually speaking, this is somewhat like a doctor lightly slapping a baby to get it to breathe for the first time once it comes out of the mother's womb. The breath in this case is the *ruach* of God, the very breath of God, a Hebrew word used to describe the Holy Spirit.[1]

THE GLORIOUS PURSUIT

Pursue being filled with the Spirit with everything in you. This is not just a one-time experience, but if you've never had a baptism experience, today is your day. If you've been praying to receive and have not yet, this is the answer to your prayers. The pursuit of the baptism is a wonderful adventure. Jesus is the guide, and the only currency needed to go on this trip is your faith.

> Pursue being filled with the Spirit with everything in you.

Right now, in Jesus' name, if you believe in faith as you pray the following prayer, the glory of God will begin to fill your room and fill your soul, and the Holy Spirit is going to touch you powerfully. *Know that Jesus is going to baptize you with the Holy Spirit right now!* Open your heart in faith, keep your eyes on Jesus, and let the Holy Spirit in! Begin to speak with new tongues as the Holy Spirit gives you utterance.

IMPARTATION

Read these words in faith:

> *I receive in Jesus' name His precious gift of the baptism of the Holy Spirit in my life. Holy Spirit, I long for you. Jesus, You are the author and finisher of my faith. I want to receive Your power to be a witness. Baptize me in Your Spirit as You will. I believe. You are worthy. You are holy.*

> The hungrier you are for Jesus and the more you embrace this gift in faith, the easier it is to receive.

There is no method; this is a unique experience to you. But in all my experiences of praying for dozens to receive this gift for the first time, I've seen that the hungrier you are for Jesus, and the more you embrace this gift in faith, with your heart and not your head, the easier it is to receive. Let the Scriptures ignite your faith; then be filled with the Holy Ghost and be baptized in fire in Jesus' name!

If God is touching you in power, you have had an amazing encounter with the Lord, you have felt empowered to witness, and you have been filled with His Spirit, congratulations! You're halfway there. Being baptized in the Spirit is not an end, but a means to an end.

If you are still believing for your heavenly prayer language and have not yet received it, know that it is a gift from God.

> *Now you are the body of Christ, and members individually. And God has appointed these in the church: first apostles, second prophets, third teachers, after that miracles, then gifts of healings, helps, administrations, **varieties of tongues*** (1 Corinthians 12:27-28 NKJV).

Know also that this is a very important tool for building yourself up in the Lord.

> *But you, beloved, **building yourselves up on your most holy faith, praying in the Holy Spirit,** keep yourselves in the love of God, looking for the mercy of our Lord Jesus Christ unto eternal life* (Jude 20-21 NKJV).

I don't believe there is always a cut-and-dried answer when it comes to questioning whether speaking in tongues is the initial evidence that somebody is baptized in the Spirit. Although, in most cases, those baptized in the Spirit will speak in tongues and it is a powerful and glorious experience that is obviously from God alone, I believe that some people who speak in tongues are not necessarily baptized in the Spirit, and some who have been baptized in the Spirit may not speak in tongues. Some people may be speaking in an unknown tongue, not as led by the Spirit, but rather out of their own or even demonic babblings. This isn't common, but satan tries to counterfeit everything that is good from God. If you are saved and surrendered to God, you should have no problem knowing if this experience is from God or not. Subsequently, I believe that there are people throughout history who have been obviously baptized in the Spirit, but not necessarily with the evidence of speaking in tongues.

Revivalist Charles Finney had a wonderful Holy Spirit baptism experience as documented in his autobiography, but he doesn't talk about himself speaking in a heavenly language at this point:

> But as I turned and was about to take a seat by the fire, I received a mighty baptism of the Holy Ghost. Without any expectation of it, without ever having the thought in my mind that there was any such thing for me, without any recollection that I had ever heard the thing mentioned by any person in the world, the Holy Spirit descended upon me in a manner that seemed to go through me, body and soul. I could feel the impression, like a wave of electricity, going through and through me. Indeed it seemed to come in waves and waves of liquid love, for I could not express it in any other way. It seemed like the very breath of God. I can recollect distinctly that it seemed to fan me, like immense wings. No words can express the wonderful love that was shed abroad in my heart. I wept aloud with joy and love; and I do not know but I should say, I literally bellowed out the unutterable gushings of my heart. These waves came over me, and over me, and over me, one after the other, until I recollect I cried out, "I shall die if these waves continue to pass over me." I said, "Lord, I cannot bear any more;" yet I had no fear of death. How long I continued in this state, with this baptism continuing to roll over me and go through me, I do not know. But I know it was late in the evening when a member of my choir—for I was the leader of the choir—came into the office to see me. He was a member of the church. He found me in this state of loud weeping, and said to me, "Mr. Finney, what ails you?" I could make him no answer for some time. He then said, "Are you in pain?" I gathered myself up as best I could, and replied, "No, but so happy that I cannot live."[2]

Despite Charles Finney's undeniably powerful experience of receiving the Spirit's baptism, I have not found it to be recorded or documented that this experience resulted in or was confirmed by the evidence of speaking in tongues. *Remember, it is the Lord and the precious Holy Spirit that we seek, not tongues.*

TONGUES FOR MISSIONS

Remember that tongues can also be used for effective missionary work. If God calls you to be a missionary to another country, it is quite possible that He will allow the Holy Spirit to speak through you in the language of the people you are sent to. On the day of Pentecost, they spoke not in a heavenly language and a miracle took place in those who heard this language. The language of the Spirit was coming from the 120, but the crowd all heard the words of their own native tongue!

Every tribe and every tongue have the right to hear the glorious message of the Gospel of Jesus Christ and His Kingdom!.

We can also pray for God to open up the ears of those who hear us even if their native language isn't the language we are using. The reason is because every tribe and every tongue have the right to hear the glorious message of the Gospel of Jesus Christ and His Kingdom!

Utterly amazed, they asked: "Are not all these men who are speaking Galileans? Then how is it that each of us hears them in our native language? Parthians, Medes and Elamites; residents of Mesopotamia, Judea and Cappadocia, Pontus and Asia, Phrygia and Pamphylia, Egypt and the parts of Libya near Cyrene; visitors from Rome (both Jews and converts to Judaism); Cretans and Arabs—we hear them declaring the wonders of God in our own tongues" (Acts 2:7-11).

It is possible for God to actually allow the Holy Spirit to minister through you in a tongue that a listener can understand. The miracle in this case would be on your end, not the hearer. My own father-in-law, a pastor for many years, on one occasion prayed in the Spirit in an unknown tongue. That tongue, he later found out from some brothers at their church meeting, was English! He was pastoring in Mexico and didn't speak English at all, not even enough to know that's what this other language was. God used this language to minister to those there who knew English, as confirmed by a bilingual patron who came up to him after the service and asked him how long he had known English.

Charles Parham was a leader in the Body of Christ during the days of the Asuza Street Revival. He taught, and many believed, that the Lord would give people the tongues of the mission fields where He was calling them.[3] Some revivalists, in fact, did have God give them the tongues of the mission field where they were to go to. Revivalist A.G. Garr was the first white Pastor to be baptized in the Spirit in the Asuza Street Revival, and he started speaking in Bengali after he was baptized in the Spirit. This was his sign that God was calling him to be a missionary to India. He, in fact, did become one of the first Pentecostal missionaries to India and made a huge difference on that continent and later during his years of tent revivals in the United States.[4] Like my father-in-law, Mr. Garr was not able to speak fluently in the language of the people that God was calling him to when he got there, but the fact that he spoke in it once was a sign, wonder, and supernatural confirmation, nonetheless.

ONGOING INFILLING

The most important aspect of being filled with the Spirit is the fact that it is a continual, ongoing process in the spiritual life of anyone who desires to live in revival and to be an effective servant of our Lord. Paul wrote, *"Be not drunk with wine, wherein is excess; but **be filled with the Spirit"*** (Eph. 5:18 KJV). *Filled,* in the Greek, is defined as the following:

πληρόω,ν {play-ro'-o} 1) to make full, to fill up, i.e. to fill to the full 1a) to cause to abound, to furnish or supply liberally 2) to render full, i.e. to complete 2a) to fill to the top: so that nothing shall be wanting to full measure, fill to the brim 2b2) to carry through to the end, to accomplish, carry out, (some undertaking) 2c2) of sayings, promises, prophecies, to bring to pass, ratify, accomplish 2c3) to fulfill, i.e. to cause God's will (as made known in the law) to be obeyed as it should be, and God's promises (given through the prophets) to receive fulfillment.[5]

This one word is pregnant with meaning and purpose! Not only does God want to fill you completely *full to the brim* with the Holy Spirit, but He also gives this infilling experience as the very oil that will fuel the vehicle of your destiny to the point of fulfilling God's promises for your life! God's intention through this Scripture is to let us know that we are always supposed to be filled with the infilling of the Holy Spirit.

How else can your life be poured out as a drink offering to a generation that needs Jesus? I almost daily come back to the Holy Spirit recharging station of His glory and grace that fills me to the brim so that when God moves me I am sure to spill out His Spirit everywhere He leads me!

Revivalists don't go to the well to get a drink and then fill up a bucket of water to give to those around them. If they did, their water would run dry and they would have to stop ministering until they went back to the well. This is the case with many pastors who pray to prepare a sermon, preach the sermon, and then find themselves empty again and in need of more prayer.

The spiritual truth is that all of us who are filled with the Spirit have a river inside of us that will always sustain us and give us refreshment when they are thirsty, spiritually speaking. This is the life of Christ inside of you, refreshing you, and giving you life more abundantly—the same life and virtue that will come forth through you as you minister to those in spiritual need. This river never runs dry; it simply must be accessed by faith! You don't need formal prayer time or an impartation from another minister to be filled; you can be filled again and again by just focusing your mind's eye on Jesus and saying sweet prayers to Him under your breath at anytime throughout the day.

You can be filled as you worship; you can be filled as you pray in the Spirit during work; you can be filled anytime you ask Jesus to allow this river to run in and through your life. As you live with the knowledge that a never-ending Holy Spirit river of life is always flowing through you, you won't need to do anything to access this except believe. It's up to you, in faith, to open up the floodgate of this spiritual source of life to fill your soul and body.

> *Jesus answered and said to her, "Whoever drinks of this water will thirst again, but whoever drinks of the water that I shall give him will never thirst.* ***But the water that I shall*** *give him will become in him a fountain of water springing up into everlasting life." The woman said to Him, "Sir, give me this water, that I may not thirst, nor come here to draw"* (John 4:13-15 NKJV).

The Holy Spirit is our source, and He is a spiritual mighty rushing river that never runs dry. The baptism of the Holy Spirit has great value and should be pursued by all of us for the edification of our souls and the empowerment to preach the Gospel. Tongues are a sign, a wonder, and a spiritual tool to be used for God's glory. Let Him fill you, and fill you again to overflowing! Don't be afraid to speak aloud in other tongues to edify your spirit and to be a sign to unbelievers. Don't be afraid of His wonder-working power consuming your life and energizing your faith. When I was ready to receive the baptism, I asked some pastors from my church to pray with me to receive. They did, and I did. I was crying, and I remember I could hardly stand up; I was holding almost all of my weight from the shoulders of two of the pastors who were on either side of me. Although this was the first and only time I needed to receive the initial baptism, I enjoy almost daily fellowship with the Holy Spirit who fills me with God's love, power, and grace.

Gloriously pursue the person of Jesus and His beautiful Holy Spirit, not just once, but daily, and the rivers of eternal life will flow through your body, soul, and spirit. Do this and not only will you be refreshed and revived, but you will be well on your way to living as the revivalist and world changer whom God has destined you to be!

QUESTIONS

1. Do you believe the baptism of the Holy Spirit is a necessary tool for every believer? Why or why not?

   _____

   _____

   _____

   _____

2. What are some of the reasons why fellow saints do not receive the baptism of the Holy Spirit? What tips would you recommend for them to get over this mountain?

   _____

   _____

   _____

   _____

3. Did you know that we as Christians are supposed to receive a continual infilling of the Holy Spirit? Have you ever felt dry and burned out? That's because you need to take a fresh drink from the river!

   _____

   _____

   _____

   _____

PRAYER (YOU TO GOD)

God, thank You for Your precious Holy Spirit who is with us always. I believe that I received Him when I accepted You as my Savior; however, I want more—more of You and more of Him. You are One—Father, Son, and Spirit. I long to be filled afresh with Your Spirit so I can be a witness and a burning one full of oil in my lamp. Thank You, Father.

PRAYER (ME TO GOD, FOR YOU)

Lord, baptize this reader afresh with Your power, the power that comes from the Holy Spirit! Amen!

Endnotes

1. *NAS Exhaustive Concordance of the Bible with Hebrew-Aramaic and Greek Dictionaries,* Hebrew definition; http://strongsnumbers.com/hebrew/7307. htm, accessed September 8, 2010, s.v. rauch. Copyright © 1981, 1998 by The Lockman Foundation.

2. Charles Finney, *Memoirs of Charles G. Finney* (New York: A.S. Barnes and Company, 1876), 20-21.

3. Pentecostal millennialism: The Second Comers, *At first, the gift of tongues meant one thing: Jesus was returning soon.*Vinson Synan, posted January 1, 1999, http://www.christianitytoday.com/ch/1999/issue61/61h038.html (last accessed, September 8, 2010).

4. Steve Thompson, "A.G. Garr and the Pentecostal Revival," *Holy Trinity New Rochelle,* http://www.holytrinitynewrochelle.org/yourti18138.html (accessed July 21, 2010).

5. Thayer and Smith. "Greek Lexicon entry for Pleroo," *The New Testament Greek Lexicon,* http://www.searchgodsword.org/lex/grk/view. cgi?number=4137. Accessed September 8, 2010.

A Word From the Holy Spirit

I don't go where I'm not welcome.

I don't dance alone.

You must be in the Spirit to communicate with Me.

I want you to know Me.

I convict you and warn you of sin.

I don't want to be separated from you.

I make clear to you what the Father is saying.

I give to you what belongs to Jesus.

I love Jesus and the Father and love to worship them with you.

I search out the deepest things of people's souls.

I don't care about accomplishments.

I care about your heart.

I see you as God does.

I live to see you succeed in who you were created to be.

I give power to creation.

I wrote the Bible, and I'm still writing it in your heart.

Chapter 12

THE ANOINTING

And they cast out many demons and healed many sick
people, anointing them with olive oil (Mark 6:13 NLT).

To change the world you don't need God-given
talent, you need God-abiding anointing.

The Holy Spirit is my best friend.

The anointing is one of my favorite subjects to talk about, and this
had to be one of the last chapters that I wrote due to the fact that the
anointing (the person, power, and presence of God) would hit me just
thinking about writing this, and I would be baptized with a fountain
of glory and incapacitated to write.

Even while writing this chapter, I had to take multiple breaks to
just weep and worship. In all my efforts, even if I wrote a whole book
about this subject, I would never be able to do justice in explaining
the person of the Holy Spirit. *The Holy Spirit **is** the power and pres-*
ence of God. I pray that through me He will at least give you a taste
of Himself, but if you want more than a taste, you must go straight
to the source!

The anointing is highly misunderstood, but often talked about. The anointing is really a person. His name is Holy Spirit. In addition to receiving the Holy Spirit upon being born-again, when we are made holy, consecrated, and set apart for God's good use (as in the Old Testament when people or things were anointed), we immediately are attached to the Holy Spirit. This closeness with Him is necessary if we want to properly function in that which we were set apart for.

When we stay close to the Holy Spirit, His very presence rubs off *on* our spirits. We begin to carry an awareness of His presence, and others can sense the presence of God around us due to this closeness. The seal of the Holy Spirit is in all who believe in Jesus (see Eph. 4:30); the baptism of the Holy Spirit is typically a one-time experience of great empowerment and sanctification (see Acts 1:8); the infilling of the Holy Spirit should be ongoing (see Eph. 5:18); but getting to know the very person of the Holy Spirit is what sets men and women of God apart as anointed. The power of God working mightily through someone's life is what many ascribe to as the anointing. This can be power from the Spirit of God to heal the sick or cast out demons (see Matt. 10:1; Mark 16:17-18), for example, thus destroying some of the works of the devil on earth as Jesus did (see 1 John 3:8b). This demonstration of the Kingdom in power should be essential in the life of a believer so that men do not put their wisdom in our words only, but in the power of God (see 2 Cor. 2:4).

People sometimes use the term *anointing* to communicate that God has chosen a person—almost as if by some sovereign divine intervention. However, it is out of relationship with Him that He gives the anointing, not from some predestined calling on a life. If we are "called" to be Christians, I believe we are also "called" to be anointed. The anointing comes with a great price and is not free nor completely sovereign. The anointing is birthed from a relationship with the Holy Spirit that takes effort to cultivate. This is the main reason why we can observe some Christians which appear to have more power of God working through their lives. They have the same God, same Holy

Spirit, the only difference is they have spent more time with Him, letting Him rub off on them more.

All relationships take two people communicating and getting to know each other. The closer we are to the Holy Spirit and His working in and through us, the more power of the Kingdom will be made manifest through our lives and the more Heaven can show up where we are.

Technically the definition of *anoint* is "to apply, to put or rub on oil, typically in a religious ceremony"; this represents sanctification or consecration.[1]

The notes in my Spirit Filled Life Bible eloquently say this of the anointing oil used in the Old Testament:

> Prophets, priests and kings were initiated into office by the anointing with oil, symbolic of the inner working of the Holy Spirit. Since God's blessing comes upon His people when the kings, priests, and prophets are faithful in their functions, Isaiah prophesies of that day when *woes would end, revival would come* and *these offices would properly function again.*[2]

> The closer we are to the Holy Spirit and His working in and through us, the more Heaven can show up where we are.

This is still true today when anointed saints embrace their proper function in the Body of Christ! We are God's present-day prophets, priests, and kings. If we are to fulfill God's will in bringing revival wherever we go, the anointing is an essential.

GUARD THE GIFT

If we want the anointing in our lives, we have to be willing to be consecrated and set apart for God's holy purposes. We must be enemies of evil and fight to keep from grieving the Holy Spirit! We have to rebel against the culture of sin in the world and the worldliness in the Church! *Revivalists value the anointing and depend on it.* Revivalists do everything they can to not hurt the Holy Spirit, and if they do, to quickly repent and restore that relationship.

If I had all the money and accolades in the entire world and was world-famous with the most revered ministry, I would trade it all in two seconds if my lifestyle meant that I would lose even half of this cherished relationship I have with this sweet but fiercely passionate person named Holy Spirit. I would rather be a no-name homeless bum living in a park with no family and no friends, but with the Holy Spirit as my friend. I would be the happiest bum in the world, and surely many of my bum acquaintances would get healed and set free! This is just a guaranteed extension of my relationship with the Holy Spirit.

Revivalists value relationship and closeness with the Holy Spirit above anything and everything else. Anytime the Holy Spirit begins pulling back from me for some reason, all of my internal spiritual alarms go on red alert! If I sin or grieve Him, I hurt with a deep, unexplainable anguish. However, He is always there to comfort me when I repent and cry out to Him. God is truly faithful when we are not, but we must never take our relationship with Him for granted.

> Revivalists value relationship and closeness with the Holy Spirit above anything and everything else.

When it comes to ministry of any kind, from ministering to coworkers, to leading a massive outreach crusade or preaching a sermon, revivalists *must* have the wisdom, guidance, and relationship with the Holy Spirit or their efforts are futile. Revivalists don't just partner with the Holy Spirit; they let Him have full control! If He's not there, we have no business being there, either. In true revival, God is not our copilot; rather, we're His passengers!

FRUITS OF THE ANOINTING

Since the anointing is a person, we must understand who this person is. Who is this Holy Spirit? The Bible says we will know a tree by its fruit (see Matt. 7:16). Thus, we know the Holy Spirit by observing His fruit.

Revivalists don't just partner with the Holy Spirit; they let Him have full control! The fruit of the Spirit are attributes of a person's heart who has been transformed by God.

But the fruit of the Spirit is love, joy, peace, forbearance, kindness, goodness, faithfulness, gentleness and self-control. Against such there is no law (Galatians 5:22-23).

The Holy Spirit perfectly encapsulates each of the character attributes just listed. Likewise, we will recognize people who spend a lot of time with the Holy Spirit because the fruit (observable results) of their lives will also share these same attributes. People do not necessarily have the anointing just because they see signs and miracles happening through their ministries. People also are not necessarily anointed just because they share a level of worldly success in their ministry (for example, they have a big church or have lots of money or popularity). The fruit of the Spirit are attributes of a person's heart who has been transformed by God. Spending time with God (beholding His glory) transforms our hearts and conforms us more into the image of Jesus (see 2 Cor. 3:18).

Only when we spend enough time with others to see whether they interact with people in love, kindness, and the other attributes on a regular basis will we know if they are really anointed. By this observation will we know that they have spent time with God and are continuing to spend time with God. Remember that, no matter how anointed people may seem, they must have the fruits of the Holy Spirit or they may be wolves in sheep's clothing simply moving in a level of gifting, but not anointing. The Bible warns us of such people (see Matt. 7:21-23).

THE SEVEN SPIRITS

The Bible makes multiple references to the Holy Spirit as the "seven spirits of God," referring to Him as looking like blazing lamps before the throne of God (see Rev. 4:5). I believe the seven Spirits really represent one perfect or complete Spirit, the Holy Spirit.

These seven Spirits are represented by seven horns (symboliz-ing authority) and seven eyes (symbolizing revelation) (see Rev. 5:6). Furthermore, in Isaiah, we find a key to this revelation of the Spirit of God. He is clearly mentioned as seven Spirits in the following passage.

> *The Spirit of the LORD shall rest upon Him, the Spirit of* **wisdom** *and* **understanding,** *the Spirit of* **counsel** *and* **might,** *the Spirit of* **knowledge** *and of the* **fear of the LORD** (Isaiah 11:2 NKJV).

These names represent both revelation and power. At first glance it may seem like there are only six spirits mentioned; however, the very Spirit of the Lord God is worthy of His own name and attri-bute because of His unique individuality and personality from the six other spiritual names. A powerful revelation about the sevenfold Spirit of God is that our resurrected Christ is right in the middle of the seven Spirits of God (see Rev. 1:13). This signifies that He stays one with the Father and the Spirit and always is in the center of the Father's will. Furthermore, the seven lampstands are known in Jewish culture as the Menorah. The very center candle of the seven is known as the "servant candle." The Spirit of the Lord, the very Spirit of Jesus, is the greatest servant we could ever know! To be at the center of God's will, we must let His Spirit make us servants. Then we must be balanced by the other attributes of God's Spirit.

> To be at the center of God's will, we must let His Spirit make us servants.

The Holy Spirit doesn't have wisdom, understanding, counsel, and might; He *is* wisdom, *is* might, *is* revelation, *is* understanding, *is* counsel, and *is* the knowledge of the fear of the Lord. In the same way that God *is* love, the Holy Spirit *is* all of these attributes. Personally, this revelation helps me appreciate Him that much more.

In the Book of the Acts of the Apostles (really the Acts of the Holy Spirit), we continually see these very same attributes revealed. Wisdom was revealed when the Spirit led the apostles to choose godly men to serve the widows (see Acts 6:1-4). The Spirit of Counsel was with the Church at Antioch, advising them to separate and send out Paul and Barnabas (see Acts 13:2). Might was demonstrated in shaking open the gates of the prisons (see Acts 16:26) and through many other signs, wonders, and miracles. Revelation occurred when the Holy Spirit gave Peter a dream about the unclean food and God's will to take the Gospel to the Gentiles (see Acts 10:9-15); almost right away God gave Peter understanding in this matter so that he could properly explain it to the other Jews. Lastly, the knowledge of the fear of the Lord manifested on multiple occasions, most notably, when Ananias and Sapphira were stricken dead (see Acts 5).

The Holy Spirit perfectly demonstrated all of who He is through His acts 2,000 years ago, but that was just supposed to be the beginning. Certainly, He will once again demonstrate His acts today through us! A lifetime of study will not reveal all of who the Holy Spirit is; we can only pray and ask Him to reveal Himself more to us each day.

THE ANOINTING OF JESUS

In the Old Testament, priests and kings were anointed for service to God for the ministry that He had for them. This actually happened with Jesus as well when God sent the dove upon Him to abide with Him when He was baptized by John.

When He had been baptized, Jesus came up immediately from the water; and behold, the heavens were opened to Him, and He saw the Spirit of God descending like a dove and alighting upon Him (Matthew 3:16 NKJV).

Furthermore, John documented that this anointing represented by the Holy Spirit actually remained on Jesus' life during His ministry.

And John bore witness, saying, "I saw the Spirit descending from heaven like a dove, and He remained upon Him (John 1:32 NKJV).

Jesus must have looked like a pirate with a bird on His shoulder because He never offended the dove, which would have caused it to fly away. The Bible says that He (God, the Holy Spirit) remained on Jesus. A dove is an extremely peaceful and sensitive creature. It is also very loyal; doves mate for life.[3] It is representative in many ways of the character of the Holy Spirit.

> The Holy Spirit anointing is to empower us to accomplish the tasks God has set before us.

The Bible says that the Holy Spirit is our comforter, counselor, and teacher (see John 14:15-16). Jesus made it a point to not offend the Holy Spirit, and so should we. This is one of the most critical points of this book.

The Holy Spirit anointing is to empower us to accomplish the tasks God has set before us. The anointing breaks every yolk of bondage that the devil can possibly use to take a person captive (see Isa. 10:27). This "set-the-captives-free" anointing is the anointing of Jesus (see Isa. 61:1). The anointing set apart and empowered Jesus for His initial three years of ministry, but Jesus was also separately anointed for His greatest test of all time, *the cross*. This included His burial and resurrection (see John 12:1-8).

THE ANOINTING TEACHES

The anointing is further equated with the Holy Spirit in this passage:

> The anointing teaches us all things.

But the anointing which you have received from Him abides in you, and you do not need that anyone teach you; but as the same anointing teaches you concerning all things, and is true, and is not a lie, and just as it has taught you, you will abide in Him (1 John 2:27 NKJV).

The anointing teaches us all things. This anointing matches with the mission statement of the Holy Spirit in John 16, which speaks about the Spirit of truth that will guide us into all truth (see John 16:13).

The subject of the anointing and the person of the Holy Spirit are truly inseparable. Every man or woman who believes in Jesus can and should be taught by the Holy Spirit. It is the experiences of learning, falling, and picking ourselves up, with the Holy Spirit helping along the way, that solidifies our relationship with Him and helps yolk us together with Him. This is much like when a man fights beside another man in combat. There's something about surviving the journey that builds camaraderie and lasting friendships. In many ways the anointing on people's lives comes only with experience.

LEVELS OF THE ANOINTING

There are measures of the anointing to meet the present position of responsibility. David was anointed on three separate occasions. First, he was anointed privately at Bethlehem—the initial consecration of God's chosen man for the destiny of his future Kingship:

> *Then Samuel took the horn of oil and anointed him in* [or "from"] *the midst of his brothers; and the Spirit of the LORD came upon David from that day forward....* (1 Samuel 16:13 NKJV).

Too often, young saints are anointed and called to ministry, like David, but fail to pursue and steward the responsibilities of the steps and seasons they must go through before that prophetic word can be fulfilled. This is where David's other two anointings came into play. It may appear that God worked in reverse in this matter, but He had to first give David a picture of His destiny and let him know by this symbolic act that His hand would be on his life and protect him until the fulfillment of the prophet's words. Not only that, the fact that David received such a strong calling and confirmation by the prophet Samuel gave him great confidence and faith in time of trial. He knew God would not break His word so He knew that he wouldn't die by Goliath's hand, but that an uncircumcised Philistine had no chance against an anointed servant of the Lord who was destined to be King!

The second anointing was by the men of Judah when David became the King of Judah (see 2 Sam. 2:4). The third anointing was by the elders of Israel when he became King of all of Israel (see 2 Sam. 5:3). It would take too long to chronicle the powerful and turbulent life of this Biblical hero, but we honor his journey and learn from his failures. God anointed him along the different stages of the journey of his life, and He will anoint us as well.

PERSONAL ANOINTINGS

In my own life, I have had a couple of divine appointments where other saints anointed me. The first happened years ago on the day when I sensed a call to the ministry. Later, when God sent my wife and I to Tucson to begin our tent revival meetings after living and working in the Southeast, I sensed that God had anointed us with power and a new level of regional authority to declare that revival is here and even go to battle with the spiritual "strong man" of the city that is hindering God's move. Later, I was anointed and released to a whole new level of nation-wide ministry on the day when God commissioned me to work for Him full-time. He called this my graduation day. Not coincidentally, it was exactly seven years, *to the day,* since He had first called me to preach, the day of the visitation that I discuss in the Introduction of the book!

Seven is the number of perfection and completion in the Bible (God laid the foundation of its meaning when He introduced this number in the context of His finished Work of Creation (see Gen 2:2). Seven was again used as a Biblical symbol when He revealed the *end of time,* described as the completion of the "mystery of God," in Revelation 10:5-7). There are no coincidences with God. Eventually, God will anoint me powerfully to take the message of the Gospel to the nations!

There are no coincidences with God.

The Holy Spirit is represented with many different symbols in the Bible: a dove, the wind, fire, oil, and even water. Oftentimes in church or prayer meetings, the leaders may have with them a bottle of anointing oil. This oil is a physical representation of the Holy Spirit that, when applied in the proper spiritual context, can provide a powerful tool in the hands of a minister (see James 5:14). This physical oil can be one of many various kinds; it doesn't have to be extra virgin olive oil or the exact recipe from the Old Testament, just like the Lord's supper doesn't have to be fresh bread and real wine.

I have many times prayerfully anointed people's heads by putting some oil on my hands and applying it to their heads to set them aside for the service and calling of God, to receive the baptism of the Spirit, or to receive healing in accordance with Scripture. Here you see that this is a New Testament commandment:

> *Is anyone among you sick? Let him call for the elders of the church, and **let them pray over him, anointing him with oil in the name of the Lord**. And the prayer of faith will save the sick, and the Lord will raise him up. And if he has committed sins, he will be forgiven* (James 5:14-15 NKJV).

REVELATION OF THE ANOINTING

No matter how dependent I am on the Holy Spirit to work in and through me to receive supernatural power to overcome and the grace to minister His love and power, it is humbling to realize that He is also dependent on me. I have heard great revival teacher, Bill Johnson, say that the Holy Spirit is trapped inside unbelieving believers. His works are released by faith, which comes through revelation. Revelation is like a new door opened in our minds, enabling us to receive a greater level of truth and a picture of what is possible with God.

No matter how strong our spirits are and no matter how anointed we may be, if we fell and hit our heads and got amnesia, it would all appear to go away! We would have to relearn everything that we had learned about God and life. In this case, the anointing doesn't really go away. I think it's like all

Revelation is like a new door opened in our minds, enabling us to receive a greater level of truth and a picture of what is possible from God.

the gifts of God and like His precious Holy Spirit who is the seal of our salvation—they have always been there, but it just takes a while sometimes for us to acknowledge them and receive them. *One of the only things that hinders us from tapping into the unlimited resources of God's Kingdom and wonder-working power in and through our lives is a lack of revelation.*

Revival is in your head—not a figment of your imagination, but a byproduct of the revelatory doors that can open to the real, unlimited possibilities of a heavenly spirit realm that is more real than the natural realm. The doors of revelation and revival are limitless, and God has given us one master key to open them all. It starts with the answer to one major question. The subject of this question was a major turning point for the disciples.

> *When Jesus came to the region of Caesarea Philippi, He asked His disciples, "Who do people say the Son of Man is?" They replied, "Some say John the Baptist; others say Elijah; and still others, Jeremiah or one of the prophets." "But what about you?" He asked. "**Who do you say I am?**"* (Matthew 16:13-15)

We are all faced with this same question. *Who do you say that Jesus is?* Your ability to receive and walk in revival rests solely on the answer to this question. There is still one more question that you must now answer: *Who is the anointing?* Your answer to that question is the only way you'll be able to see a sustained revival in and through your life.

Revival starts with the knowledge that Jesus is the Messiah, the original Anointed One, and revival is continued by knowing the anointing for yourself. Jesus is the door that opens the Way to the Kingdom; the Holy Spirit is the One who leads us along the way.

Whether you're willing to go on this journey is completely up to you. Once you make that decision, I strongly encourage you not to camp out at the door of salvation but to let the Holy Spirit guide you to a wonderful life of excitement, faith, mystery, and the supernatural.

QUESTIONS

1. Do you long to know this person named Holy Spirit? Why is He so important to the life of a believer, especially somebody who wants to see the supernatural?

_____

_____

_____

_____

_____

_____

2. What can you do today to make your home, prayer closet, or business more Holy Spirit friendly?

_____

_____

_____

_____

_____

_____

3. What happens to somebody who tries to minister
    or tries to understand the truths and mysteries of the
    Kingdom without the anointing?

_____

_____

_____

_____

_____

_____

PRAYER (YOU TO GOD)

*Lord, I pray that you would teach me Your ways. I long to
honor and reverence your Holy Spirit like never before. I
will do my best to rest in His presence, learn to hear from
Him, and let Him teach me Your Word. God, I long for an
anointing on my life that can break every yolk of the enemy
and bring refreshing to the people around me. You are the
giver of all good gifts, and I worship You and thank You
for sending us Your Holy Spirit to guide us in everything
we do.*

PRAYER (ME TO GOD, FOR YOU)

*God, I release in Jesus name a special anointing for this
everyday evangelist and revivalist to thrive spiritually in
any environment they walk into. God I pray Your Spirit
touches Your servant powerfully right now. I pray You
would flood Your children's soul with Your love and grace.*

Mess them up in a good way, Jesus. Mess them up for You. Anoint and equip this everyday evangelist for this new season of power and closeness with You. May Your servant steward Your presence wherever he or she goes. In your name I pray, amen.

Endnotes

1. *The American Heritage® Dictionary of the English Language,* Fourth Edition copyright ©2000 by Houghton Mifflin Company. Updated in 2009. Published by Houghton Mifflin Company. All rights reserved, s.v. *anoint,* http://www.thefreedictionary.com/anoints. Accessed September 8, 2010.

2. Jack Hayford, Litt.D. (Gen. Ed), *Spirit Filled Life Bible,* New King James Version (Nashville: Thomas Nelson Publishers, 1991).

3. "Mourning Doves Mate for Life," Songbird Protection Coalition, http://www.savethedoves.org/misc/mateforlife.html. Accessed July 21, 2010.

SOUND THE ALARM

Sound the alarm
Gather the people
Gather the elders
Let the ministers wail
God, take back the years that the enemy's stolen
Lord, You are coming
Holy Visitation
We return to You
With fasting and weeping and mourning
Oh, my Lord, You're returning
We lie here weeping between porch and altar
Pour out Your spirit on Your sons and Your daughters
We lie here weeping between porch and altar
Pour out Your spirit on Your sons and Your daughters

Sound the alarm
Awaken the watchmen
Open their ears
Let their voices be loud
We prophesy,
You'll come to this nation
Touch this generation
Holy Visitation
We dance, and we shout and we lift up our voice
Let your kingdom come down.

—CHARLIE HALL[1]

Chapter 13

PRAY WITHOUT CEASING

Keep on asking, and you will receive what you ask for.
Keep on seeking, and you will find. Keep on knocking,
and the door will be opened to you (Matthew 7:7 NLT).

You can have prayer without revival, but you
can't have revival without prayer.

Revival people are praying people.

Revival is carrying the glory of God you experience in
your personal prayer time with you wherever you go.

In Brother Lawrence's timeless book written in the 1600s, *Practicing the Presence of God,* he taught that we can hear from Heaven and commune with the Lord at any time throughout our day, regardless of our job or life situation. Brother Lawrence worked in a kitchen most of his life, but was well regarded as one with great wisdom because of his ability to communicate with the God who created the Universe.[2] When we do this, we can receive from the Lord's wisdom and direction and have a calm and peace about us that surpasses all understanding. These things are found in this place of rest under the shadow of the wings of the Almighty.

Prayer is about much more than just making your requests known to God. This is part of prayer, but for the purposes of living a life in revival, we need to consider a deeper level of walking with God in a continual state of prayer.

Our whole day can be our "alone time" with God, as I will explain as we go on throughout this chapter. We need to understand what prayer really is in order to be able to make requests to the Father that can change lives and shape the destiny of our nation.

HOLY PERSPECTIVE

Prayer gives us proper perspective. Even when there is chaos going on around us, God's perspective is what separates spiritual from soulful Christians. Soulful Christians react to situations and circumstances around them rather than responding to situations and circumstances from a place of heavenly perspective.

> Soulful Christians react rather than respond to situations and circumstances from a place of heavenly perspective.

The road of Christendom is full of peaks and valleys. When we are on our peak, when we see from a bird's eye view, from God's perspective, we will be aware of coming valleys and not be afraid. *"Yea, though I walk through the valley of the shadow of death, I will fear no evil, for You are with me..."* (Ps. 23:4 NKJV).

When we are in our valleys, but we live from God's perspective, we can see our hills up ahead. God gives and takes away; He rains on the just and on the unjust (see Matt. 5:45). Valleys (tough times) in this life are inevitable, yet trials and persecutions build perseverance and strength, and without them we would not be able to be the triumphant Church that God so earnestly intends.

> *Consider it pure joy, my brothers and sisters, whenever you face trials of many kinds, because you know that the testing of your faith produces perseverance. Let perseverance finish its work so that you may be mature and complete, not lacking anything.* (James 1:2-4).

HOW TO NEVER STOP PRAYING

Paul commanded the Thessalonians—and in essence, all who would read his letter to that church—to *"Pray without ceasing"* (1 Thess. 5:17 NKJV).

How on earth is that possible? It isn't. But then again, we're not from earth, are we? We are N.O.W.—not of this world (see John 17:16). We are peculiar people (see Deut. 14:2; 1 Pet. 2:9), and we are ambassadors from another land (see 2 Cor. 5:20).

I believe Paul intended two meanings when he made that request. First, he really did intend for us to pray whenever we could for whomever we could as often as we could. Second, I believe there is a deeper truth than simply making verbal prayer requests that is hidden in this command. *The truth is that such a request to "pray always" is really possible, but only through an abiding unbroken place of communion with our Lord.* Brother Lawrence figured this out 350 years ago, but the Church has been having problems figuring this out for themselves since the days of Paul.

To pray without ceasing is a state of being that comes from a place of peace and rest, despite the surroundings, through staying in a state of communion with God. It is listening, not just making petitions known to our Father. When we listen, truly listen, we'll be surprised at the wonderful things God will speak to us about. He'll talk to us about ourselves, our futures, those around us, His heart for people, His wisdom, and potential warnings for things in the future. First, to do this, we must find a quiet place; Jesus calls this our prayer closet (see Matt. 6:6).

The Bible says, *"Be still, and know that I am God..."* (Ps. 46:10). It is through this stillness that we can *know* God. In that place of knowing God is the secret source of all spiritual power in the life of a believer. The enemy desperately wants to take this away from us by bringing as many disruptions and distractions into our lives as possible. If the enemy can steal our peace, he can steal our place of power.

WE CAN DO IT

We, being human, continue to make things harder than they really are. A lot of times the Kingdom is so very simple. Jesus, Himself, said that we must receive the Kingdom as a child. *"Truly I tell you, the truth, anyone who will not receive the kingdom of God like a little child will never enter it"* (Mark 10:15).

We can truly become childlike in our faith and hear the voice of our daddy for ourselves. *If we are saved, we can talk to God for ourselves, and we should.* We don't have to wait on our pastor, priest, prophet, or spouse to hear from God for us. They have the same access to and relationship with God as all other Christians. Look at parents and their children. Good parents do not love and favor one child over another. And God would never do this with His children either; He loves us all the same and wants to talk to us all the same.

> *If you, then, though you are evil, know how to give good gifts to your children, how much more will your Father in heaven give good gifts to those who ask Him* (Matthew 7:11).

Let's learn to talk to our Father and listen. Here are some problems with prayer that I believe hinder some from experiencing this wonderful opportunity in all its fullness.

FOUR PROBLEMS OF PRAYER

1. *We've made prayer too hard.* As I stated, prayer is a state of mind and is as easy as waking up in the morning and saying, "Good morning, Holy Spirit."[3]

2. *We haven't given prayer the attention that it needs.* A nonpraying church is like a car with no engine.

3. *People are let down when we "beat the wind."* We need to target something specific, pray for it, document and celebrate the miracle for a "win," and then go on to the next thing.

4. *We need to add fasting to our prayers.* This is discussed in
   much more detail in Chapter 14.

In a world full of darkness and death and an ungodly culture that
tries to steal our time and sabotage our minds so that we would compromise our morals, it is imperative that we as a people, as the Body of
Christ, pay extra special attention to praying for the needs around us.

Nobody should pray because they feel like they have to; we should
want to. Furthermore, we are not to waste our breath with vain rep-
etition (see Matt. 6:7), and we are not to shoot prayers aimlessly into
the wind in hopes that they'll hit some bull's-eye on some target
somewhere.

If we are making prayer requests to God, we must first *"...believe
that He is and that He is a rewarder of those who seek Him"* (Heb. 11:6
NASB). Then we must be diligent and steadfast about our prayers (see
James 5:16), knowing that anything we ask for or seek in Jesus name,
according to the will of the Father, *will* be granted (see John 16:23).

PRACTICAL TIPS

With these truths in mind, it is OK to set for yourself specific
prayer targets. Put God on the spot. He doesn't mind. He likes it even
more when we put ourselves on the spot for His sake but the Bible does
say we can ask anything in Jesus' name and the Father will answer our
prayers:

> *Ask and it will be given to you; seek and you will find; knock
> and the door will be opened to you. For everyone who asks
> receives; the one who seeks finds; and to the one who knocks,
> the door will be opened* (Matthew 7:7-8).

Certainly these requests must be in alignment with God's will and
His Word. As the Lord leads, you can give God a specific prayer and the
answer that you and the world need to know that this was truly Him;
you can even ask Him to reveal a date so that you can be looking for the
answer. God doesn't get mad at you for needing proof sometimes, like

Thomas the disciple (see John 20). However, he does commend those who believe without it. This gives you a prayer target to aim at. If we pray and believe, all things are possible (see Matt. 21:22)!

Do the fleece test with God if necessary to build your faith. The fleece test was modeled when Gideon tested the word of the Lord with a fleece that God left dry or made damp with the dew of the ground (see Judg. 6:36-40). Of course, your situation will be different, but *God doesn't have a problem confirming His Word to you*. God does long to encourage you to believe that He truly does answer prayer, that He is willing to, and that He wants to answer your prayers even more than you want Him to!

Lastly, document the answers to your prayers in a journal. Start with small things and work your way up. This is a way for God to strengthen your faith and for you to gain confidence in your wonder-working God.

When we do these things, our prayers will be dripping with purpose, and our prayers will be a lot easier and lot more effective. The Bible says the *"effective, fervent prayer of a righteous man avails much"* (James 5:16b NKJV).

INTERCESSION

To this point I have talked mostly about personal prayer, which is focused primarily on our own lives and needs and relationship with God. However, true God-led intercession for the world around us is a necessary byproduct of our intimacy with God. It just happens. The Holy Spirit will lead us to pray for others' needs. Even if we don't feel led per se, we should still pray for our leaders, our spouses, our families, our friends, and our enemies.

> True intercession comes from a place of intimacy with the Lord.

True intercession comes from a place of intimacy with the Lord, a place of resting our heads on His chest and listening to the concerns of His heart. We shouldn't get overburdened or overwhelmed by trying to pray for every request under the sun, but we must give some time daily to addressing the burdens on God's heart by asking Him what is on His mind and if there is anything we can pray for.

There's a story I heard once of a Christian missionary from China that visited the United States. When asked about what impressed him the most about the States upon his return, he said, "It's amazing to me that in America, Christians can do church without God." If we really meditate on this and think about what we have observed, could this be true? Certainly it doesn't apply to all churches, but in some churches, is it true? Are we doing church in the natural wisdom of man or in the power of God? If so, how dare we! A church that emphasizes prayer is the exception to this. A prayerful church is a church that is dedicated to dependency on God. It is very apparent to someone with spiritual discernment upon entering a church, whether or not they have a vibrant prayer life as a group of believers in general. Not everyone in every church prays like they should, but there is certainly a spiritual substance evident in a service that would not be there without the prayers of the saints. Likewise, there is a shallowness and lack of power when a church lacks prayer and when even the most charismatic of preachers preaches an unanointed sermon. I'm not pointing fingers at anyone in particular; this is simply a spiritual fact that can happen to any of us if our prayer life is falling short.

PERSONAL PRAYER CONFESSION

Because I value my relationship with God above all else, when I'm missing the mark, it is very apparent to me (as it should be). During one three-week season in my life, while I was the main pastor and leader of a young adult ministry at a large, spirit-filled church in Tucson, I attended a particular Sunday night worship service around Christmas time. At the end of the service, the pastor had us pray for one another. I can even now, years later, remember exactly where I sat and what songs we sang. A man next to me, who was obviously bothered by something, had me pray with him. I prayed the typical Christian "bless him, Lord," prayer and let him pray for me.

The story behind the story, however, is that I had been slipping up in my walk with God. I was attempting to date a non-Christian woman and was going through a lot of confusion and resentment toward God for my own reasons. I was truly out of alignment with Him and was actually fighting Him.

Usually when I pray for people, I am able to read their hearts very easily—especially if I'm walking closely with the Lord, which by His grace and power alone, is most of the time. In this particular circumstance, the man's brother just died earlier that evening. He had come to the church for answers and at least a temporary ointment for the pain! The devastating thing to me was that I had no idea. You may say, well, who would have had an idea? That's not the point. The point is that, with my walk with the Lord, I hold myself to a high standard. Revivalists always hold themselves to the highest standards.

*I **must** be able to hear from God; my whole life is dependent upon it.* Had I been solid in my relationship with God, I most definitely would have felt the pain of his heart because God felt it, too. The fact that I couldn't tell one thing that was wrong in his spirit and that I prayed a shallow, insulting prayer over him that night made me feel like I had really let God down—something I never want to do.

Thank God for good friends; shortly after that incident, some friends came over to my house, who obviously knew something was off in my relationship with God, and they anointed my head and prayed over me. We wept and worshiped together. I was brought back into alignment. Sometimes we need a good Holy Spirit chiropractic adjustment! I am so thankful for friends who bear one another's burdens. I never again want to not be there for someone in spiritual need who comes to me for prayer.

> Sometimes we need a good Holy Spirit chiropractic adjustment.

PRAYER REQUESTS

We never intend to pray in vain. Every prayer we pray is intended to have an answer; otherwise we wouldn't pray it. However, praying for an answer is a peculiar paradox because oftentimes we are driven to intense prayer by an emotional situation and it's our very emotions that block our spiritual level-headedness and ability to hear clearly from God. However, *I have never seen someone who truly pressed in for their answer in prayer be let down.* They either had the answer or had peace about the situation, one or the other.

When in doubt, engage other prayer partners, take your time, and lay your request on the altar of God many times if necessary. I've always said, when it comes to a feeling of spiritual confirmation, that what is from God will grow stronger over time. What originates in self or is just a good idea (not God's idea) will diminish almost as fast as it entered into our heads and tried to confuse our spirits.

REVIVAL PRAYER

Without prayer, you cannot have revival in your life or in any corporate setting. It just can't happen, not a true revival at least. It can't happen because God moves through prayer. If there is no prayer, there is no move of God. You may be able to stir people to an emotional frenzy and try to call it revival, but it will surely die off as quick as it started. Prayer should truly be a lifestyle.

> Without prayer, we cannot have revival in our lives or in any corporate setting.

We desperately need to transition from request-based prayer (which views God as being far off) to presence-based prayer (which is conversations in the presence of a close by God). Even more, we need to understand that prayer is about a continual state of open communication between us and the Father. Anytime throughout the day, He can talk to you and you to Him; it's like you having a Bluetooth earpiece in that has a direct connection to God's cell phone, and He never hangs up! To be revivalists, we need to understand the dynamics of walking in this ceaseless state of prayer. Also, we must know that revival isn't just about praying for something; it's also about being an answer to prayer.

QUESTIONS

1. Do you pray without ceasing? Could you explain what this means if somebody asked you?

    _____

    _____

    _____

    _____

2. Have you made prayer requests and just felt like God was not answering? Is it possible that you weren't praying specifically enough?

    _____

    _____

    _____

    _____

3. Have you had a time when you thought you heard from God, but were dead wrong? I have. Was it possible that your emotions were a little too involved? What can you do to guard against this happening again?

    _____

    _____

    _____

    _____

PRAYER (YOU TO GOD)

God, I thank You and worship You for who You are and what You have done for us. Jesus, thank You for Your sacrifice, Holy Spirit thank You for Your guidance. I desire to learn how to abide in You in such a way that I always have Your perspective, an eternal perspective, and not my own. I want to listen to You, not just ask You for things. I want Your heart, not just Your hand.

PRAYER (ME TO GOD, FOR YOU)

Please, Lord, help this friend to hear You and to pray in such a way to know You will answer all of Your saint's requests as they are prayed into Your will.

May You and this friend have a wonderful prayer partnership together so Your servant can see Your will be done on earth. Thank You, my lovely Father, lover, and boss.

Endnotes

1. Charlie Hall, from the album, "Porch and Altar," track 6, c 2001, EMI Christian Music Group.

2. *The Practice of the Presence of God* is a text compiled by Father Joseph de Beaufort of the wisdom and teachings of Brother Lawrence, a seventeenth-century Carmelite monk. It is a collection of his letters, and records made, by other participants in them, of Brother Lawrence's conversations. Publisher: Ics Pubns; Critical edition (December 1, 1994).

3. That's my shameless plug for Benny Hinn's revival classic, *Good Morning, Holy Spirit* (Nashville, TN: Thomas Nelson, 1997).

Why Do We Fast?

We fast because God wants us to and few others are doing it. We fast because of injustice and murder and strife. We fast because our own souls become polluted by the world. We fast because nations are under the siege of secularism. We fast because there is still human trafficking in the world. We fast because Christians are being martyred daily. We fast because our enemies need Jesus.

Why do we fast? We fast because we must. It wasn't a suggestion. Neither was the cross. Neither was the Great Commission.

We fast to show ourselves as good soldiers of the cross, to lay down our lives, ambitions, and carnal appetites for spiritual riches the eye cannot comprehend and the mouth cannot explain.

We fast for deeper fellowship with Jesus.

We fast because we've cluttered our minds with distractions and we need to hear Jesus. We fast because we're surrounded by crazy people in a crazy world and we need to get a little more crazy for Christ.

We fast because Jesus did it and He said to do it.

We fast because the disciples, apostles, and just about every significant man or woman of faith in history did it. Do they know something we don't?

We fast because satan doesn't want us to—just to get on his nerves.

We fast because there is great evil that can only be overcome by an overcoming Church! We're just crazy enough to believe we are that Church.

We fast and pray because fellowship with the King is the ultimate reward.

We fast so we can fix our eyes on the Author and Finisher of our faith.

We fast because we are an army. No substance can control us, but the substance of His presence. No food satisfies more than the daily bread of the Word, and we've never been thirstier for a drink of the Holy Spirit!

We fast because we don't have all the answers or the solutions—but we know who does.

Chapter 14

FASTING

*And Jesus said to them, "Can the friends of the bridegroom mourn as long as the bridegroom is with them? But the days will come when the bridegroom will be taken away from them, and **then they will fast**"* (Matthew 9:15 NKJV).

When you fast you lose wait.—ZANE ANDERSON[1]

Not only does fasting appear to be a lost art form in the modern Church, in my observation, but a lack of prayer and fasting is one of the single greatest reasons why I believe the Church isn't the overcoming Church God intends us to be. The overcoming Church is another name for what I call a revival Church. For various reasons, I will discuss in this chapter how fasting, when done properly and in the right spirit, can be a great source of power in an individual's life and in a church. Next to our intimate relationship with God, I believe fasting is the greatest weapon in the arsenal of a revivalist.

Fasting is defined typically as abstinence from food. We will also discover together a few types of fasts that don't necessarily mean abstaining entirely from food.

> Next to our intimate relationship with God, fasting is the greatest weapon in the arsenal of a revivalist.

As a practice, I fast a few times a year for 3 to 21 days at a time, trying to stick to mostly water. I know of many other revivalists who do even longer fasts than that. Hopefully I'll one day work my way up to a 40-day water-only fast. However, *it's not the length of the fast that really matters—it's all about your heart when you fast and the reason why you're fasting.* Fasting greatly increases the acceleration of your spiritual growth and has a number of other spiritual benefits.

It would take two books to write down all of the amazing things God has done with me through fasting. He gives me strong visions and dreams, speaks to me very clearly, and encourages me. I have valued every single fast I've done as a wonderful time of bonding with my Lord, and I have always emerged with a stronger faith, fully encouraged in the Lord. *He has blessed me with His presence and His direction in such beautiful ways when I encounter Him with fasting.* Just talking about this makes me want to fast again starting tomorrow!

Fasting should be a lifestyle. Those who have never fasted before will need to change their mindsets or false assumptions regarding fasting in order to change their behavior and begin fasting.

For one, we must understand that fasting is not an option. *"But you, **when** you fast, anoint your head and wash your face"* (Matt. 6:17 NKJV). Yes, it says "when," not "if." We will not die if we fast! We need first air, then water, then sleep, then food. Any of us can literally live off of just juice. Think about someone who's bedridden and gets fed intravenously through tubes; they're obviously not eating solid foods, yet getting all the nutrients they need. There are, of course, a few different types of fasts that vary in their execution, but not necessarily in effectiveness.

TYPES OF FASTS

1. *A beginner's fast*—This is a fast from television, candy bars, and other minor distractions or vices. If this fast is quite a challenge and sacrifice for you, we bless it in Jesus' name. However, mostly this type of fast works for kids to help teach them the point of discipline and

fleshly denial for the sake of the Kingdom. Adults can do better than this.

2. *A partial fast*—This is fasting from caffeine, meat, sodas, sugar, and any other food or drink stimulants that you feel led to abstain from. This can also include a juice and/or smoothie fast.

3. *A Daniel fast*—A Daniel fast is so named because of the Babylonian diet that Daniel and his comrades rejected in order to be consecrated to the Lord. Read Daniel 1:8-21 for more details.

   A Daniel fast or juice fast can be effective when you're training your body to fast and can be a good idea when you have a labor-intensive job. A Daniel fast can have value in conditioning your body to get used to water-only fasts and is also valuable in times where God is calling you to a less physically intense fast for whatever reasons.

4. *A regular fast*—When we talk about regular fasting, it is by definition a water-only fast, a total flesh denial of sugar, caffeine, food (hard and soft), and anything with taste that can stimulate your flesh.

5. *An Esther fast*—This fast is with no food and no water. Biblically, this fast is practiced only for three days maximum (see Esther 4:15-16). Moses spent 40 days in the glory without food or water (see Exod. 34:28), but this is an extremely rare case that should not be emulated without a major supernatural encounter with the glory of the Lord.

6. *A sleep fast*—Jesus fasted from sleep on a number of occasions in order to give Himself to prayer with the Father (see Luke 6:12). Sometimes the greatest peace and revelation with God comes when you pull spiritual all-nighters. This happens to me often when I get caught up in praying, reading, and writing. Sometimes I'm not even tired the next day.

7. *A lifestyle fast*—The early Church fasted every Wednesday and Friday per tradition.[2] Many wonderful men and women of God fast for one day per week to keep their flesh in alignment with their spirit and to press in with an extra level of urgency and consecration on the day they are fasting. All of these methods of fasting are wonderful. Whatever works best for you, as long as you're giving God your all, will no doubt have great results.

SET THE STANDARD

It is unfortunate that, at times, the world puts us to shame in the area of fasting, and they're not even doing it with the power of God! Even Oprah (famous talk show host) ate only veggies grown from her own garden for 21 days![3]

I was in a gym one time and overheard a guy talking about his tree-hugger friend up in Oregon who fasted without food for 60 days in protest. I don't say this to be offensive; he literally strapped himself to a tree in protest of logging or some other cause. I take this as a spiritual challenge to the causes that we fight for. We must be willing to strap ourselves to God in protest of the worldly culture around us for the sake of souls!

> We must be willing to strap ourselves to God in protest of the worldly culture around us for the sake of souls!

Fasting should always be a spiritual thing. It's not a diet, so we shouldn't act like it is. We must stay focused on God and God alone. If we're spending too much time thinking about what kind of new foods we are going to eat as soon as we end our partial or Daniel fast, then we've lost the focus of why we are fasting in the first place. This should be a time of prayer, worship, reading the Word, and consecration (being set apart) to our Lord Jesus. Certainly we can fast in the flesh as well as eat ice cream in the Spirit.

Now that I've established the importance of fasting, let me share with you some really important things you need to know that will help you to start living a lifestyle of fasting.

FASTING REMOVES UNBELIEF

Unbelief hinders God's spiritual work in and through our lives. Look at the story where the disciples struggled to heal this common disease and then were taught a very valuable lesson:

> *And when they had come to the multitude, a man came to Him, kneeling down to Him and saying, "Lord, have mercy on my son, for he is an epileptic and suffers severely; for he often falls into the fire and often into the water. So I brought him to Your disciples, but they could not cure him." Then Jesus answered and said, "O faithless and perverse generation, how long shall I be with you? How long shall I bear with you? Bring him here to Me." And Jesus rebuked the demon, and it came out of him; and the child was cured from that very hour. Then the disciples came to Jesus privately and said, "**Why could we not cast it out?**" So Jesus said to them, "**Because of your unbelief**; for assuredly, I say to you, if you have faith as a mustard seed, you will say to this mountain, 'Move from here to there,' and it will move; and nothing will be impossible for you. However, **this kind does not go out except by prayer and fasting**" (Matthew 17:14-21 NKJV).*

The one time in Scripture when the disciples truly failed at delivering someone, Jesus rebuked them and then gave them the solution to their problem. *How wonderful is our Savior for not just bringing correction, but also giving direction and imparting the grace to see it through!* He told them that if they only would pray and fast more, they would be able to handle the situation better. This passage says, *"This kind does not go out except by prayer and fasting."* What was "this kind" that Jesus was talking about?

Possibly upon first glance it may seem that He was talking about an extra-powerful devil, saying that kind of powerful devil could only be overcome by believers with the authority and relationship with God born through prayer and fasting. However, I don't believe Jesus was talking about *this kind* of devil at all. I believe He was talking about *this kind* of unbelief.

Jesus rebuked the disciples for their unbelief, not for their lack of executing on any method of healing or deliverance that He had shown them. He said throughout the Gospels that all things are possible to those who believe (see Mark 9:23.). This includes casting out one demon or a hundred, no matter how strong they are. *The thing that was hindering the disciples wasn't the power of this devil; it was their lack of belief in the overcoming power of God, despite this scary situation.* They let fear come in when they saw how violent this devil was, and possibly they got nervous because everyone was looking at them as the solution to the problem. These emotions could have hindered the power of faith at work in their lives.

> The more we protect our hearts to believe what the Word says over what the enemy suggests, the more we will walk in faith and not unbelief.

Even for those who do think this passage is talking about *this kind* of devil, the power and anointing on their lives will be stronger after a fast and will undoubtedly give them bigger guns to shoot at the enemy with. Nonetheless, *the power of our lives is short-circuited by one thing—unbelief.* That's what I believe Jesus wants us to understand in the above passage.

They were presented with a crazy situation, a boy flailing around on the ground and having violent seizures while a crowd watched; we can imagine the nervousness or fear that may have caused their hearts to beat faster, may have even caused them to think twice about why they were even there. This is likely what happened to the disciples.

The Holy Spirit pricks our hearts to convict us of sin or to convince us to do something. However, satan also pricks our hearts with fear. I know from experience that the more we fast, the less this emotion of unbelief can come into our hearts. Faith is truly a shield blocking our hearts. The more we protect our hearts to believe what the Word says over what the enemy suggests, the more we will walk in faith and not unbelief. Fasting purges this unbelief from our hearts and prepares us to walk in greater levels of faith and power

When my wife and I began tent revival meetings in Tucson, I distinctly remember asking God why I had no fear and nervousness when witnessing and praying for the sick like I had had in the past. God then revealed the power of this principle to me by speaking to my heart and spirit that this was due to the fact that I had just come out of a season of a 21-day fast. Something about this fast broke off the power of the emotion of fear.

NEW WINESKINS

Wineskins are animal-skin pouchlike containers that were used to carry wine during the days when Jesus walked the earth. Spiritually speaking, God wants our lives to be these containers that contain more of God's anointing, preferably new containers to carry the new wine of His Spirit.

> *Then the disciples of John came to Him, saying, "Why do we and the Pharisees fast often, but Your disciples do not fast?" And Jesus said to them, "Can the friends of the bridegroom mourn as long as the bridegroom is with them? But the days will come when the bridegroom will be taken away from them, and then they will fast. No one puts a piece of unshrunk cloth on an old garment; for the patch pulls away from the garment, and the tear is made worse. Nor do they put new wine into old wineskins, or else the wineskins break, the wine is spilled, and the wineskins are ruined. But they put new wine into new wineskins, and both are preserved"* (Matthew 9:14-17 NKJV).

Clearly in this passage, Jesus is emphasizing that the new and the old do not go together. The same is true spiritually.

I heard from a Messianic Jewish Rabbi that the Jews used to recycle their wineskins. After the wineskin was used, it would be left out to be picked up, thrown on a truck, and taken to a wineskin facility, where some ladies would anoint and rub oil into the old, dry skin. After they had pressed and rubbed this oil into the leatherlike material long enough to know that the skin would be supple and flexible, the wineskin was ready to be redistributed.

The old, dry wineskin would break if you poured new wine into it. *The same goes for old, dry churches when it comes to receiving the new wine of the Holy Spirit!* This is a wonderful analogy of what God can do in our lives. When our theology, traditions, mindsets, patterns, and actions regarding our spirituality become old and stiff, we must go before the Lord to receive a fresh rubbing in of His anointing.

Only then will our hearts, minds, and spirits be ready to receive new revelation and the new wine of God's Spirit to take us from one season to the next. God longs to anoint us and stretch us to contain more of His Spirit so we can be equipped to make more of a difference in the world. God's process is to *anoint us, fill us (which causes a stretching)*, and then *pour us out*. Once He pours us out, He runs back through the same process again. If we do not allow this process to work itself out, we will likely just stay stuck in the same cycles of life and feel like we're never going to graduate from this particular season with the Lord. *Fasting is a way to keep our spirits flexible to be filled with more of the Holy Spirit and the fullness of God.*

He can take what is old and make it supple again; however, if we truly want *more of God* and a *new move of the Spirit* in our lives, we must not simply ask the Holy Spirit to anoint what is old. God wants to do far more in His Kingdom Church! *I believe God wants us to understand a greater truth about Him desiring to separate the old from the new entirely.*

He wants to completely destroy the old wineskin and give us the new so that we truly can handle the new wine of the Spirit. Sometimes the old just isn't enough for the next level of anointing, authority, and ministry that God wants us to move in. If God wants to give us more, He must replace our old "recycled" wineskins and give us new, *bigger* ones. This comes by fasting.

When we let God break us, shatter us, and destroy the old through fasting, God will then insert more of Himself into the mix and add His fire to melt and refine our spirits. Through this process, God can then re-form (reshape) us to be greater vessels who are able to contain more of the new wine of the Holy Spirit. Fasting has accelerated me to new levels of faith and love and has been a positive tool in my own personal growth and maturity.

A true revival ministry will not just let God anoint them, but will let God break them and transform them so that they can be filled with more of God and can contain more of the new wine of His anointing.

CAN YOU HEAR ME NOW?

The true power of the Christian life comes in our ability to walk in unbroken communion with our Lord so we can hear and act upon what He is speaking to us in any given situation. If a situation like the one in Matthew 17, when the disciples could not cast out a demon, presents itself, we should be able to receive clear direction for what steps to take to truly cast that demon out as we walk in the Spirit and listen to the Lord, despite the present circumstances.

Fasting is an excuse to tune out the world and tune in God. To fast properly, we really should watch as little television and get on the Internet as little as possible during this time. Just those things alone will help us hear more clearly from God. Fasting really does heighten our spiritual "sixth sense." In fact, it also heightens our minds and our eyes; and, contrary to popular belief, I feel like I have more energy and need to sleep less when I fast. Certainly I do feel weak, have headaches, and experience other side effects at times, but much of that is just a result of our bodies breaking our food addictions.

> The true power of the Christian life comes in our ability to walk in unbroken communion with our Lord so we can hear and act on what He is speaking to us in any given situation.

The vision and dream realm is more clear and vibrant when I'm fasting. God talks to me in visions quite often. But we're all different, and we all hear God differently. God will probably speak to you during a fast in the way He normally speaks to you, only it will appear much clearer because your spiritual ears can now hear Him better! In faith, if you open up to hear from Heaven for God to answer your prayers, He *will* show you new gifts and new levels of anointing, favor, and breakthrough!

FASTING IS TRUE SPIRITUAL WORSHIP

> *I beseech you therefore, brethren, by the mercies of God, that you present your bodies a living sacrifice, holy, acceptable to God, which is your reasonable service* (Romans 12:1 NKJV).

Fasting is an act of worship. God tunes in to the fasting prayer because He loves the smell of the sacrifice of our flesh. Fasting shows desperation and urgency, two prerequisites to answered prayer and the ability to successfully pull down the promises of Heaven.

At the risk of sounding like an Alcoholics Anonymous meeting, we must repeat this truth until we believe it: *My flesh is not my friend.* Our flesh continually is working against our spirits. It has carnal tastes and desires that beg for immediate satisfaction. Wise stewards value delayed gratification, and revivalists value beating down our flesh, knowing that it is a virtue to withstand that which works against our spirits.

Paul said it this way:

> *That the righteous requirement of the law might be fulfilled in us who do not walk according to the flesh but according to the Spirit. For those who live according to the flesh set their minds on the things of the flesh, but those who live according to the Spirit, the things of the Spirit. For to be carnally minded is death, but to be spiritually minded is life and peace* (Romans 8:4-6 NKJV).

Good athletes know that they must work out hard and train, even when they don't want to. People with food, sex, and substance addictions give their flesh what it wants when it wants it. The only way for us to break addictions and kick out our flesh devils is by prayer, abstinence, and filling the void left by that fleshly desire with the Holy Spirit. Fasting with prayer accomplishes all three of those things, which means it will most certainly strengthen our spirits and our spiritual walk.

If we want greater spiritual strength in our lives, if we want greater works to occur through our lives, and if we want a greater anointing, *fasting is essential!*

SIDE EFFECTS

Fasting has physical and emotional side effects that we must be aware of if we hope to persevere.

The first few days to a week of fasting, we will have physical side effects. Our bodies are purging poisons and freeing our internal healing qualities to work harder at fixing things that are wrong. Our bodies can now work overtime doing much needed maintenance since they can get a rest from the constant task of digesting and processing physical foods. Fasting has many proven health benefits.[4]

When on extended periods of fasting, we will also have emotional and psychological challenges, such as a deep internal longing for food that goes beyond a physical craving; we may even have dreams about food.

There is also a social impact that fasting also brings to our lives that we all need to be ready for. In many cultures, sitting down to have a cup of coffee and dessert with some friends is a natural part of our social life. Sitting down to dinner with the family is also a valued tradition. I have not heard anybody mention this before, but I think one of the hardest things about fasting is rejecting the social aspects of food, not just the physical aspects of food. *This is just another test to see if we will pay the price to pray and spend the necessary time with God to strengthen our spiritual walks so that we will be bright, shining ones for Jesus, full of love and power, full of the Holy Spirit!*

When fasting for longer than a week or two, emotionally we may get worn down by just the endurance aspect of a fast. At this point, we must continue to feed ourselves spiritually by reading the Bible and surrounding ourselves with godly people.

Whether God has spoken to you to fast or you are just doing it because you feel like it is a great spiritual discipline, I encourage you to give it your all! However, if you fall and eat something, it's OK. Just pick yourself up and keep going; don't be discouraged. Sometimes a "mixed" fast may work for you as well—in which certain days you fast from all food and other days you just eat a vegetarian diet. The point of a fast, more than the full fleshly denial of any food or drink stimulants, is really the consecration aspect of the fast through which you truly dedicate to drawing near to God so He can draw near to you. God wants your heart above all else. Relationship with Him is far more important and valuable than just another method of growing spiritually

A CULTURE OF FASTING

Never forget that fasting is a time of consecration. Matthew 6 talks about anointing our heads with oil when we fast. That is important because God uses the anointing oil throughout Scripture as a symbol of being consecrated or set apart.

> Those who live a fasted lifestyle will walk in such surrender and relationship that they will often know and sense the heart of God.

Oftentimes in Christendom, we seek the face of Jesus and God's glory and have powerful moments of visitation. There are times of desperation when we cry out to God and hear His voice. However, there is so much more to Christianity that just those special moments. Those who live a fasted lifestyle will walk in such surrender and relationship that they will often know and sense the heart of God. They will walk in faith and power, which at the root is knowing their identity in Christ and their personal relationship with God. They will also be able to hear the Holy Spirit clearly at any time, on any day.

When we decide to *be* revival, we are choosing to walk in the Spirit (surrender to the Holy Spirit) 24/7, 365 days a year. There are no days off for the flesh, and there shouldn't be.

Living a life of fasting and praying not only sets us apart for God's good purposes (see 2 Tim. 2:20-22), but it allows us to live a life of habitation rather than just visitation. Only then will we be able to touch lives wherever we go, thus bringing full glory to God and being the salt and light to the earth that Jesus says we're to be (see Matt. 5:13-14).

A lifestyle of separation and consecration, like that of the Nazarites (see Num. 6), is more important than any other spiritual discipline. Fasting should just be an extension of this lifestyle.

Even if we did one 40-day fast a year, but spent the rest of the year living like the world—eating anything we want and gorging ourselves on ungodly television, music, and other influences—we would not be doing ourselves much good. However, I am fully convinced that once we taste and see how good God is, we will hardly have the taste buds for the things of this world! Nothing in this world impresses me like just one small glimpse of the face of Jesus.

> Nothing in this world impresses me like just one small glimpse of the face of Jesus.

Whether we fast one day per week, one day per year, or 200 days a year, we must stay focused on Jesus and choose to always walk in the Spirit so that our Christian walk will be one of power and glory. When more and more of us start doing that as individuals, then and only then will we see God's powerful move of revival spread throughout the world like fire on a windy day!

QUESTIONS

1. Do you have fears about fasting? Are these fears rele-
    vant, or are they based on preconceived misconceptions
    or discouragement from others who may be deceived or
    in ignorance?

    _____

    _____

    _____

    _____

    _____

2. Have you fasted before? If not, are you encouraged to
    begin this wonderful lifestyle of consecration? If you
    have fasted previously, are you encouraged to travel even
    deeper with the Lord on this journey?

    _____

    _____

    _____

    _____

    _____

3. What makes fasting truly effective for the spiritual life
    of a believer?

    _____

    _____

_____

_____

_____

PRAYER (YOU TO GOD)

God, help me to continue to take new steps of faith in my walk with You. I do not want to be a slave to self, a slave to food, or a slave to this world. I want to hear You more clearly and learn how my life can be more of a blessing to You. Give me the grace and strength to fast and even greater grace and strength to let my life be a blessing to others around me. God, stretch our faith and keep our hearts softened to be able to receive more of Your anointing. You are holy and worthy. Amen.

PRAYER (ME TO GOD, FOR YOU)

God give my friend a special grace to live the fasted lifestyle, and bless this person in the pursuit of going to greater depths in his or her spiritual walk. Provide a special grace to fast, even a special grace for the 40-day fast with no food. Provide open visions of Your supernatural realm and let the Lord Jesus visit Your child in person if it is Your will. Let Your words and Your will shape this person's spiritual life more than any discouragement from any person. Bless this servant and send Your servant to others to encourage them in the deeper things of Your Kingdom. Amen.

Endnotes

1. Zane Anderson, preached during a Sunday morning sermon at Victory Worship Center, Tucson, Arizona, sometime in early 2010.

2. St. Nikodemos the Hagiorite, "Concerning Fasting on Wednesday and Friday," 2006, http://www.orthodoxinfo.com/praxis/exo_fasting.aspx, last accessed, September 8, 2010. Also Timothy Ware, *The Orthodox Church* (London: Penguin Books, 1964), 75-77.

3. http://www.oprah.com/food/The-21-Day-Cleanse-Oprahs-Blog-1.

4. http://www.fitnessthroughfasting.com/fasting-health-benefits.html.

It will cost you everything if you want to know God and see His glory. Like Paul, you will have to lay down all your knowledge and become like a little child before Him. You will have to sign your own death certificate on the cross of obedience and in daily surrender of your life, your agenda, and your priorities in prayer and fasting. Then, as you trust Him to strip your "filthy rags of manmade righteousness and religious credentials," God will give you His own righteousness and "new credentials" that have everything to do with His presence and nothing to do with the approval and pleasure of men.

—MAHESH CHAVDA,
The Hidden Power of Prayer and Fasting[1]

Chapter 15

ANYONE CAN PREACH

*You see, we are not like the many hucksters who preach
for personal profit. We preach the word of God with
sincerity and with Christ's authority, knowing that
God is watching us* (2 Corinthians 2:17 NLT).

*...Woe to me if I do not preach the
gospel* (1 Corinthians 9:16).

*The purer the Word of the Gospel is preached, the
purer the power of the Gospel will be manifested.*

*Revivalists are not scared of giving a hard word;
they're scared of not speaking the truth.*

There is a book on my bookshelf entitled, *How to Prepare Bible
Messages.* It came with a prepackaged kit that, once completed, would
allow me to be a "Certified Minister." I don't know in what exactly
I'd be certified, other than reading a few books and passing a few
tests. I think I proved I could read and take tests when I graduated
with my BSBA from Northern Arizona University. *That book and
that certification won't help me to preach anymore than reading about
Pavarotti would teach me to sing opera.*

God's hand is either on someone's life or it isn't. God's message through His servants is either anointed or it isn't. Today, more than ever, we need unction over knowledge and power over preparation!

When it comes to preaching a sermon, preparation isn't bad, but we must be careful that we don't spend time with God with an agenda. God long ago convicted me of reading the Word or praying just to prepare a message (instead of just to be with Him). God's message through us should come from His daily revelations and teachings to us, not from something we dig up just because we need to. Then instead of us just "getting a word" we will "*be* the word!"

> Today, more than ever, we need unction over knowledge and power over preparation!

Seeking God's heart and will for the audience ahead of time is certainly not wrong, but my goal here is to demonstrate how to be a revival preacher, not just another so-called "professional" minister. We have too many of those and too few *fire-filled, Holy Spirit compelled, messengers of God's pure Gospel!* I believe that God is raising up a mighty generation who will learn how to depend on the Holy Spirit to be burning revivalists who preach a pure Gospel because they know the living Jesus.

Jesus instructed His disciples to go and preach the Gospel. The Greek word for preach in this case is *kerysso*, which literally means "to cry like heralds."[2] This is similar to Isaiah's commission in Isaiah 58:1 (NKJV) to *"cry aloud"* and is a word meaning "to lift up their voice like a trumpet."

True preachers are watchmen on the wall, intercessors concerned and compelled by the well-being of the souls of their hearers.

> *The word of the Lord came to me: "Son of man, speak to your people and say to them: 'When I bring the sword against a land, and the people of the land choose one of their men and make him their watchman, and he sees the sword coming against the land and blows the trumpet to warn the people, then if anyone hears the trumpet but does not heed the*

warning and the sword comes and takes their life, their blood will be on their own head. Since they heard the sound of the trumpet but did not heed the warning, their blood will be on their own head. If they had heeded the warning, they would have saved themselves. But if the watchman sees the sword coming and does not blow the trumpet to warn the people and the sword comes and takes someone's life, that person's life will be taken because of their sin, but I will hold the watchman accountable for their blood.'" (Ezekiel 33:1-6).

Where are our modern-day watchmen? Who will blow the trumpet? Who will warn the people that their blood is required of them to pay for their sins if they don't accept Jesus' sacrifice?

Who will take on the burden of a generation that is going to die an everlasting death if they are not warned? May God release us all to preach and preach like life or death is at stake—because it is. If we do this, God won't hold us accountable for their blood.

FIRST SERMONS

It was spring of the year 2003. My former pastor in San Manuel, Arizona, asked me to preach a Sunday morning service. This happened after I had boldly proclaimed that I knew God was calling me to be a pastor and preacher. He extended the invite and said that we would take out an ad in the city newspaper, *The Miner,* and invite everyone in town who used to know me or who was curious about my testimony as a prodigal son. Immediately when I hung up with him, a sense of nervousness and worry filled my heart. *Oh, Lord,* I thought, *I've never preached a sermon in my life. I have no idea what to do.*

Then the Holy Spirit reminded me of the great passage from Paul to Timothy: *"For God has not given us a spirit of fear, but of power and of love and of a sound mind"* (2 Tim. 1:7 NKJV). At that moment, I laid face down on my bed and began to pray. The Lord then showed me a vision of me preaching and what I would preach about. I got up and knew it was done. I experienced no more fear and no more nervousness.

The day came for me to preach, and I think the pastor was the one now getting nervous. It was a packed house! He sat me down in his office and had a serious talk with me, saying that if I was not moving under the power of the anointing and I preached one minute past noon, he would get up and pull the plug on me. He said that if people weren't crying and God wasn't touching people, then he would intervene and pull me down from the pulpit. This talk could have made any newbie preacher nervous, but not me—not because of anything great in me, but because of the mindset that God had taught me. I knew that when we're doing any kind of spiritual ministry, like praying, preaching, or prophesying, the Holy Spirit will be the one doing it through us—at least that's how it should be.

I began to preach and flow under the power of God. I had ten pages of notes and don't know if I used more than one in my sermon. *The power of God hit that place and people were weeping.* I went almost a half hour past noon, and only one couple walked out. I was so full with the Holy Spirit that God had to actually take me over, turn me around, and put me on my knees at the altar to make me stop. It's quite hilarious now that I think back. But I had no idea how to close out a message, do an altar call, or anything like that. I just saw in my head the vision, relied on the Holy Spirit, and stayed prayed up and in Christ, and God did the rest.

> When we do any kind of spiritual ministry, like praying, preaching, or prophesying, the Holy Spirit will be doing it through us.

To this day, if I'm invited to preach anywhere, I simply let God show me in a vision what I'll be talking about and then I prepare accordingly. I don't think I've been nervous once.

David Yonggi Cho's book, *The Fourth Dimension*, must have affected me in a positive way. I heard him say that before he learned to partner with the Holy Spirit, he used to listen to and copy every single one of Billy Graham's sermons until he ran out. He was lost and had only one choice left, to hear from Heaven and deliver a Word that God gave him directly.[3] What a beautiful example that all young preachers *must* learn from.

Years ago (coincidentally around the same time I preached my first sermon), my wife was asked by her brother to preach at the youth service at her parents' church. She immediately said, "No way!" Her brother persisted and said that God had revealed to him that she would be the one to preach that upcoming service. She again said "No." He said, "OK, I'll give you ten minutes and call you back for a final answer." Again she said, "That is my final answer." Of course, God had other plans. He convicted her, and His anointing hit her hard as a confirmation that she was in fact the one to preach this message.

She said that when the time came it was an amazing experience. She flowed in the power of God, hardly used her notes, and preached a powerful, prophetic message for the church; many people responded to the altar call. She realized at that time what I also had learned—any man or woman filled with the Spirit of God is capable of carrying the message of Christ and preaching with great unction and power. If I can do it and my wife can do it, so can you!

ANYTIME'S A GOOD TIME

Famous historical revivalist Charles Finney amazed the religious leaders of his day because He could preach anytime, any day, at a whim. The same was said of other historic revivalists like John Wesley and George Whitfield. Not only that, Finney did this out of pure inspiration of the Holy Spirit, as documented in his autobiography:

> When I first began to preach and for some twelve years of my earliest ministry, I wrote not a word; and was most commonly obliged to preach without any preparation whatever except what I got in prayer. Oftentimes I went into the pulpit without knowing upon what text I should speak, or a word that I should say. I depended on the occasion and the Holy Spirit to suggest the text, and to open up the whole subject to my mind; and certainly in no party of my ministry have I ever preached with greater success and power than I did when I preached in that way. If I did not preach from inspiration, I don't know how I did preach."[4]

FOOLISH OR WISE?

You may call me presumptuous, naive, or even foolish, but preaching solely from Holy Spirit inspiration has worked for me from day one, and I'm sure it will work for you as well.

I've heard preachers say that God helps us with things until we learn to do it ourselves, referring specifically to God's special grace in preaching powerful sermons when we've had relatively little experience. This method of teaching is true with good fathers, such as when a dad is teaching his daughter how to ride a bike or his son how to shoot a gun. It is true with God, too, to an extent. The problem with this theory is that, if we're not careful, we can subconsciously divorce ourselves from the dependence on the Holy Spirit in our spiritual preparations. *The special raw moments of depending on His anointing above our own efforts and those glorious tangents we may go off on while preaching just because one person in the audience had to hear that could slowly start to vanish!*

We may begin substituting prayer time for preparation. We may get so refined in presenting our thoughts that after a while the power of the purity of the Gospel has slipped out the back door and we didn't even notice. We certainly over time learn how to properly study the depths of His Word, the historical context, and the original Greek and Hebrew meanings of words, phrases, and passages. This is a wonderful adventure in itself. We may even get really good at generating an altar call response at the end of our messages. However, if we're not careful, we will stay at this soul level, simply touching emotions, but not separating the thoughts and intents of the heart by the true power of the Word (see Heb. 4:12) and truly leading others into repentance and salvation. If you are called to preach, pray earnestly that you don't fall into this deception, and I will do the same for myself.

ACTIVATION

At one home Bible study for men, I felt led by the Lord to activate some young men as prophets and preachers in our midst. It's always been a particular gift of mine to see the gifts in others, and it brings special joy to my heart to see others moving in their God-given gifts.

Without prior notice and with only an emphasis on hearing from the Holy Spirit, I pulled out my Bible, turned to a particular passage, and passed the Bible over to this unsuspecting friend. I asked him if he would get up in the middle of the room and preach a sermon on that passage. He stared at me with a frightened look. I encouraged and prodded. He began to pray, then shake, then cry as he stood because the Spirit had dropped a bomb of glory and anointing on him.

What happened next was quite amazing. As he opened his heart in faith to receive this special grace to preach from God, God filled Him with so much of Himself that my friend started actually speaking out the very voice of God in first person! God, Himself, was preaching to us and encouraging us. All the while my friend was shaking under the power. This was his first sermon, and since then, he has preached and taught wonderful messages when he's had the opportunity. Hopefully he will never lose the lesson he learned that day—that *"I can do all this through him who gives me strength"* (Phil. 4:13), even when we're afraid.

This activation happened because of my encouragement, his faith, and God's grace. Let the words of this book and the testimonies encourage you to step out in faith knowing that *if you have a full dependence on God, He **will** come through!*

ANY IDEAS?

For those who can't think of what to preach about, a good place for them to start is sharing what they know about Jesus, what He has done in their lives. Our testimonies are powerful. And we must share with the people the fact that God loves them and cares for their souls enough to send His Son Jesus Christ to take their place on the cross of

Calvary and be brutally murdered so that we wouldn't have to spend eternity in hell because of our sins.

Pure preaching of the Gospel and a clear call to repentance are the prerequisites to any true revival. Repentance is also the only way you can understand and walk in the revelation of God's Kingdom. Jesus clearly preached repentance, which preceded the Kingdom (see Matt. 4:17). So if we care for people's spiritual growth, we will surely do them a huge favor by preaching repentance.

> Pure preaching of the Gospel and a clear call to repentance are the prerequisites to any true revival.

If you are called on to preach and feel like the Holy Spirit hasn't shown you what to preach yet, the bottom-line, when in doubt, is to preach first Jesus and to then preach what He preached, repentance. You can also borrow the title of my first sermon ever, "Wake up, Church!" That was my first sermon, but I have discovered, many years later, that it is really the theme of my life's message.

In all things spiritual, in all commandments of the Word, we know that it is not by our strength that we will be successful in any of these things. The Bible says that God's strength is made perfect in our weakness.

> In all things spiritual, in all commandments of the Word, it is not by our strength that we will be successful.

But He said to me, "My grace is sufficient for you, for My power is made perfect in weakness." Therefore I will boast all the more gladly about my weaknesses, so that Christ's power may rest on me (2 Corinthians 12:9).

If you're ever called on to preach in faith, know that all you have to do is open your mouth and God will surely give you the right words to pierce hearts and change lives. But when it comes to sermons, please pull no punches; my life is at stake! Please don't water down the message to try and protect my feelings. If you don't offend me, how will I be moved to change? If my pride doesn't rise up in offense, how will I know that it's there and that it needs to be dealt with?

The Bible clearly states that *"faith comes by hearing, and hearing by the word of God"* (Rom. 10:17 NKJV). No matter how big or cool your church is, that will not generate faith in someone's heart. No matter how perfect your worship music may sound at church, that won't generate faith in someone's heart. All the toys, food, games, prizes, dances, dramas and any other creative method to get peoples' attention are just gimmicks if the Word of God is not followed. You can grab someone's attention with various means, but they won't be birthed into God's Kingdom without the Word of God preached. In some ways, true Bible preaching is a lost art form, replaced by positive, motivational messages that don't help anyone into the Kingdom any more than watching a political speech would.

I, myself, am a motivational speaker to high school students and in other secular arenas where I know I am not supposed to mention Jesus or anything to do with Christian faith. In these cases, I let God's anointing on my life shine through positive messages and encouraging words. However, I am praying that these messages gain credibility and favor with my hearers so that an open door with them may be opened up for me to really share the Gospel message to them personally or through another means of them connecting with me afterward such as by social media or buying one of my books. If and when I am allowed, you can bet I am preaching the full Gospel of Jesus Christ, not a watered-down version that hardly generates faith in the hearer's hearts.

Lastly, the Gospel must always be preached with a demonstration of power. If the Gospel we preach is not accompanied by demonstrations of power, then it is only half of the equation, sadly incomplete.

QUESTIONS

1. Do you believe that you can preach? You don't need to know much, a simple, "Once I was lost, now I am found" will do just fine when you have the power of the Holy Spirit behind it.

   _____

   _____

   _____

   _____

2. What are you doing now that you could surrender at an even greater level to our Lord and to the working of His Spirit instead of relying your own efforts?

   _____

   _____

   _____

   _____

3. Do you attempt to "do" ministry and prepare for ministry rather than just have intimate fellowship with the Lord and let your life be the ministry extension of that relationship? If so, what can you do to change that?

   _____

   _____

   _____

   _____

PRAYER (YOU TO GOD)

God, I surrender all of my talents and gifts to You for Your glory. I come to You with a childlike heart, wanting to learn how Your Spirit longs to reach the people You allow me to minister to. God, teach me Your ways and empower me with Your presence so that I may help spread the Gospel around the world through my actions and words. Praise be to You! May Your name be lifted high throughout every remaining generation on this earth. Amen.

PRAYER (ME TO GOD, FOR YOU)

God, anoint this precious saint to preach Your words with power and authority, even when no words are used. Let Your warrior's life be an extension of power from Your throne. Provide visions and visitations from Your Spirit to encourage Your servant to be dependent on Your supernatural power to preach messages that can come from inspiration from the Holy Spirit alone. Bless this precious saint and bless his or her words to reach thousands and tens of thousand for the sake of the Gospel of Jesus Christ and for Your glory! Amen.

Endnotes

1. Mahesh Chavda, *The Hidden Power of Prayer and Fasting* (Shippensburg, PA: Destiny Image Publishers, 1998).

2. Gerhard Kittel, Gerhard Friedrich, Geoffrey William Bromiley, *Theological Dictionary of the New Testament, Volume 1* (Grand Rapids, MI: William B. Eerdmans Publishing Company, 1985), available at http://books.google.com/books?id=ltZBUW_F9ogC&pg=PA432&lpg=PA432&dq=kerysso+Hebrew&source=bl&ots=4zWEMOrPcB&sig=vN4MwZZNsvo1fFtFJifzeHtCDuI&hl=en&ei=wgV-TJChNpKCsQOoz4iXCw&sa=X&oi=book_result&ct=result&resnum=1&ved=0CBcQ6AEwAA#v=onepage&q=kerysso%20Hebrew&f=false.

3. David Yonggi Cho, *The Fourth Dimension, Vol. 1,* (Alachua, FL: Bridge-Logos Publishers, 1979).

4. Charles Finney, *The Original Memoirs of Charles G. Finney* (New York: A.S. Barnes and Company, 1876), 75-76.

YOU'RE AN ARMY

You're an army dressed for battle

Take the land

The weapons of our warfare

They are mighty through our God

We cut off the giants head

We eat giants for our bread

—RICK PINO[1]

Chapter 16

POWER TOOLS

But if I cast out demons by the finger of God, surely the
kingdom of God has come upon you (Luke 11:20 NKJV).

My message and my preaching were not with wise and
persuasive words, but with a demonstration of the Spir-
its power, so that your faith might not rest on human
wisdom, but on God's power (1 Corinthians 2:4-5).

A tool has no glory; it simply is used to help fix or build
something much grander than itself. The greatness
of the finished product then will point to the one
who created it, not to the tools that were used.

There is a saying in Christendom, "God doesn't call the equipped;
He equips the called." More than just some cliché, there is a great
truth to this quote. A major spiritual battle is waging war against
our souls and the souls of those we love, and we are recruits in
God's army to fight against His and our enemy, satan, and his spiritual forces. We cannot ignore this spiritual reality, and we better
be equipped to handles the realities of the spiritual battle at hand.
Revivalists are always on the frontlines, fighting for the things
nearest to God's heart.

Paul taught the church at Ephesus how to properly be prepared for this spiritual battle:

> *Put on the full armor of God so that you can take your stand against the devil's schemes. For our struggle is not against flesh and blood, but against the rulers, against the authorities, against the powers of this dark world and against the spiritual forces of evil in the heavenly realms. Therefore put on the full armor of God, so that when the day of evil comes, you may be able to stand your ground, and after you have done everything, to stand. Stand firm then, with the belt of truth buckled around your waist, with the breastplate of righteousness in place, and with your feet fitted with the readiness that comes from the gospel of peace. In addition to all this, take up the shield of faith, with which you can extinguish all the flaming arrows of the evil one. Take the helmet of salvation and the sword of the Spirit, which is the word of God. And pray in the Spirit on all occasions with all kinds of prayers and requests. With this in mind, be alert and always keep on praying for all the Lord's people* (Ephesians 6:11-18).

> Revivalists are always on the front-lines, fighting for the things nearest to God's heart.

Satan's servants have power. It's not much and not like God's, but if we are battling against an enemy that isn't entirely powerless, God knows we need some tools, some weapons to go with us into battle.

Like any good army, we are not meant to go to war with no armor and no weapons. Any army you fight for will send you to the battlefield with the right equipment to succeed. If God is calling us to fight for Him, He wants us armed and loaded!

Remember, Jesus came to earth not to just provide the once-and-for-all sacrifice for our sins, but also to destroy the works of the devil (see 1 John 3:8). We should desire to follow in His footsteps. His spiritual power gifts, when we learn how to use them, can provide a great resource for God's Kingdom advancement on earth and a great blow to the enemy.

In addition to administrative gifts, talents, and other roles and functions that we may have in the Body of Christ, there are also nine gifts of the Spirit that we label, in contemporary Christianity, as the nine "power gifts" (see 1 Cor. 12:7-11). These are Spirit-empowered Kingdom weapons that are spiritual in nature and, when manifest, are obvious signs that point to a God of the impossible who can do things beyond our natural interpretations and explanations. These gifts are documented in Paul's letter to the Corinthians and were manifested in various places throughout Scripture by Jesus and His apostles.

As we study this, it's important to remember that there are no gifts of the Spirit that you cannot also pray to receive and move in yourself. The Holy Spirit distributes the gifts of the Spirit as He sees fit (see 1 Cor. 12:7-11); however, I have seen in my own life and in others that when we properly manage the gifts He has given us, we can pray to receive others that God will allow us to function in. The provision for each gift has already been given to us by the finished work of Jesus on the cross. However, God also will give us gifts/tools distributed according to God's will to accomplish a certain task at hand (see Heb. 2:4). Certainly, some require varying degrees of spiritual authority to operate in, but as you prove to the Lord that you are faithful with little, He can and will continue to bless you with more. Also, as your level of spiritual responsibility grows, your capacity and need to operate in certain gifts will become more apparent.

> There are no gifts of the Spirit that you cannot also pray to receive and move in yourself.

Jesus, Paul, and Peter all moved in the nine power gifts of the Spirit listed here:

> *But the manifestation of the Spirit is given to each one for the profit of all: for to one is given the **word of wisdom** through the Spirit, to another the **word of knowledge** through the same Spirit, to another **faith** by the same Spirit, to another*

*gifts of healings by the same Spirit, to another the **working of miracles**, to another **prophecy**, to another **discerning of spirits**, to another **different kinds of tongues**, to another the **interpretation of tongues**. But one and the same Spirit works all these things, distributing to each one individually as He wills* (1 Corinthians 12:7-11 NKJV).

It would take too long to try and explain each in detail, but I will list each gift with a brief description and a couple of biblical examples.

WORD OF WISDOM

A word of wisdom is a divinely inspired wise response to a question or situation in order to bring ultimate glory to God, the only one from whom such a response may originate.

Jesus often had great responses to any question the religious Jews asked Him as they continued to try and stump our Master teacher. One of the top examples of a word of wisdom is the wise response Jesus gave when the chief priests tried to challenge His authority.

When He entered the temple, the chief priests and the elders of the people came to Him while He was teaching, and said, "By what authority are You doing these things, and who gave You this authority?" Jesus said to them, "I will also ask you one thing, which if you tell Me, I will also tell you by what authority I do these things. The baptism of John was from what source, from heaven or from men?" And they began reasoning among themselves, saying, "If we say, 'From heaven,' He will say to us, 'Then why did you not believe him?' "But if we say, 'From men,' we fear the people; for they all regard John as a prophet." And answering Jesus, they said, "We do not know." He also said to them, "Neither will I tell you by what authority I do these things" (Matthew 21:23-27 NASB).

As you can see by Jesus' response, He baffled the spiritual leaders by giving them a question for their question, knowing that they would not want to answer it because either way they would be in trouble with the people.

Another great example of this gift is found in the Old Testament story of Solomon resolving a conflict between two mothers by commanding that the baby they were fighting over be cut in two. As the story goes, he knew who the true mother was because she conceded the child to the other woman rather than having him cut in two (see 1 Kings 3; 2 Chron. 1).

WORD OF KNOWLEDGE

A word of knowledge is information that only the Spirit of the Lord would know. He reveals it to us in order for us to share it with people in a way that shows them that God knows all things and cares for them enough to share this information with one of His servants. A word of knowledge can be any divinely inspired information ranging from a sickness in someone's body to a future prophetic event or revelation about something in someone's life that we wouldn't know by human knowledge. This is seen in these two examples with Nathanael and the Samaritan woman.

> *Jesus saw Nathanael coming to Him, and said of him, "Behold, an Israelite indeed, in whom there is no deceit!" Nathanael said to Him, "How do You know me?" Jesus answered and said to him, "Before Philip called you, when you were under the fig tree, I saw you"* (John 1:47-48 NASB).

With Nathanael, Jesus told him details of an event that had just happened in his life that Jesus could not have known about in the natural. Later in His ministry, Jesus encountered the woman at the well, and though He had never met her before, He knew that she had been with multiple men.

> *The woman answered and said, "I have no husband." Jesus said to her, "You have correctly said, 'I have no husband'; for you have had five husbands, and the one whom you now have is not your husband; this you have said truly." The woman*

said to Him, "Sir, I perceive that You are a prophet" (John 4:17-19 NASB).

In both cases, Jesus used the opportunity to share this divinely revealed knowledge to reveal to both Nathaniel and the woman at the well that He was not only a prophet, but also the Christ.

Another excellent example happened when Jesus met Zacchaeus in Luke 19. The Bible says that Zacchaeus wanted to see who Jesus was, inferring that He and Jesus had never met (see Luke 19:3). Nonetheless, Jesus called him by name, *"Zacchaeus, come down immediately. I must stay at your house today"* (Luke 19:5). Jesus knew who he was because God had revealed this to Him prior to them meeting, even showing Jesus that He must stay at Zacchaeus's home. *I pray that we will be able to call out strangers by name as God strengthens the word of knowledge gift in our lives.*

FAITH

The gift of faith descends on a believer in the time of need like a supernatural mantle. The gift of faith removes unbelief, causes boldness, and empowers the person to declare or act in such a way to cause atmospheric shift in a situation. It is so powerful that Jesus says this of faith:

> The gift of faith removes unbelief, causes boldness, and empowers.

...If you have faith the size of a mustard seed, you will say to this mountain, "Move from here to there," and it will move; and nothing will be impossible to you (Matthew 17:20 NASB).

Examples of such faith include the times when Peter walked on water and when Paul raised a child from death, as we see in the following Scriptures:

And Peter answered Him and said, "Lord, if it is You, command me to come to You on the water." So He said, "Come." And when Peter had come down out of the boat, he walked on the water to go to Jesus. (Matthew 14:28-29 NKJV).

Peter's faith was taking Jesus at His word, much in the same way that the Centurion took Jesus at His word for the healing of his son and was commended for it (see Matt. 8:10). When Paul grabbed the boy who fell from the window and died, his certainty that the boy would live was a manifestation of the gift of faith.

> *And in a window sat a certain young man named Eutychus, who was sinking into a deep sleep. He was overcome by sleep; and as Paul continued speaking, he fell down from the third story and was taken up dead. But Paul went down, fell on him, and embracing him said, "Do not trouble yourselves, for his life is in him"* (Acts 20:9-10 NKJV).

Paul's faith in this case was likely a Holy Spirit inspired mantle of faith that descended on him as he encountered this urgent emergency situation.

Revivalists like Smith Wigglesworth moved in gifts of faith; it was documented that many people were raised from the dead by his prayers and commands of faith empowered by God's Spirit. Maria Woodworth-Etter and many others throughout history also consistently demonstrated the working of this gift.[2]

GIFT OF HEALING

Healing is a virtue of Christ and a demonstration of Christ to illustrate the fact that the Kingdom has come, and it is greatly emphasized throughout Scripture.

It is well documented throughout the Gospels that Jesus healed those who came to Him from all manner of sickness and disease (see Matt. 4:23; 9:35). It was one of the missions of our wonderful Savior that He healed all who were oppressed by the devil. Sickness and disease are oppressions from the devil. Anything that fits in this category would be healed.

> *God anointed Jesus of Nazareth with the Holy Spirit and with power, who went about doing good and healing all who*

were oppressed by the devil, for God was with Him (Acts 10:38 NKJV).

A release of healing virtue, or power, even went out from Jesus in a way that He could actually feel when the woman with the issue of blood touched His cloak.

> *And a certain woman, which had an issue of blood twelve years, and had suffered many things of many physicians, and had spent all that she had, and was nothing bettered, but rather grew worse, when she had heard of Jesus, came in the press behind, and touched His garment. For she said, If I may touch but His clothes, I shall be whole. And straightway the fountain of her blood was dried up; and she felt in her body that she was healed of that plague. And Jesus, **immediately knowing in Himself that virtue had gone out of Him**, turned Him about in the press, and said, Who touched My clothes?* (Mark 5:25-30 KJV)

This story proves the timeless truth that our faith pulls on Christ's healing power. When the two are combined, no matter of sickness or disease can stand! This wasn't just for Jesus of Nazareth's day, but for our day, too!

It is also documented that all were healed during the time of the early Church when the apostles were ministering healing. *"Also a multitude gathered from the surrounding cities to Jerusalem, bringing sick people and those who were tormented by unclean spirits, and they were all healed"* (Acts 5:16 NKJV).

John G. Lake provides a good historic example of a very strong healing ministry. And Benny Hinn is a good present-day example.

WORKING OF MIRACLES

Miracles are rarer than the gift of healing, which can be defined more as accelerated natural healing. A miracle is typically instantaneous and undoubtedly supernatural in nature.

Acts 19 shares a fascinating picture of the miracle anointing. There was so much power, authority, and anointing in Paul that he even prayed over handkerchiefs that were used to carry God's power and authority to set people free:

> *Now God worked unusual miracles by the hands of Paul, so that even handkerchiefs or aprons were brought from his body to the sick, and the diseases left them and the evil spirits went out of them* (Acts 19:11-12 NKJV).

> Miracles are rarer than the gift of healing, which can be defined more as accelerated natural healing.

These unusual miracles were performed in the context of Paul *"arguing persuasively about the kingdom of God"* (Acts 19:8) and having *"discussions daily"* about the Kingdom of God (see Acts 19:9).

The Bible documents another example of miracles in the ministry of Philip, the evangelist; when the people heard and saw the miraculous signs he did, they all paid close attention to what he said (see Acts 8:6). These miracles got people's attention so they could hear about the Kingdom.

Jesus performed a miracle for the man with the withered hand so that He could teach the religious leaders about God's true heart for the Sabbath day.

> *Now when He had departed from there, He went into their synagogue. And behold, there was a man who had a withered hand. And they asked Him, saying, "Is it lawful to heal on the Sabbath?"—that they might accuse Him. Then He said to them, "What man is there among you who has one sheep, and if it falls into a pit on the Sabbath, will not lay hold of it and lift it out? Of how much more value then is a man than a sheep? Therefore it is lawful to do good on the Sabbath." Then He said to the man, "Stretch out your hand." And he stretched it out, and it was restored as whole as the other.*

Then the Pharisees went out and plotted against Him, how they might destroy Him (Matthew 12:9-14 NKJV).

When the Gospel message of Jesus Christ was going throughout Jerusalem, God even used Peter's shadow as a trigger mechanism for people's faith, causing them to believe in the authority of the name of Jesus and the authority of the apostles as God's representatives of the Kingdom.

And believers were increasingly added to the Lord, multitudes of both men and women, so that they brought the sick out into the streets and laid them on beds and couches, that at least the shadow of Peter passing by might fall on some of them. Also a multitude gathered from the surrounding cities to Jerusalem, bringing sick people and those who were tormented by unclean spirits, and they were all healed (Acts 5:14-16 NKJV).

Lord, I pray that You would once again confirm your teaching about the Kingdom through miracles performed by me and all those reading this book, all through the name of Jesus and for Your glory and Your Kingdom.

PROPHECY

Prophecy is the gift that Paul encouraged us to desire above all others (see 1 Cor. 14:1). I discuss this in much greater detail in Chapter 17, "Prophets by Default." A quick summary of the gift is that it is used for edification, comfort, and encouragement of the Body of Christ (see 1 Cor. 14:3). Those who prophesy speak things that are to come into the present so that we can align our spirits and actions with these divinely inspired words of revelation as we receive them in faith.

Philip was so full of the Holy Spirit that he even had four daughters who were prophets! Here in Acts we see an example of the prophetic word acted out by Agabus, who came down to connect with the believers and prophesy over Paul. There was a lot of prophetic activity going on in Caesarea!

> *And when we had finished our voyage from Tyre, we came to Ptolemais, greeted the brethren, and stayed with them one day. On the next day we who were Paul's companions departed and came to Caesarea, and entered the house of Philip the evangelist, who was one of the seven, and stayed with him. Now this man had four virgin daughters who prophesied. And as we stayed many days, a certain prophet named Agabus came down from Judea. When he had come to us, he took Paul's belt, bound his own hands and feet, and said, "Thus says the Holy Spirit, 'So shall the Jews at Jerusalem bind the man who owns this belt, and deliver him into the hands of the Gentiles'"* (Acts 21:7-11 NKJV).

The prophetic is such a powerful tool that when utilized by the leading of the Holy Spirit and through relationship with the Holy Spirit, it can enable us to discern people's hearts and allow us to pray and declare God's specific will over people, places, and nations.

DISCERNING OF SPIRITS

Discernment is discussed in more detail in Chapter 18; however, discerning spirits is found often in the New Testament as another revelatory gift that the Lord imparts upon believers, enabling them to supernaturally know what spirits are involved in a certain situation. In the below examples, Peter rebukes a man and discerns the spirits at work in his life and Paul also rebukes the spirits enslaving a slave girl.

Remember, we have authority over any spirit that is not of God. God desires to reveal to us what the spiritual situation is by showing us what spirits are involved and how to deal with them, as we see in the following two examples.

> *And when Simon saw that through the laying on of the apostles' hands the Holy Spirit was given, he offered them money, saying, "Give me this power also, that anyone on whom I lay*

hands may receive the Holy Spirit." But Peter said to him, "Your money perish with you, because you thought that the gift of God could be purchased with money! You have neither part nor portion in this matter, for your heart is not right in the sight of God. Repent therefore of this your wickedness, and pray God if perhaps the thought of your heart may be forgiven you. For I see that you are poisoned by **bitterness** *and bound by* **iniquity**" (Acts 8:18-23 NKJV).

Highlighted in bold, the spirits involved in these situations were spirits of bitterness and iniquity. In addition, here is a documented case where Paul had to go up against a different spirit:

It happened that as we were going to the place of prayer, a slave-girl having a **spirit of divination** *met us, who was bringing her masters much profit by fortune-telling. Following after Paul and us, she kept crying out, saying, "These men are bond-servants of the Most High God, who are proclaiming to you the way of salvation." She continued doing this for many days. But Paul was greatly annoyed, and turned and said to the spirit, "I command you in the name of Jesus Christ to come out of her!" And it came out at that very moment* (Acts 16:16-18 NASB).

How interesting that this evil spirit was proclaiming the truth, but in a way that distracted from the real message of the Gospel. On multiple occasions while I was evangelizing, people with evil spirits would argue with me regarding the Gospel and Bible, although they were essentially agreeing with every point I was making. It was simply a method of the enemy to bring in a distracting spirit to annoy and disrupt. In these cases I would rebuke them to leave or simply just walk away myself.

DIFFERENT KINDS OF TONGUES

While Peter was still speaking these words, the Holy Spirit fell upon all those who heard the word. And those of the

circumcision who believed were astonished, as many as came
with Peter, because the gift of the Holy Spirit had been poured
out on the Gentiles also. For they heard them speak with
tongues and magnify God (Acts 10:44-46 NKJV).

The gift of *glossolalia,* or speaking in a heavenly tongue, appears
to have been around as long as Pentecost. As in Acts 10, we see that
God gave no partiality to who could receive the gift; these Gentiles
received even while Peter was speaking! There are a few vital points
to consider when discussing tongues.

Tongues are a sign to unbelievers (see 1 Cor. 14:22), a witnessing
tool to people of other languages (see Acts 2), and a prayer language
to build ourselves up in the faith (see Jude 1:20). Praying in the Spirit
is also a weapon of warfare, as documented at the beginning of this
chapter in Ephesians 6:18! The gift of tongues can be our spirit praying
and worshiping God in a heavenly language when we don't even have
the words to speak. In such a way, tongues can greatly assist with our
own private prayer and worship life.

Furthermore, tongues can be observed sometimes in corporate set-
tings in relation to the gift of interpretation, which edifies the entire
body of believers within listening distance.

INTERPRETATION OF TONGUES

Interpretation of tongues is meant for a corporate setting (I
suppose this can be defined as any fellowship of more than one person)
so that whomever speaks in tongues may utilize that gift to edify those
around them. Paul aptly explains in the following Scripture that if you
are speaking in tongues loudly enough for others to hear, you should
also be praying for interpretation. Often God uses those who pray or
speak a message aloud in tongues to a body of believers to interpret
that message, but God may also and often does have others around
who can interpret for the edification of those listening.

There are, it may be, so many kinds of languages in the world,
and none of them is without significance. Therefore, if I do

not know the meaning of the language, I shall be a for-
eigner to him who speaks, and he who speaks will be a for-
eigner to me. Even so you, since you are zealous for spiri-
tual gifts, let it be for the edification of the church that you
seek to excel. Therefore let him who speaks in a tongue pray
that he may interpret. For if I pray in a tongue, my spirit
prays, but my understanding is unfruitful. What is the
conclusion then? I will pray with the spirit, and I will also
pray with the understanding. I will sing with the spirit,
and I will also sing with the understanding. Otherwise, if
you bless with the spirit, how will he who occupies the place
of the uninformed say "Amen" at your giving of thanks,
since he does not understand what you say? For you indeed
give thanks well, but the other is not edified (1 Corinthians 14:10-17 NKJV).

DESIRE GOOD GIFTS

Paul groups the following gifts with the fivefold ministry roles of apostle, prophet, and teacher and orders them in a list of "the best gifts."

It is actually selfish and prideful to not go after a desire that God has put in your heart, so don't you dare say you're not worthy!

And God has appointed these in the church: first apostles, second prophets, third teachers, after that miracles, then gifts of healings, helps, administrations, varieties of tongues (1 Corinthians 12:28 NKJV).

If you have a desire to see God use you more in one of these gifts, then likely God put that desire there! It is actually selfish and prideful to not go after a desire that God has put in your heart so don't you dare say you're not worthy!

If you have had inclinations toward God using you in one of the areas and have seen some results, I encourage you to read more about these gifts and how they work and to hang around those who may be moving in those similar gifts. This is how you will learn and grow.

WALK IT OUT

That's the reason for miracles. No miracles for miracles' sake, but to lead nonbelievers to faith in—and commitment to—the Lord Jesus Christ. —KATHRYN KUHLMAN[3]

When we minister out of the right intentions and with the heart of God, we must know that He wants to show up in power in people's lives to heal them, help them, and love on them. The power gifts are just an extension of God's character. We must not seek the gifts for the sake of the gifts, but for the sake of Jesus.

God gives gifts to those who will steward them; it is a principle of the Kingdom. We must prove ourselves in character—in how well we manage money and our own families—before God will let us be stewards over great heavenly riches, such as His anointing (see Luke 16:11; 1 Tim. 3:12). The Bible says that *"from the one who has been entrusted with much, much more will be asked"* (see Luke 12:48). We must not stop ministering in our gifts or stop pursuing more of God if we want Him to show us how to receive, open, and use His heavenly power tools for His glory and for the advancement of His spiritual Kingdom influence!

We should also surround ourselves with others who move in great spiritual authority and in God's supernatural power tools. If we honor and learn from these men and women of God, we will quickly learn how these same gifts can be activated in our own lives as well. And we must pray that the Holy Spirit will show us through progressive experience the working of His mighty gifts, while also relying on His direction and His anointing above His gifts.

Last but not least, we need to just start doing them in faith! *Faith activates all of the promises of God.* The more people we pray for, the more results we will have simply because of the law of averages. Once we get real breakthrough and authority in one area, we can consider that another city conquered in our Promised Land and go after another gift. God desires us to feel free to continue to pick up the gifts and use them when the opportunity arises.

Humility wants to move in every power gift for God's glory. False humility is thinking and acting like we are not supposed to have any of the gifts because we are not worthy.

If you have a strong desire in your heart to change the world and spread the Good News about Jesus Christ, then God must have put it there. As you come into alignment with Heaven's will for your life, God's gifts will grow stronger in your life and you will become more and more of a force to be reckoned with in His heavenly army!

QUESTIONS

1. Do you desire to move in power? Why do you think this is important for God's Church?

_____

_____

_____

_____

_____

_____

_____

2. Which of the power gifts have you seen at work in your life, even partially?

_____

_____

_____

_____

_____

_____

_____

3. Go back and reread the Scripture with the nine power gifts again. Which ones stand out to you as gifts you

think God would like you to move in? This is the Holy
Spirit illuminating His Scriptural will for you.

_____

_____

_____

_____

_____

_____

_____

PRAYER (YOU TO GOD)

*God, we long to help You build Your Kingdom. Break us
from any "unworthiness" mindsets that would hinder us
from using Your heavenly power tools. It doesn't matter how
weak we are in the flesh or what our backgrounds are; we
know You give us Your Holy Spirit and power to be faithful
witnesses for You, telling others of the full Gospel, the Gospel
of Your Kingdom and power led by Your Son, Jesus. May we
move in power ten thousand times greater than any witch,
warlock, shaman, or deceiving devil in the world. May the
world see Your powerful Church moving in Your gifts of
power, all to the power of Your Son's name, Jesus. We honor
You with our lives. Amen.*

PRAYER (ME TO GOD, FOR YOU)

*God, impart every major spiritual power gift to this reader
in Jesus' name according to Your will for Your glory. Equip
the reader with the power and process needed to know and
activate every one of the Holy Spirit's gifts in his or her life,*

and give the wisdom to steward such power and authority. In
Your name we pray. Amen.

Endnotes

1. Rick Pino, "You're An Army," *Songs For an End Time Army* (Cedar Hill, TX: Fire Rain Music, 2009), track 8.

2. See Smith Wigglesworth, *Greater Works: Experiencing God's Power* (New Kensington, PA: Whitaker House, 1999), and Maria Woodworth-Etter, *Signs and Wonders*, (New Kensington, PA: Whitaker House, 1997).

3. Katherine Kuhlman, taken from article, "I Believe in Miracles," accessed via, http://www.bennyhinn.org/articles/articledesc.cfm?id=6962. Accessed September 8, 2010.

The Lord says, *"Who will cry out for mercy?"* on a throne of mercy. *"I am enthroned on the very seat of mercy. I desire mercy not judgment, grace not punishment. But I am just and righteous and hate sin like a father despises His son's foolishness. I hate evil and pray for you that you would not succumb to it. Yet My very heart, My very being, is love and mercy, grace and truth. You can find rest in My arms. I will not judge you once you cry out for mercy and repentance. You will find refuge in My peace."*

Chapter 17

PROPHETS BY DEFAULT

...If your gift is prophesying, lthen prophesy in ac-
cordance with your faith (Romans 12:6).

All should desire to prophesy... (see 1 Corinthians 14:5).

When are we going to learn to "be" ministry
rather than "do" ministry?

In the Bible, I believe the greatest description of a revival church that we can find was written about by the Apostle Paul to the Corinthians. He described a church where, when nonbelievers walked in the door, they would almost immediately fall on their faces and repent before God and then become instant witnesses for Jesus! What an atmosphere that would be, and truly it would be an answer to prayer! No preaching would even be necessary.

> *But **if all prophesy**, and an unbeliever or an uninformed person comes in, he is convinced by all, he is convicted by all. And thus the secrets of his heart are revealed; and so, **falling down on his face, he will worship God and report that God is truly among you*** (1 Corinthians 14:24-25 NKJV).

All of that is due to the prophetic gift. Paul says we all should desire to prophesy above all other spiritual gifts. *"Pursue love, and desire spiritual gifts, but especially that you may prophesy"* (1 Cor. 14:1 NKJV). After seeing the above description of revival breaking out in a church because of prophecy, you can see why! But, as Paul explains, this gift is for the following purpose: *"But he who prophesies speaks edification and exhortation and comfort to men"* (1 Cor. 14:3 NKJV).

Every believer can and should have some innate ability to prophesy. This is an extension of our relationship with God and in the simplest definition is simply being able to hear and respond to God, something we all should do. I don't believe this makes us all prophets, but it does make us prophetic people.

God is timeless and ageless. When we seek His face, He can reveal to us truths past, situations present, or events to come. He does these things for a purpose, not so we can become God's sideshow circus act. Prophesy, like all of the gifts of the Holy Spirit, is given for one reason and one reason only—God loves people and wants to express His love to them in its many facets.

The modern-day prophet is not one to proclaim judgment all the time. It has been said that if you prophesy bad things long enough, you're almost sure to be found true. The modern-day prophet sometimes has to bring correction related to God's near judgment, but this is always done in the most loving way. The Bible says God disciplines those whom He loves (see Heb. 12:3-11). God has spoken to me on a number of occasions, guiding me (though I was reluctant) to bring correction to someone with whom I had relationship and trust. God lovingly does this to get us back on the right track. God has even spoken to friends about certain things in my life when I wasn't walking according to His expectations for my life. However, I believe God always does this out of love and the proper relational authority. *Only if you have the right relationship with people do you have the right to speak into their lives.*

MORE THAN WORDS

The role of a modern-day prophet, however, is far more extensive then just giving prophetic words or bringing people into correction. A modern-day prophet releases regional, national, and global words of encouragement, correction, or the future destiny of the regions addressed. A modern-day prophet values intercession and is on God's 24/7 pager to be called out to pray for things at any time. For more information on the prophetic, reference these great books from John Sanford[1] and Graham Cook.[2] There are many other wonderful books out there on this subject as well.

A prophet simply speaks God's Word into a person or situation. We live not on bread alone, but by every Word that precedes from the mouth of God (see Deut. 8:3). We, as God's prophetic people, are speaking the very oracles of God (see 1 Pet. 4:11). The word itself carries with it such a weighty authority that it can align people's minds, bodies, and destinies to get them on the right track with God's intentions.

Prophetic people must not go by what they see, but by what God has said. At a young adult conference years ago, I was leading a small group session and I had a strong sense that a girl on my left had been trying to have a baby, but could not. The crazy thing in the natural was that she already had a child who was about four years old!

I released the prophetic word, stating that God had shown me that she was trying to have a baby and could not and that God was going to give her a child very shortly. I said other encouraging things to her also as she wept and wept. A girl from her church e-mailed me a little over a month later with word that she was pregnant! The child is happy and healthy to this day, glory to God! I know some prophets who have spoke life into barren wombs on over 50 different occasions!

ACTIVATE THE GIFT

Simply praying for people activates the prophetic gift in our lives. God once in a while may use us to speak in the first person to somebody. I was very surprised the first time God started speaking first person through me; it freaked me out. God was telling the guy through me, "I this...and I that...." I wanted to politely explain to the person I was praying for that I was not trying to play God and wouldn't dare speak on His behalf on my own accord. But he was so touched by the words of God that he needed no such explanation.

Greater steps of faith, while depending on God, can help activate that gift to another level. A great brother of mine in the Lord challenged me when he saw this gift of God in my life. He purposely put me in situations that would challenge the gift to come out when he knew it would be useful for it to manifest.

On one occasion he was going to lead worship for chapel at a local radio station. He asked me to come along specifically to minister in the prophetic when he was done. I had never been called on to do anything like that before! A healthy nervousness that led to dependence on God swept over me. I thought, if he's putting me on the spot, I guess I'm going to put you on the spot, God.

The room was full of people from different churches and denominations, from Catholic to Calvary Chapel. As the worship went on, I was spiritually anxious to see if God would show me anything to say prophetically or let me know when it was time to begin to minister. I remember looking around the room and then bowing my head again to pray. At that point, God showed me faces of three or four different people in my head whom I had just seen when I glanced over the room. All of a sudden I knew certain information about their lives that God was revealing for me to speak to them, as well as God's specific word and direction for each of them.

As the worship was subsiding, I stood up shaking and a little teary eyed (that's how I get often when I feel the Holy Spirit's strong anointing). I looked at a woman and said I believed God wanted her to pick up a particular gift in her life that she had laid down. I mentioned that I knew she was going through a divorce and subsequently released encouragement. To another man, a prodigal in the back row of the meeting, I said that God wanted him to know that He loved him, and

I encouraged him to stop running from the Lord. I did this with about four people until I knew it was time to sit down. *The whole atmosphere in the place had shifted!* People were in teary-eyed astonishment all over that place! The people came up to me afterward and asked how in the world I knew that private information about them. I simply shrugged my shoulders and gave God the glory.

STAY HUMBLE

One of the most important things young prophets of the Lord can do when starting out is to stay humble about the gift. The Bible says the spirit of the prophet is subject to the prophet (see 1 Cor. 14:32). This means that we can control the gift. This requires much responsibility.

We must not only learn to hear from God, but also to ask Him when is the appropriate time to release a word. Furthermore, no matter how much or how little success we may appear to be having, we must keep the following Scripture in mind and refuse to be discouraged:

> *For we know in part and we prophesy in part. But when that which is perfect has come, then that which is in part will be done away. When I was a child, I spoke as a child, I understood as a child, I thought as a child; but when I became a man, I put away childish things. For **now we see in a mirror, dimly**, but then face to face. Now I know in part, but then I shall know just as I also am known* (1 Corinthians 13:9-12 NKJV).

We're never going to always "get it right," so to speak, and even if we do "get it right," we only know in part. We should try to never interpret and explain a prophetic word for somebody else unless God wants us to and gives us revelation. We just say what God said and that's it.

It's important to always stay humble and rely on the Lord when ministering in any of the power gifts, lest we fall into pride; then God will do the humbling. *When we need it, God will humble us by lifting*

His protection over an area of our lives that may not be fully consecrated to Him, thus embarrassingly revealing imperfections in our own hearts.

He only does this out of love for us, to lead us to repent and give this area over to Him completely. I much prefer humbling myself then being humbled by our Almighty God!

PROPHETIC INTERCESSION

Knowledge of a pending disastrous event is one fruit of the spirit of prophesy. This comes with a great burden or perceived need to pray immediately. This can include groanings that can and can't be uttered, Holy Spirit travail, and partnership with God in ushering in His will in advance through prayer (see 1 John 5:14-15). These are all forms of prophetic intercession. Prophetic intercessors rest their heads on the bosom of Jesus, like John did at the Last Supper (see John 13:23). They press their faces into His chest to hear His heartbeat. With their heads on His chest, their ears are not far from His mouth. He can then whisper to them the mysteries of His Kingdom or the burdens of His heart.

> When He shares His burdens, it means He trusts us and would like us to help Him intercede for these needs.

When He shares His burdens, it means He trusts us and would like us to help Him intercede for these needs. Intercessors consider this a wonderful privilege and honor. Those who think they're intercessors should keep in mind that true intercessors don't just pray for anything, but only for what the Spirit of God reveals for them to pray about.

Multiple times in the Book of Acts the Holy Spirit warned the people of something so they would be ready or so they could pray against such an event from occurring. Here is one occurrence of that:

> *During this time some prophets came down from Jerusalem to Antioch. One of them, named Agabus, stood up and through the Spirit predicted that a severe famine would spread over the entire Roman world. (This happened during the reign*

of Claudius.) The disciples, as each one was able, decided to provide help for the brothers and sisters living in Judea. This they did, sending their gift to the elders by Barnabas and Saul (Acts 11:27-30).

Paul was also warned of chains and beatings when he arrived in Jerusalem. I don't know if the Holy Spirit wanted to stop the event, but for sure He wanted to prepare him emotionally for it.

TERRORIST WARNINGS

It was late January or early February of 2004. In my quiet time with the Lord, throughout the day, as I prepared Bible messages, worked from home for IBM, and did whatever else I normally do, I started seeing numbers popping out at me on the clocks around the house and in other places in a way that appeared to be God trying to show me something. Nothing like this had happened to me before. As a result of this, and the leading of the Spirit, I typed the following message to my notepad on my laptop, *"A catastrophic terrorist attack similar to 9/11 will happen on 3/11."* I typed this and despite the severity of the message, I must have taken it for granted.

It was about March 14 or 15 when I received my weekly subscription of *Newsweek*. At that time I didn't own a television and wasn't up with the latest news. The cover of *Newsweek* said, "Spain's 9/11" and had a picture of a woman holding someone on the ground, and they were both bloody. I vaguely remembered that I had typed something on my PC about a terrorist attack. When I found and opened the text file, I read it and started to cry in agony. I was crying, first, because I was completely shocked that the Holy Spirit would reveal to me such a drastic message. Second, I was crying because I had done nothing about this to help in some way stop or divert such terror.

Shortly after receiving this revelation, I called the youth pastor I was serving under and left him a message. Next I called my mom and cried on the phone to her. Anyone who knows me knows that I never cry for anything except when the anointing hits me—then I seem to cry all the time. I made the decision in my heart that if God ever revealed something like that to me again, I would do more about it.

It was November or December of 2007 and once again I felt a strong sense of evil or darkness over what I knew was Arizona Stadium in Phoenix, Arizona. It wasn't that I had driven by and had this feeling; it was just something I felt as I was at my computer doing my daily work in Tucson. Anyway, I remembered that the Super Bowl in 2008 was supposed to be played in Arizona, and I immediately knew that there was going to be some sort of terrorist attack at the Super Bowl. This time, instead of ignoring this prophetic premonition, I called my best friend and told him about it and began to pray.

The conversation must have sounded crazy, but like any good friend, he listened and agreed with me in prayer nonetheless. Again I didn't think much of this as the Super Bowl came and went. It wasn't until about six months afterward that I found out that a disgruntled Tempe man had gone to the stadium with an AR-15 rifle and a car full of ammunition to essentially unload on the crowds of people outside of the stadium. Apparently just before he began shooting, a compelling force came over him and he stopped and turned himself into the authorities. This is what happened, as documented by the *Phoenix Tribune:*

> Before kickoff, Havelock went to a parking lot of Jobing. com Arena, which can be seen from the University of Phoenix Stadium. But Havelock told authorities he lost his nerve after about a minute, the newspaper reported. "He was very upset, he was sobbing hysterically," Frank Havelock told the Tribune. "He said, 'I've done something terribly, terribly wrong'"[3]

I found out later that there was at least one prophetic pastor in Phoenix whom God had revealed this to ahead of time; he had his whole church praying and fasting about it. And there was one traveling prophet, my friend Bob Griffin, who came to Phoenix shortly before the Super Bowl and was prophesying regarding this attack, commanding the man to "disarm." Glory to God for revealing such things to those willing to listen in order to avoid calamity!

God saved the day through people's prayers. How much more does He want to do the same thing all the time? He doesn't want others to suffer. If you get a similar word or hear that there is going to be some disaster or nuclear attack, pray, pray, pray! God doesn't want us to know these things just so we can boast about them or write a book. He wants to prophetically warn us and prepare us for what's to come so we can divert disaster.

PROPHETIC EVANGELISM

When we hear from Heaven and release specific words of God to people, words that pertain to their situation and to things that we wouldn't know without supernatural revelation, it is a great demonstration to them of God's love and the truth of the Gospel. Because of this demonstration of God's love and power, they will have no argument that God is not real. Lord willing, they will be humbled as their hearts are exposed, and they will surrender their lives fully to Jesus. This is what we define as prophetic evangelism. Sean Smith[4] and Patricia King[5] have both written good books on this subject.

THE TREASURE HUNT

A phenomenon is happening among evangelistic groups all over the country—something called a treasure hunt. In youth and college groups, treasure hunts are a popular way of searching for a number of things on a list until the search is fulfilled. The team who finishes with everything on the list first, wins.

These new evangelistic treasure hunts are similar, but for an altogether different purpose. The participants get together to pray, asking God to give them hints and tips about people they will come into contact with on their "treasure hunt" for the purpose of witnessing to them. Then they take these clues to a public place and use them to find the people God wants them to pray for. When they witness to strangers whom the Lord leads them to through specific clues, they are showing these people that *they* are God's treasure and that now is their time to receive prayer for healing, salvation by faith in Christ, or both.[6]

God will certainly honor any form of prophetic evangelism when done in the right spirit, and God loves when we dedicate time to share His heart with the lost. I always have a great time when I train and activate new everyday evangelists through following the Holy Spirit on these treasure hunts. I have seen good results with this method, and it's a wonderful way to break people into prophetic evangelism. Of course, as with anything, we must be careful to not get stuck with one method and must try not to limit God. We need to focus on people and the fact that God loves them. Whenever I see a wheelchair, some crutches, a cast, a limp, or another injury, those are the people I will almost always go up to and offer my prayers of faith for.

> God will honor prophetic evangelism when done in the right spirit.

I want to see God's power heal people in public! Anytime we share God's love and power with people, we shift the atmosphere. The looks on people's faces when they see us really living our faith are classic—and most importantly, when we share our faith, it makes God smile.

We must keep our focus on people, love them, and let the Holy Spirit show us how we can minister to each individual. We also must be careful to focus our evangelistic conversations with people on Jesus, refusing to get into long talks with people who want a confrontational conversation about religion or who are trying to avoid any real talk about God. A good way to do this is to ask them straight up if they know Jesus personally and if they know without a shadow of a doubt that they would go to Heaven if they died today. If they don't know, we should simply show them the love and power of Jesus through our prayers and proclamations of the Kingdom. If we can find agreement with them that Jesus is Lord and they are willing to surrender their lives to Him, this will bring true fruit that will last.

Prophetic evangelism that is done by the leading of the Holy Spirit (in any form) is a laser-sharp tool to pierce someone's heart with the message of the Gospel. They can still refuse to accept God's message and His Son Jesus' sacrifice; however, they won't be able to deny that God is real.

We must keep our focus on people, love them, and let the Holy Spirit show us how we can minister to each individual.

WORD OF KNOWLEDGE

Word of knowledge is a form of releasing God's prophetic word. It can manifest as feelings in our bodies or as simple knowledge of things we wouldn't normally know without God's supernatural revelation. It's important for us to foster an awareness and expectation of this gift and to step out in faith when we get a prophetic inclination in our hearts or bodies.

> Prophetic evangelism done by the leading of the Holy Spirit is a laser-sharp tool to pierce someone's heart.

On one occasion, while I was leading a revival meeting, the Holy Spirit spoke to me very clearly that a certain man whom I'd never seen before had a kidney problem. When God reveals those things to me, it is usually because He wants me to address and solve the problem!

I looked around the room and asked if anyone had a kidney problem, while trying to watch this man to see his response. He didn't raise a hand or do anything so much as flinch. *Oh, well,* I thought. *I must have really missed that one.*

Toward the end of the meeting during the prayer time, he came up and said in a real monotone voice, "I'm the guy with the kidney problem." I was just thankful to the Lord that the Holy Spirit had been right, even though I questioned His voice because of what I saw in the natural. *Of course, that's ridiculous because the Holy Spirit is always right! It's when we get the earwax of the world or our own emotions in our spiritual ears that we have a problem.*

We prayed for the man and, though I haven't heard back from him and don't know his name or contact information, I believe he's completely healed.

PROPHETIC VERSUS THE PROPHET

There has been something troubling my mind for some time now regarding the prophetic. It is whether or not we can really train and raise up modern-day prophets. The answer is yes and no. The truth is that in this age of grace, we can all hear God for ourselves and respond in faith to words that He drops in our spirit. This can be a prophetic word for an individual during personal prayer, or some other divine directive for our life. This, however, does not make one a prophet. A true prophet has been chosen by God to be a prophet. That is part of the prophet's calling and gifting. This cannot be trained or taught.

We can identify those with a "prophet's anointing" and then teach them the principles of how their gift and office should function, but we cannot take somebody and impart to them what God alone can give. A true prophet does not question the Word of the Lord that comes forth through his or her lips. A true prophetic word for an individual or a group is sharp, powerful, and declarative. This is in contrast to teaching prophetic people to say things like, "I believe the Lord is saying, x, y or z," or "I think God wants you to know this or that." That is a good practice for prophetic individuals but a prophet and a prophetic individual are two different things. A true prophet will simply declare the Word of the Lord because the Spirit of God has come so fully upon him that he seemingly cannot do otherwise. When a prophet has a Word from the Lord, it's like a woman in labor...that baby is coming whether you like it or not!

I'm not saying I am a true prophet, but I know when God has a corporate word for a group of individuals that He wants to speak through me, the Spirit of the Lord comes so strongly upon me that I will shake and weep until the word gets released. The sprit of prophecy is still subject to the prophet, and I remember on one such occasion in the middle of a church service, I did not speak out because of rationalization or fear of man/embarrassment, but in that case, I know I grieved the Spirit of God.

Sometimes if God's Spirit comes upon you to deliver a Word and you don't do it, somebody else in the room will deliver that same exact word. There are usually multiple Prophets and prophetic people among us that God will use if we are fully surrendered to Him. When the "no doubt" Word of the Lord begins to come forth, my lips are no longer saying things like, "I believe the Lord wants you to know..." they are saying things like, *"thus says the Lord!!"*

The true prophetic word can shift the entire atmosphere of a building no matter how small or large! The true prophetic word actually carries with it life and creates in the spiritual realm that which is being spoken! The true prophetic word is the very Lord, Himself, speaking through an individual, not an individual trying to interpret what he or she thinks the Lord is revealing. This kind of prophetic word cannot be preempted, manufactured, or manipulated at the will of the prophet, this kind of Word comes from God alone.

In the Old Testament, you can see the contrast between the "School of Prophets" prophets and the true prophets. There was clearly a school for prophets, and many prophets around in those days, particularly in the regions of Naioth in Ramah (see 1 Sam. 19), Gilgal (see 2 Kings 4), Jericho (see 2 Kings 2), and Ephraim (see 2 Kings 5).

However, there were only a few set-apart prophets that carried the true voice of the Lord and the "now" Word of God. You can see in this case (see 2 Kings 2:16) where the prophets from the school were all saying that they should look for Elijah, while Elisha was saying something different and told them they won't find him. You can also see that Saul got connected with some prophets, likely also from a similar school and started prophesying just like they were (see 1 Sam. 19:23-24). However, God had His special prophets that penned and declared His Word with such great authority and clarity that truly separated them from the pack—prophets like Jeremiah, Isaiah, Elijah and Elisha.

There was also a time where God allowed a lying spirit to come and deceive most of the prophets to help separate out who His true prophet was (see 2 Chron. 18:1-22)! In this case, Micaiah was the only person who was able to purely declare what the Lord was saying, thus disagreeing with even his prophetic peers. Because of his consecration to the Lord and special gifting, his prophetic vision and accuracy was far greater than those who were simply saying what everyone else was saying because they were deceived. Remember, just because a lot of people are saying similar things, prophetically, to the body of Christ, this doesn't always mean they are right. Some may just be plagiarizing from another prophet, others may be legitimately deceived and their deception is getting picked up on and multiplied. You must know how to discern the Word of the Lord for yourself, which we will discuss in more detail throughout this book.

PROPHETIC FORGETFULNESS

The funny thing about delivering prophetic words is that I have rarely ever remembered anyone else's messages from God. I may know the intimate details of your heart while I'm praying for you, but God doesn't permit me to remember them, nor would I need to unless He wants me to share a testimony of something that was prophesied in order to give Him glory.

Prophetic people must divorce themselves from the conditional or nonconditional words that God releases through them. God's Word has enough power to work on its own once released. We do not need to be held responsible for every prophetic word we deliver; we would drive ourselves crazy.

We also don't need to know all the details of people's lives before ministering to them prophetically. Many times, prophetic people will just know the first one or two sentences of what they are supposed to say to a person. As they step out in faith and begin to minister, God fills their mouths with the rest of the words. This is why ministering prophetically requires more faith than tongues and interpretation of tongues. With interpretation of tongues, the interpreter hears the words fully first and then has time to process and repeat them. Prophetic people just need to step out on the tree limb until it starts cracking because that's when God likes to show up.

The prophetic is used to align people, regions, heavenly authorities, and times and seasons and get them on the right track with what God's Word is. It is a great Kingdom weapon for any revivalist! We must desire to prophesy for the glory of God and according to the measure of our faith.

QUESTIONS

1. Did you know that even today God does not do anything significant without revealing it to His servants the prophets? (See Amos 3:7.) The voice of the prophets had obvious significance in the Old Testament; why do you think the role of the prophet is equally important in the New Testament Church?

   _____

   _____

   _____

2. Did you know that God wants someone to share His heart and His secrets? Did you know you that the person He wants is you?

   _____

   _____

   _____

3. What are some practical steps you can take to help guard against abusing the gift of prophesy that is available to every believer?

   _____

   _____

   _____

PRAYER (YOU TO GOD)

God, help me hear from You and walk in such closeness of relationship with You that I can hear You anytime, any day. I long to receive and move in greater levels of the gift of prophecy. Holy Spirit, show me how to use this gift for the glory of God, but more importantly to know that I value You and Your anointing above any of Your gifts. You are awesome and holy. Amen.

PRAYER (ME TO GOD, FOR YOU)

Father God, by Your power and through the name of Jesus of Nazareth, I break off any impeding spirit that would hinder this saint from hearing from You more clearly. I break off the power of any deceiving spirits and release the Holy Spirit into this person's life in a fuller way to speak clearly to his or her spirit about Your will for Your saint and about what You would like to share with others being prayed with.

Thank You for helping this saint to hear Your voice and flow with You wherever he or she goes. I stir up the gift of prophesy right now in Jesus' name and release this saint to move in the prophetic in the marketplace, on the streets, and in the malls, bookstores, shopping centers, and anywhere else. We bless and seal this prayer with the blood of Jesus. Amen.

Endnotes

1. John Stanford, *The Elijah Task* (Lake Mary, FL: Charisma House, 2006); John Stanford, *Elijah Among Us* (Grand Rapids, MI: Chosen Books, 2002).

2. Graham Cooke, *Developing Your Prophetic Gifting* (Grand Rapids, MI; Chosen Books, 2003).

3. Associated Press, "FBI: Man planned to attack Super Bowl fans," The Tucson Citizen, February 8, 2008, http://tucsoncitizen.com/morgue/2008/02/08/76380-fbi-man-planned-to-attack-super-bowl-fans/. Accessed September 08, 2010.

4. Sean Smith, *Prophetic Evangelism* (Shippensburg, PA: Destiny Image Publishers, 2005).

5   Patricia King, *The Light Belongs in the Darkness* (Shippensburg, PA: Destiny Image Publishers, 2005).

6. For more information on treasure hunts, see *The Ultimate Treasure Hunt* by Kevin Dedmon (Shippensburg, PA: Destiny Image Publishers, 2007).

We must have a reformation within the Church. To beg for a flood of blessing to come upon a backslidden and disobedient Church is to waste time and effort. A new wave of religious will do no more than add numbers to the churches that have no intention to own the Lordship of Jesus and come under obedience to His commandments. God is not interested in increasing church attendance unless those who attend amend their ways and begin to live holy lives.

—A.W. Tozer[1]

Chapter 18

DISCERNMENT

*For if one comes and preaches another Jesus whom we have
not preached, or you receive a different spirit which you have
not received, or a different gospel which you have not accepted, you bear this beautifully* (2 Corinthians 11:4 NASB).

*The greatest deception is the thing closest
to the truth.* —UNKNOWN

There are many scenarios in life when a Holy Spirit-led "sixth
sense" experience of recognizing spirits is extremely helpful and
can guard us from harm in the spiritual or natural realm. There is
a spiritual tool that God gives us to know what spirits are at work
in any given situation so we know how to properly respond. This
is the tool of discernment. The gift of discerning spirits and the
wisdom of discernment can be different, but I will discuss both
throughout this chapter.

In personal and collective revival, we must continue to mature in
our knowledge of the Lord's Scriptures and our knowledge by experience of how to respond to different situations that we may face while
ministering. This is to guard us—and the sheep we have the responsibility to protect—from any spirits that are not the Holy Spirit.

It will also help us know how to deliver people, regions, and nations from the influence of such spirits. In addition, as revivalists, oftentimes we will face attacks or persecution from demonic and religious spirits. These typically manifest through people so it is vitally important to discern spirits in the atmosphere as well as those at work in individuals. Even Levitical priests did not always do things according to God's law and God's Scriptures, as we see with the example of Nadab and Abihu.

> *And Nadab and Abihu, the sons of Aaron, took either of them his censer, and put fire therein, and put incense thereon, and offered **strange fire** before the LORD, which he commanded them not* (Leviticus 10:1 KJV).

The Bible doesn't explain exactly why this fire was strange to God, but it was certainly out of order in regard to temple protocol. The Bible just says it was contrary to God's command. When the priests violated this command, a fire came forth from the presence of God to consume them, and they died right there before the Lord (see Lev. 10:2). This example of "strange fire" should keep us on guard to make sure that everything we do when ministering to the Lord is in accordance with His Word—and that we know how to discern if it is not. *It is also important to discern when others are playing with "strange fire" so we can stay away!*

> We are spiritual beings, and there is a spiritual world that we live in that is as real as our natural world.

Discernment can be knowing what the Word of the Lord says and knowing how to respond in maturity. Discernment can also go much deeper, to the point of knowing the thoughts and intents of a person or knowing what inner healing a person may need to experience. We are spiritual beings, and there is a spiritual world that we live in that is as real as our natural world. We are naive to ignore such a reality and ignorant to think that God wouldn't want us to understand it. Christ's Kingdom is a spiritual one; thus it would be wise to assume that He desires us to know how to usher in this spiritual rule and pray down His will from this spiritual realm.

DISCERNMENT IS AN ESSENTIAL TOOL

For everyone who partakes only of milk is unskilled in the word of righteousness, for he is a babe. But solid food belongs to those who are of full age, that is, those who by reason of use have their senses exercised to discern both good and evil (Hebrews 5:13 NKJV).

I have seen too many would-be revivalists who are ill-equipped to deal with situations where other spirits are manifesting and are even susceptible to receiving from people or church atmospheres that are entertaining spirits that are not from God at all! How it grieves my soul to see the Body of Christ deceived! Discernment is the cure. We must always be open to receiving from God in faith, but we must also know the difference when something is or is not from Him.

Due to the renewed practice of "laying on of hands," we must be wise about who we are having pray for people, and we must be careful about who we allow to pray for us. In Chapter 19, I discuss the fact that there is a spiritual transfer that takes place through the human touch. This transfer can be good or bad; we *must* know the difference.

Discernment is a tool to help us read the hearts of people and the spirits of certain circumstances and situations so that we can know when to avoid trouble, what is and isn't of God, and what God would like to speak and do in a certain situation or with a certain individual.

Discerning of spirits is discernment specifically to identify and deal with certain spirits that have influenced a person or situation. We should want to and need to discern spirits when demonic spirits have someone bound, when a familiar spirit is posing as the Holy Spirit in a church meeting or prophetic conference, or when the Lord would want us to understand what spirit is around that is not His.

We can do this by judging according to His Spirit, not according to the natural situations and circumstances.

> *But the natural man does not receive the things of the Spirit of God, for they are foolishness to him; nor can he know them, because they are spiritually discerned. But he who is spiritual judges all things, yet he himself is rightly judged by no one. For "who has known the mind of the LORD that he may instruct Him?" But we have the mind of Christ* (1 Corinthians 2:14-16 NKJV).

Because we have the Holy Spirit living in us, He is the one who will give us this ability to know right from wrong in our spirits and to know when something is wrong. We have the mind of Christ because we have the Holy Spirit. If you have any question about a situation, person, or environment you find yourself in, give it to the Lord and ask Him for guidance. Do not subject yourself to anything you are not comfortable with. It hurts my heart to think of all the foolish fake "movements" that have given true revival a bad name. If the leaders or patrons involved in such movements had discernment and administered correction, such foolish activity like making animal noises and falling over in your own power (faking truly being slain in the Spirit or being overwhelmed by the power of God to the point of falling over) could have been avoided.

> We have the mind of Christ because we have the Holy Spirit.

JESUS DISCERNED SITUATIONS

Throughout His ministry Jesus discerned thoughts and intents of people quite often. This was a gift from God that was much like a compass or an alarm clock in Jesus' life. The alarm went off spiritually and He knew He needed to get up and go. Discernment also kept Him on the right track with His God-given mission. He knew how to avoid those who wanted to kill Him when it wasn't yet time, and He knew exactly when to submit Himself to the religious leaders to be crucified. We all are *eternally* thankful!

Although people can argue that this was a prophetic word of knowledge, I believe Jesus knew where His disciples would be and how to get them to follow Him. He knew where to tell them to drop their nets in faith (see John 21:6). He knew where a donkey would be tied up on the day of His entrance to Jerusalem (see Matt. 21:1-2). Jesus seemingly knew the future of almost everything that was about to happen. Not only that, but He warned and taught His disciples about what would happen to them when they were persecuted, and what would happen during the destruction of the Jewish temple (see Matt. 24). *As the Son of Man, He could experience this level of discernment of present and future events because of the Holy Spirit living in Him who is omnipresent (all places at all time), omniscient (knows all things), and omnipotent (all powerful).*

> *But when He, the Spirit of truth, comes, He will guide you into all the truth; for He will not speak on His own initiative, but whatever He hears, He will speak; and He will disclose to you what is to come* (John 16:13 NASB).

Clearly the Holy Spirit can speak and disclose to you what is to come just like He did with Jesus. The Holy Spirit is the Spirit of discernment. In another example, Jesus perceived the false intentions of those around Him who were trying to once again put Him to the test, and He rebuked them for it.

> *"Tell us then, what do You think? Is it lawful to give a poll-tax to Caesar, or not?" But Jesus perceived their malice, and said, "Why are you testing Me, you hypocrites?"* (Matthew 22:17-18 NASB).

After multiplying the fish and loaves, Jesus discerned that the people whom He just miraculously fed wanted to make Him king. Here He discerned that He had to withdraw Himself to avoid this colossal distraction.

> *Therefore when the people saw the sign which He had performed, they said, "This is truly the Prophet who is to come into the world." So Jesus, perceiving that they were intending*

*to come and take Him by force to make Him king, with-
drew again to the mountain by Himself alone* (John 6:14-15
NASB).

Jesus discerned multiple times when the religious leaders wanted
to take Him and kill Him so He had the spiritual smarts to avoid
these situations until the time was right for Him to lay down His life.
Again Matthew documents that He discerned what was going on and
withdrew Himself:

> *But the Pharisees went out and conspired against Him, as
> to how they might destroy Him. But **Jesus, aware of this,
> withdrew from there**. Many followed Him, and He healed
> them all, and warned them not to tell who He was* (Matthew
> 12:14-16 NASB).

Jesus also purposely scared off a bunch of would-be disciples by
teaching them that, if they really believed in Him, in order to be one
with Him, they had to eat His flesh and drink His
blood (see John 6:48-58). Disgusting! This was completely against Jewish Levitical law, and cannibalism is
one of the most despised things they could think about.
We know this now to be the tradition of remembrance
that Jesus signified at the "last supper," with the bread
and the wine. Many traditional denominations call this
the Eucharist. He challenged them to the core on a religious belief to make sure that He only had the truly
committed original disciples following Him. He is
ever-challenging His present-day disciples to make sure
we also have not become too religious to receive Him.

> He is ever-challenging His present-day disciples to make sure we also have not become too religious to receive Him.

Here was the people's response: *"As a result of this **many of His
disciples withdrew** and were not walking with Him anymore"* (John
6:66 NASB).

Discernment was a vital part of Jesus' ministry (His life and
purpose) and should be of our ministry as well (our life and purpose).

God does not want us to be caught unaware and caught off guard. God prepares us in advance for what is to come.

THE SPIRIT BRINGS JUDGMENT

Discernment is a form of judgment—judging a situation to be right or not in God's eyes and taking appropriate action in response to what the Holy Spirit is revealing. Look at the scariest bit of discernment in the New Testament shown by Peter in relationship to two individuals who decided to lie to the Holy Spirit:

> *But a man named Ananias, with his wife Sapphira, sold a piece of property, and kept back some of the price for himself, with his wife's full knowledge, and bringing a portion of it, he laid it at the apostles' feet. But Peter said, "Ananias, why has Satan filled your heart to lie to the Holy Spirit and to keep back some of the price of the land? While it remained unsold, did it not remain your own? And after it was sold, was it not under your control? Why is it that you have conceived this deed in your heart? You have not lied to men but to God." And as he heard these words, Ananias fell down and breathed his last; and great fear came over all who heard of it. The young men got up and covered him up, and after carrying him out, they buried him. Now there elapsed an interval of about three hours, and his wife came in, not knowing what had happened. And Peter responded to her, "Tell me whether you sold the land for such and such a price?" And she said, "Yes, that was the price." Then Peter said to her, "Why is it that you have agreed together to put the Spirit of the Lord to the test? Behold, the feet of those who have buried your husband are at the door, and they will carry you out as well." And immediately she fell at his feet and breathed her last, and the young men came in and found her dead, and they carried her out and buried her beside her husband. And great fear came over the whole church, and over all who heard of these things* (Acts 5:1-11 NASB).

In revival there are grave consequences if you try to deceive God and spiritual leadership. In this case, they lied to God, but Peter discerned it and immediately pronounced God's judgment on them. The rest is history. I don't know about you, but I am not planning on trying to deceive God in a revival atmosphere and risking dropping dead! God knows everything and reveals things to His servants so why would we ever try to hide anything from Him?

SPIRITUAL ATMOSPHERE

Discerning the spiritual atmosphere of a new location is what I call "taking spiritual temperature." If you walk into a church for the first time or drive through a new city, it is possible to sense the spirits at work there. I remember driving through downtown Baltimore and discerning such a strong spirit of poverty. I drove through a certain part of downtown Phoenix and felt a strong spirit of sexual immorality and pornography. This was without any observance of adult stores or anything of the sort—it was just a spiritual awareness. When I evangelize in bad areas of town, my spiritual senses are always on alert. I can sometimes sense a demon-possessed person from half a block away. It is like the hair on the back of my neck stands up as the Holy Spirit is readying me for a spiritual conflict of sorts. Sometimes when people are oppressed or tormented by spirits, it takes longer for that to manifest than when they are fully possessed, and this can also take longer to discern.

One time during a technical conference I was visiting New Orleans, Louisiana. During the evening I was walking down Bourbon Street and could feel the evil spirits pulling so strongly on me that it freaked me out. The evil coming from some of the voodoo shops and strip clubs was the strongest I have felt anywhere. Bourbon Street makes Las Vegas feel like Disneyland. I went back to my hotel room and looked up an Assemblies of God Church that was in the French Quarter and went to the pastor for prayer. He prayed and prophesied over me and said that God had sent me there to do spiritual battle over that area. The strong spiritual influences that were pulling me down seemingly had no more influence; it was totally broken off! *Under the authority of that pastor and the command of the Lord, I went to the hotel room and did spiritual battle over that street for the next two or three hours!*

RECEIVING

We must have maturity in revival and be careful of who we listen to and receive from. I have listened to popular preachers or prophets who tell mistruths and exaggerations to manipulate their audiences to follow their theology and agenda. We must also be careful to discern the intentions of individuals who may come around and try to control things. I have seen laymen from the church and even spiritual leaders moving under the manipulation of spirits of religion or Jezebel spirits. I have interpreted the spirit of Jezebel as a spirit of rebellion that tries to take the place of true God-given authority. It wants to control the situation even if it hasn't been given the right to by God, just like Jezebel tried to do in the Bible. This is why we name this spiritual manipulation after her (see 1 Kings 21:25).

> If people are going to pray for you for anything, be very careful to know who they are, the spirit in them, and whose authority they are under.

If people are going to pray for you for anything, be very careful to know who they are, the spirit in them, and whose authority they are under. Even worse than people praying for you and giving you an inaccurate Word from the Lord (or those who try to push or pull you down while praying for you) is people who pray for you while being bound by some habitual sin or evil spirit themselves. I have seen New-Agers who had obvious spirits of witchcraft at prophetic conferences and revival meetings. If we learn from history, we will see that the Azusa Street Revival attracted many New-Agers and individuals in the occult. God was manifesting supernatural miracles, and they came to check it out. This is fine; bring them in and share with them the Gospel (they need Jesus as much as anyone), but don't let these people pray for you or anyone else, lest a bad spiritual transfer take place.

PREPARE FOR A BATTLE

If all Christians were living righteous, godly lives and every church was led by the Holy Spirit, why would we need revival at all? *Christians and spiritual leaders are not perfect.* People can and will make mistakes, and people can and will hurt us intentionally and unintentionally. There are also many spirits always at work trying to deceive people, hurt people, and get people to hurt each other. We must open up our spiritual eyes and ears and let God reveal to us what's going on in every situation. If we do this and have this perspective, we will not take things personally and respond in ignorance, but we will know what's going on in a situation and will be able to pray God's glorious and powerful will into that situation.

I have often discerned the wiles of the enemy when he has come in to attack my marriage. When I give the problem to the Lord, instead of trying to solve it in my own power, I can then receive truth in that situation. God shows me what spirits are attacking me and my wife and how to pray them out of my house! I take authority over them in the name of Jesus! This has even happened to me during different times of sickness in my physical body. I cast a devil right out of my own stomach one time when I was reeling in pain. I knew it was a spiritual attack; I took authority and cast it out and had to run to the restroom to finish the deal.

> Let's bring God glory by maturing as believers.

You may think that's presumptuous or overly spiritual, but not everything that happens in life is just chance or due to a natural cause and effect consequence. There are spiritual forces at work all around us that we need to discern. *This Christian walk is a battle.* If our lives are super-easy all the time, we may already be POWs (prisoners of war) so the devil doesn't need to mess with us. He already has us ineffective, without power or purpose, and locked up in some prison of comfort or religiosity.

May this book and God's Spirit break us out and equip us for the battlefield! Let's bring God glory by maturing as believers, thinking for ourselves, knowing God's Word for ourselves, and passionately pursuing a greater anointing in relationship with the Holy Spirit. If we do this, we will start to see Christians truly become Christ-followers, not just religious robots, and lovers of others, not just lovers of self.

The following prayer that Paul wrote for the church at Philippi aptly summarizes my heart on this matter:

> *And this I pray, that your love may abound still more and more in real knowledge and all discernment, so that you may approve the things that are excellent, in order to be sincere and blameless until the day of Christ; having been filled with the fruit of righteousness which comes through Jesus Christ, to the glory and praise of God* (Philippians 1:9-11 NASB).

QUESTIONS

1. Have you sensed something that was not right in the
    Spirit, but couldn't quite tell what it was? Did God later
    show you, or do you realize now that this was your spiri-
    tual "sixth sense" at work?

    _____

    _____

    _____

    _____

    _____

2. What is the first thing you should do when you feel like
    something just isn't right spiritually?

    _____

    _____

    _____

    _____

    _____

3. What is a situation or two in your life where discern-
    ment would be quite a valuable gift to have?

    _____

    _____

    _____

    _____

_____

_____

PRAYER (YOU TO GOD)

Lord, help me to not be deceived, but rather, to discern deception and free others from deception. Show me how to pray and what I can do to protect myself and others from things that are not of You and that would grieve the Holy Spirit and hinder His power from working in my life. Keep me pure in thought, intention, and action, and help me to communicate only proper doctrine and truth.

PRAYER (ME TO GOD, FOR YOU)

Jesus, please protect this wonderful person from ungodly spirits and ungodly influences. Protect this saint from the wolves in sheeps' clothing that call themselves prophets, pastors, and preachers in your Church.

Lord, impart to this saint a fresh spiritual insight to see more clearly into the spirit realm to know what is and isn't from You and how to respond accordingly. Thank you for always guiding us. We can always trust in You. Amen.

Endnote

1.   A.W. Tozer, *Keys to the Deeper Life* (Grand Rapids, MI: Zondervan, 1957).

HOLY

Here we are, God, come before the mercy seat
I can hear the voices proceeding from Your throne
Twenty-four elders bowing low, casting
down their crowns of gold
And four living creatures crying out,
day and night, night and day

Choruses:
Only one word comes to mind
There's only one word to describe
Holy, holy, Lord God Almighty
There is no one like You
You are holy, holy

—MATT GILMAN[1]

Chapter 19

Laying on of Hands

As it happened, Publius's father was ill with fever and dysentery. Paul went in and prayed for him, and laying his hands on him, he healed him (Acts 28:8 NLT).

When you confront someone's devils, you'll be greeted with hate. When you confront someone's spiritual gifts, you'll be greeted with love.

The practice of "laying on of hands" found renewed popularity almost 60 years ago in Christian circles during the time of the Latter-Day Rain movement[2] and has continued to be a common practice today. Near the turn of the twentieth century, when the baptism of the Holy Spirit was becoming more common, people would often tarry for this experience for weeks, months, and even years before God would bless them with this blessing. However, during the renewal of focus on apostles and prophets, spiritual leaders around the country began to once again find value in praying for people and laying their hands on them to speed up the experience of "spiritual blessing."

This is a practice known today in many circles as impartation. This experience of laying on of hands has gained much popularity—so much so that in nearly every revival meeting or conference,

277

preachers lay hands on believers to release prayer, blessing, and healing. Furthermore, "fire tunnels" are also common practice in some Spirit-filled churches and at conferences. This is a practice where two lines of people stand parallel to one another and have people walk between them while they lay hands on them and pray for them.

The people walking through are touched and prayed for by all of these people as they progress their way through the line. This is not always a wise practice, as we learned in the previous chapter; however, it is worthy of mentioning.

WHAT WOULD JESUS DO?

Let us look at the first documented New Testament laying on of hands impartation service:

> *And when He had **called His twelve disciples to Him**, He gave them power over unclean spirits, to cast them out, and to heal all kinds of sickness and all kinds of disease* (Matthew 10:1 NKJV).

A careful reading of this passage shows that they came *to* Jesus. This implies that they were standing close together, close enough for Jesus to touch them while He prayed. It is not presumptuous to say Jesus laid His hands on His disciples here to impart His Spirit to them to help accomplish the job He set out for them.

Jesus gave what He had to them, and then they were commanded to give this same spiritual blessing away wherever they went (see Matt. 10:8). This was a way for Jesus to multiply His Kingdom influence while not being present in person. By praying over His disciples and encouraging them to do Kingdom work with His virtue as their strength, Jesus released them to move in the same Kingdom power that He did. This was for the purpose of introducing first to the Jews the awareness and presence of God's Kingdom on earth.

*These twelve Jesus sent out and commanded them, saying:
"Do not go into the way of the Gentiles, and do not enter a
city of the Samaritans. But go rather to the lost sheep of the
house of Israel. And as you go, preach, saying, 'The kingdom
of heaven is at hand.'* **Heal the sick, cleanse the lepers,
raise the dead, cast out demons. Freely you have received,
freely give"** (Matthew 10:5-8 NKJV).

FREELY GIVE

The Bible shares a similar story of Moses, an Old Testament "type"
of Christ, when he called 70 elders to himself to also impart to them.

*...He brought together seventy of their elders and had them
stand around the tent. Then the LORD came down in the
cloud and spoke with him, and he took some of the power of
the Spirit that was on him and put it on the seventy elders.
When the Spirit rested on them, they prophesied—but did
not do so again* (Numbers 11:24-25).

What did Jesus have to give? Like Moses did with his 70 elders,
Jesus placed the same Spirit that was on Him onto the disciples. The
same power, virtue, and anointing that came out of
Him when He prayed for the sick could now come
forth from them as they acted as those with His
authority. He didn't instantaneously make them like
Him; He just filled their spiritual tanks with high-
octane super premium fuel, Heaven-style! He essentially sent them out to the battlefield with enough
ammo and fuel for their assignment.

We can administer the hand of God as ambassadors of Heaven to see people healed, set free,
and filled with the Spirit! God is introducing
people around the world to His Kingdom awareness through the same methods that He used with
the early Church. He imparts His power and virtue through us for a

> We can administer the hand of God as ambassadors of Heaven to see people healed, set free, and filled with the Spirit!

number a reasons that we've talked about. All we need to do is simply give what we have first received! We all have the Holy Spirit without limit (see John 3:34) and have our own personal measure of faith (see Rom. 12:3). I don't know what more we need? The rest is up to God.

The Lord must have thought it was a good time to teach me a little about the power of "laying on of hands" when I participated in a missions trip to Mexico one time as a young preacher. The trip had been exhausting and I was preaching one or two times a day and doing evangelism in the barrios during the day. The second to last day we were there, I felt so dry and empty. I felt like I truly had maxed out my ministry potential and just wanted to turn over the service to the local pastor or somebody more capable than me. I just felt like I had nothing left to give. After my sermon, I asked people who wanted to come down to the altar for prayer to come forward. I hardly knew how to even give an altar call let alone what to do afterward. Anyhow, I, in my emptiness, and now complete dependency on God, began to pray for individuals who were standing in a horizontal line at the front of the church. I remember coming up to one man and lifting my hand to place it on his head to pray. Before my hand could even touch his head, the guy flew a few feet backward and landed flat, smack on the concrete (the church had no carpets)! While trying to keep my cool on the outside, I was thinking to myself, "Wow, is this guy OK? What just happened?" I surely thought he must have been "faking it" regarding being slain in the spirit (what we call it when people fall out under the power of God).

The Spirit of the Lord then came upon me and I began to weep. Immediately, I, myself, headed to the altar on my knees, ignoring the rest of the people I was supposed to pray for. There, God spoke to me and taught me a very valuable lesson. He said that power in the Spirit always comes from Him. There is nothing we can do to initiate it or generate it out of our own power. I learned that in our weakness His strength is truly made perfect (see 2 Cor. 12:9). The pastor of the church then came up and prayed for me and I felt a rush of the spirit of love and grace on me. I was just so thankful to God for His won-der-working power to set people free and change lives. Such learning experiences are priceless when God disciples His children. May we all stay fully dependent on the source of all revival experience.

KNOW THE SOURCE

Throughout the New Testament, the apostles realized the power of laying on hands for impartation and that they could accelerate the process of igniting people's faith to receive the gift of the Spirit by laying hands on them. In the New Testament Church, laying on hands was commonly utilized, not just as a spiritual tool, but as a doctrine as well. It is included with the list of beginner items of the faith in Hebrews 6:2.

The apostles laid their hands on believers to impart to them the gift of the Holy Spirit:

> *Now there was a man named Simon, who formerly was practicing magic in the city and astonishing the people of Samaria, claiming to be someone great; and they all, from smallest to greatest, were giving attention to him, saying, "This man is what is called the Great Power of God." And they were giving him attention because he had for a long time astonished them with his magic arts. But when they believed Philip preaching the good news about the kingdom of God and the name of Jesus Christ, they were being baptized, men and women alike. Even Simon himself believed; and after being baptized, he continued on with Philip, and as he observed signs and great miracles taking place, he was constantly amazed. Now when the apostles in Jerusalem heard that Samaria had received the word of God, they sent them Peter and John, who came down and prayed for them that they might receive the Holy Spirit. For He had not yet fallen upon any of them; they had simply been baptized in the name of the Lord Jesus. Then **they began laying their hands on them, and they were receiving the Holy Spirit**. Now when Simon saw that the Spirit was bestowed through the laying on of the apostles'*

*hands, he offered them money, saying, "Give this authority to
me as well, so that everyone on whom I lay my hands may
receive the Holy Spirit." But Peter said to him, "May your
silver perish with you, because you thought you could obtain
the gift of God with money! You have no part or portion in
this matter, for your heart is not right before God. Therefore
repent of this wickedness of yours, and pray the Lord that,
if possible, the intention of your heart may be forgiven you"*
(Acts 8:9-22 NASB).

Simon, the sorcerer, tried to pay for the power that comes from
impartation and was rebuked! *Simon didn't know the source, but
wanted the power.* How in error he was—like many today who want
to minister in the power of God without spending the necessary
time soaking in prayer in the presence of God! Revivalists want
God more than the power that comes from knowing Him.
Revivalists also know and value the gift of God on their lives and
know without a doubt that it can and will bring refreshing to all
who are willing to receive.

STIR UP THE GIFT

Timothy was encouraged to stir up the gift that was first given
by the laying on of hands by Paul: *"...I remind you to
kindle afresh the gift of God which is in you through
the laying on of my hands"* (2 Tim. 1:6 NASB). I
don't believe that Paul imparted his gift onto or into
Timothy, but, rather, that he activated by the laying on
of his hands the gift of God that was already inside of
Timothy. The same is true when you pray for others.

> You cannot
> just lay
> hands on
> someone
> and, "Poof!"
> they have
> your
> anointing
> out of the
> blue.

God made you unique. There are gifts on your life
and an anointing that is learned by stewardship and
personal relationship with God. You cannot impart this
gift to others. It is arrogant and ignorant to believe that
we can give something that is not ours to give. God is
the source of all good gifts. You cannot just lay hands on someone and,

"Poof!" they have your anointing out of the blue. You can, however, pray for people with spiritual power that breaks open their faith to receive the gifts of God that He has already destined for them. The anointing is always unique to an individual because it comes through your individual relationship with the Holy Spirit. *If anyone is selling their anointing, don't buy it; you're wasting your money!*

We should follow Christ's and Paul's examples and lay holy hands on others, along with prayer, to see people receive a touch from God and see their gifts activated as the Lord leads. Many times I have laid my hands on people for God to impart something to them like a touch of healing grace or power in their lives. God knows what people are praying for and sometimes, through being obedient to pray over our brothers or sisters, we can help release the faith and gift into their lives at that moment.

PRAYER TEAMS

As I mentioned previously, we must be careful about who we allow to pray for others in a revival meeting. When somebody prays for someone else by laying on of hands, a spiritual deposit tries to take place. The undiscerning sheep will simply receive from anyone whom we have allowed to be in front of them praying for them. On the other side, the Lord has shown me over the years that demonic influences in people can try to jump out at the person praying for them. We must take authority and not be afraid to pray for anyone, but at the same time protect ourselves by using discernment.

Despite the need for caution, praying for one another is important and extremely encouraged. Personal prayer for others, accompanied by laying on of hands, can break off spiritual hindrances and bring a flood of the Holy Spirit's power and God's grace into someone's life. Laying on of hands is a powerful tool to break people free from any doubts or demonic spirits, and it can even stir up the smoldering ashes of their internal revival fires so they can once again be burning ones shining brightly for the glory of our Lord, Jesus! We must not neglect this important foundation of our faith.

QUESTIONS

1. Has anyone prayed for you by laying hands on you before? What did you observe from this experience?

   _____

   _____

   _____

   _____

   _____

2. What must you do to be ready and be full of power when the time comes for you to lay hands on others to stir up their spiritual gifts or cast out their spiritual hindrances?

   _____

   _____

   _____

   _____

3. What can you do to help discern who to pray for and when?

   _____

   _____

   _____

PRAYER (YOU TO GOD)

God, thank You for Your power and the gift of Your Holy Spirit here on earth with us showing us all things. I desire to be used by You and to pray for others to release Your healing virtue to those in need and to activate the gifts in other revivalists. Let me not neglect the gifts in my own life, but stir them up as I move in them in faith. Give me the wisdom to know when and how to pray for others, and put the right people into my life to pray for me when the time calls.

PRAYER (ME TO GOD, FOR YOU)

*Please stir up **all** of the gifts in my friend right now, Lord Jesus. May these words carry a powerful anointing to break off any hindrances and to stir up an internal fire. Release a fresh fire right now, Jesus. Impart a faith that overwhelms this saint to be confident in the gifts and calling You have for the person. Thank You, Lord.*

Endnotes

1. Matt Gilman, "Holy," *Holy* (Kansas City, MO: Forerunner Music, 2008), track 7.
2. L. Thomas Holdcroft (1980), "The New Order of the Latter Rain," *Pneuma: The Journal of the Society for Pentecostal Studies* 2 (2): 48. Reference taken from http://en.wikipedia.org/wiki/Latter_Rain_ (post-World_War_II_movement)#cite_note-PneumaLatterRain48-7).

Into the Fire

I've been here a thousand times
And a thousand times I've failed
But as life comes crashing round me
Still I know Your love prevails

CHORUS

Into the fire
Into the furnace
To the ends of the earth I'll go
For Your name is holy
And Your love is mighty
It's the only love I know
Please won't You send me
Cause my soul is burning
And I'm yearning for You Lord
And I want to know You more

And I swear I'll seek Your face and not Your hand
Though they say it's not as I should
And I can't let them pull me down
Though they try, cause You know they try
In the end I know you win
Just like you said You would

—Kelsey Bowen and Corey Robinson[1]

Chapter 20

TRANSLATION

*...the Spirit of the Lord snatched Philip
away...* (Acts 8:39 NKJV).

*We need to view things from a spiritual perspective,
through the lens of the Bible, rather than from a
natural perspective, through the lens of ourselves.*

Translation is possible for any believer. No I'm not talking about
Spanish to English or Italian to Chinese. I'm talking about Spirit-led
"jumping" from one place to another with no natural regard for the
laws of time and space. This may sound like science fiction, but it's
completely biblical! It's evangelism, "Beam me up, Scotty," style, and
can be a great tool to advance the message of the Kingdom! Think
about it, we wouldn't even need to pay for airfare or waste many
hours traveling from place to place.

Translating (being supernaturally transported by the Holy Spirit)
occurs in multiple places throughout the Bible. I've also heard many
present-day stories of people driving to a destination and getting there
in a fraction of the time due to an apparent acceleration in time and
space that's not necessarily noticeable while it's happening, but very
apparent once they see how much time seemed to have disappeared in

getting to their destination. People can also be transported while sleeping or taken up in visions to be at multiple places at the same time. I even heard a story of entire groups of intercessors getting transported in their sleep to Africa to help rescue some children. They fell asleep in their homes at different locations, but God transported them spiritually to Africa to be an answer to the prayers they were praying! Praise God that *all things truly are possible* if we would only believe!

In a primary New Testament example of this private method of spiritual transportation from the Holy Spirit, Phillip was translated (transported) after he ministered the Gospel to the Ethiopian.

> *So he commanded the chariot to stand still. And both Philip and the eunuch went down into the water, and he baptized him. Now when they came up out of the water,* **the Spirit of the Lord caught Philip away,** *so that the eunuch saw him no more; and he went on his way rejoicing. But Philip was found at Azotus. And passing through, he preached in all the cities till he came to Caesarea* (Acts 8:38-40 NKJV).

If God wants something done, He will use every supernatural means necessary!

The possibility of translating was apparent in Philip the Evangelist's life for the sake of advancing the Gospel. God did this specifically for the purpose of winning souls, regions, and nations. If God wants something done, He will use every supernatural means necessary!

LORD, TAKE ME AWAY

Enoch was taken up to Heaven without seeing death (see Heb. 11:5), as was Elijah (see 2 Kings 2:11-13). Elijah had also a bionic moment when he could run as fast as a chariot; that's one of my favorite stories in the Old Testament: *"...So Ahab rode away and went to Jezreel. Then the hand of the LORD came upon Elijah; and he girded up his loins and ran ahead of Ahab to the entrance of Jezreel"* (1 Kings 18:45-46 NKJV).

Philip may have done the same: *"Then the Spirit said to Philip, 'Go near and overtake this chariot.' So Philip ran to him, and heard him reading the prophet Isaiah, and said, 'Do you understand what you are reading?'"* (Acts 8:29-30 NKJV).

In both cases, some biblical translations say that what came upon these men of God to allow for supernatural transport was the "hand of the Lord" (NKJV) or "Power of the Lord" (NIV). The point is that with the Spirit of the Lord all things are possible, even things that we think are physically impossible. The moral of walking in the Spirit is to believe that the impossible is possible. *Translation is no more impossible than being able to live a sinless life after surrendering your life to Christ, healing the sick, or preaching a powerful sermon—yet the Holy Spirit gives you power to do all for the glory of God!*

> The moral is to believe that the impossible is possible.

LIMITED PERSONAL EXPERIENCE

My only potential experience with this, to date, happened one morning, years ago, when I was running late for work. My clock on my laptop, my clock on the wall, my watch, and my clock in my vehicle all said it was about 10 minutes until 8.[2] I was late for an 8 A.M. meeting. My natural reaction was to speed to work, but God wanted me to strictly obey the speed limit. He was teaching me obedience. With much reluctance, I submitted to Him and slowed *way* down. I just accepted as inevitable the fact that I would be late for the meeting. But when I got to the office to set up my stuff, I realized that people were not in the meeting yet, but were just about to walk into the conference room. To my surprise, I had gotten to the office just in time!

This would have been impossible if I had not obeyed God. Somehow, my timeless Father gave me 20 minutes along the way. I thought perhaps He just slowed down time for me, like He did with Joshua when he was fighting the Philistines (see Josh. 10:13). Would God slow down time in the entire world just for me? Why not? *Revivalists don't ask, "Why," when it comes to the supernatural; they ask, "Why not?" The point is to trust always in God first and foremost and follow His leading. Because I obeyed God in the natural, something impossible in the natural happened. When we follow His leading, the impossible will begin to be a part of our everyday lives!*

THE DISCIPLES GOT JUMPED

The spiritual truth in supernatural things, such as translating, is that God is timeless and omnipresent. His Spirit can be at any place at any time. If His Spirit is living in us, it makes such things possible for us as well. Jesus could oftentimes see into the future because of His close relationship with God, and because of this timeless aspect of God's character, God could easily show Him things to come.

Jesus proved that Spirit-filled, Spirit-led people are not bound by physical laws of nature when He walked on water. He then proved that Christians are not bound by space and time by "jumping" the boat and all the people in it directly to the shore (instantaneous transportation of the boat from one physical location to another)! It is the largest-scale translation that I've read about in the Scriptures.

> When the disciples received Jesus, He accelerated them to their destination.

*Now when evening came, His disciples went down to the sea, got into the boat, and went over the sea toward Capernaum. And it was already dark, and Jesus had not come to them. Then the sea arose because a great wind was blowing. So when they had rowed about three or four miles, they saw Jesus walking on the sea and drawing near the boat; and they were afraid. But He said to them, "It is I; do not be afraid." Then **they willingly received Him into the boat, and immediately the boat was at the land where they were going** (John 6:16-21 NKJV).*

The Bible says that when Jesus got into the boat it *immediately* was at the other side on shore! This journey seemed long and treacherous until Jesus got on board. When the disciples willingly received Jesus, He changed their day and accelerated them to their destination. Let this be a life lesson for all of us. No matter how hard or long the journey of life may appear, when Jesus gets on board, all can be calm and well. Not only that, but I know from personal experience that, even if we feel we have wasted many years of our lives not living a Spirit-filled life of revival, once we embrace the fact that Jesus is Lord of the impossible, as the disciples did when they let Him on their boat, He can in fact accelerate our lives to our destination in a way that would be impossible without Him. He speeds up our spiritual growth and reclaims our wasted years! For those of us who were prodigals and may have felt that we let God down, we can simply let our wonder-working Savior on board our ship and watch Him take us to places of destiny that we thought were unreachable due to our limited time or resources.

A doctrine in the Word is solidified when it is mentioned in two or more places and especially cemented when found in both the Old and New Testaments. "Translation" is a doctrine as real as anything else in Scripture. If you have a problem with this, you have a problem with God. You need to open your mind up to believe the Scriptures. Take them for what they truly say, not just as some crazy stories from thousands of years ago. Today, all over the world, Christians are experiencing similar supernatural occurrences in their lives—just like those found in the Book of Acts and all throughout Scripture.[2]

If God did something once, of course He can do it again! This includes tongues of fire and sounds of rushing wind (see Acts 2), translating in the Spirit (see Acts 8:38-48), walking on water (see Matt. 14:22-33), stopping storms with a command (see Mark 4:35-41), and so forth.

To be revivalists, we must at the least be open to believing that what happened in the Scriptures is also possible for today. The only things God won't do are lie, go against His Word, or undo what was already accomplished through Jesus Christ on the cross. I pray that this book gives you permission to ask God to do the impossible in and through your life so He can get the glory from your supernatural testimonies.

QUESTIONS

1. Do you believe that you can also be translated like the examples we see in the Bible? Why or why not?

_____

_____

_____

_____

2. Why do you think some people have a problem with the belief in translation? Can this error of unbelief also carry over to other commandments and doctrines in the Word?

_____

_____

_____

_____

3. What must you do to be translated?

_____

_____

_____

_____

PRAYER (YOU TO GOD)

God, I believe that all things are possible for those who believe in You. I believe You are who You say You are and You can do again what You have done before. If You can translate Philip to share your Gospel with an Ethiopian, I know you can translate Your servant today to witness to kings and presidents all over the nations. I believe it and receive it, in Your name.

PRAYER (ME TO GOD, FOR YOU)

God, impart Your faith right now to enable this reader to believe everything Your Word says. Let the readers of this book know, that they know, that they know, that if You have done something through one person in history, You can and will do it again if You so choose. Lord, give this saint the opportunity to be translated in sleep and when awake. Give the person the grace to be in multiple places at once, and to get from one destination to another in a supernatural way that goes beyond the laws of space and time—all for the advancement of the Gospel of Jesus. Thank You, Father.

Endnotes

1. Kelsey Bowen and Corey Robinson, "Into the Fire," (Victory Productions, 2006), Fourtwelve, part of the Youth Ministry at Victory Church, http://www.victorychurch.tv.

2. My meeting was at 8 A.M. with my team from IBM. I lived at Fountain Village Apartments at the time at Kolb and 22nd. The office was at 9000 S. Rita Rd, at I-10 and South Kolb road. To drive to the office, park, and walk all the way to the office took at least 25 to 30 minutes.

The growth of the Christian life is, in reality, the increasing manifestation of His life. "He that believeth in (into) Me, out of his innermost being shall flow rivers of Living Water." The outpouring of this divine flow of resurrection life will cover body, soul, and spirit—and the divine virtues of our Lord will nullify and abrogate absolutely everything we have received under the curse of the Law. This provision includes healing. It means more than healing, it means the perpetuation of health. It means the continuous operation in us of the resurrected life of Christ.

—CHARLES PRICE[1]

Chapter 21

RAISING THE DEAD

*Heal the sick, cleanse the lepers, **raise the dead**,
cast out demons* (Matthew 10:8 NKJV).

*A Christian with no power is like a car with no
engine—useless and just taking up space.*

Through the example that Jesus gave when He walked the earth and
the subsequent command that He gave to His disciples, and their
example after He was gone, the Bible clearly implicates that raising
the dead should be a part of normal Christianity. Allow me to explain
through a few Biblical and present-day examples.

We must read the Scriptures and let them consume us, and we
must shape our lives around what they say. Jesus said to raise the dead
(see Matt. 10:8). The original Greek translation of this passage still
means "raise the dead." This means that if a man dies, we should pray
for him and command him to live.

This command to raise the dead was not reserved just for the
original disciples. They were just regular people like the rest of
us, full of imperfections. Not only that, but the synoptic Gospel
version of this story in Luke documents that Jesus gave resurrection power and authority to 70 believers (see Matt. 10:8), not just

His 12 disciples (one of whom was Judas, Jesus' betrayer). Jesus command for His disciples (including us) to raise the dead is absolutely undeniable. If we ignore such commands, we are no better than the religious people Jesus rebuked: *"Jesus answered and said to them, 'You are mistaken, not knowing the Scriptures nor the power of God'"* (Matt. 22:29 NKJV).

The command to raise the dead is for anyone who will believe; it is not just a one-time, special occasion commandment relegated to the time when Jesus physically walked the earth. The apostle Paul, who was not an original disciple of Christ, also moved in resurrection power at a much later time:

> *Now on the first day of the week, when the disciples came together to break bread, Paul, ready to depart the next day, spoke to them and continued his message until midnight. There were many lamps in the upper room where they were gathered together. And **in a window sat a certain young man named Eutychus**, who was sinking into a deep sleep. He was overcome by sleep; and as Paul continued speaking, **he fell down from the third story and was taken up dead**. But Paul went down, fell on him, and embracing him said, "Do not trouble yourselves, for his life is in him." Now when he had come up, had broken bread and eaten, and talked a long while, even till daybreak, he departed. And they brought the young man in alive, and they were not a little comforted* (Acts 20:7-12 NKJV).

I've heard of people falling asleep in sermons, but "falling dead," now that's extreme! But Paul quickly gained back momentum and attention to his teaching through this resurrection.

The same thing that happened here with Paul can happen with any of us. The Word says that the same Spirit that raised Christ from the dead lives in *me!* We must either believe all of the Scriptures or none of them. Revivalists believe that if it was possible before, it is possible now.

And if the Spirit of Him who raised Jesus from the dead is living in you, He who raised Christ from the dead will also give life to your mortal bodies because of His Spirit, who lives in you (Romans 8:11).

The Scripture here doesn't say that He will give life to our resurrected bodies or that we should wait around for our new spiritual bodies; it says our *mortal* bodies. The Holy Spirit gives life to our mortal bodies! How true this is! When it comes to raising the dead, this is just like any promise in Scripture. If we know it and continue to pray for it, one day it will happen!

> The Holy Spirit gives life to our mortal bodies!

This command is attached to the Great Commission and should be a regular occurrence throughout Christianity. Throughout history, many past and modern-day revivalists have prayed for dead people and seen them come alive.

COMMAND LIFE

Raising the dead is no more impossible than someone getting "saved." Both are by the Spirit of life, the Spirit of Jesus, who leads and guides us daily, not by our own holiness, righteousness, or works.

Any believer can raise the dead! The difference is that salvation is received by the faith of the individual. When the dead are raised, there is no such cooperation. Instead, God requires *us* to take control and take action by His faith. This means that, as we sense His miracle mantle and strong anointing to intervene in any given situation where the dead need to be raised, He actually requires us to then do something about it. People's spirits must be revived by God's Spirit.

If people are alive in the flesh, but dead spiritually, they cannot receive eternal life. When they believe in Jesus, their spirits come alive by the breath of God's Spirit breathing life into their spirits! This is what it means to be "born again." When people are dead in the natural, their spirits have left them entirely. In this case, we must command that the spirits of these people come back into their mortal bodies. The method and model for this in the Scripture can be found in Ezekiel, in the famous passage about the dry bones:

> Then He said to me, *"Prophesy to these bones and say to them, 'Dry bones, hear the word of the LORD! This is what the Sovereign LORD says to these bones: I will make breath enter you, and you will come to life. I will attach tendons to you and make flesh come upon you and cover you with skin;* **I will put breath in you, and you will come to life. Then you will know that I am the LORD.'"** *So I prophesied as I was commanded. And as I was prophesying, there was a noise, a rattling sound, and the bones came together, bone to bone. I looked, and tendons and flesh appeared on them and skin covered them, but there was no breath in them. Then He said to me, "Prophesy to the breath; prophesy, son of man, and say to it, 'This is what the Sovereign LORD says: Come, breath, from the four winds and breathe into these slain, that they may live.'"* **So I prophesied as He commanded me, and breath entered them; they came to life and stood up on their feet—a vast army** (Ezekiel 37:4-10).

Ezekiel prophesied that the breath (spirit) come into the bodies to give them life. The same can work today when we pray, prophesy, and speak life into the bodies of those who are ailing from disease, broken, sick, or even deceased with no apparent life.

Jesus commanded Lazarus to come out of his tomb after being dead for four days! When Jesus spoke to Lazarus' dead body to come out, by His authority, Lazarus's spirit had no choice but to enter back into the body and respond to the words spoken by our Savior:

> *Jesus, once more deeply moved, came to the tomb. It was a cave with a stone laid across the entrance. "Take away the stone," He said. "But, Lord," said Martha, the sister of the dead man, "by this time there is a bad odor, for he has been there four days." Then Jesus said, "Did I not tell you that if you believed, you will see the glory of God?" So they took away*

*the stone. Then Jesus looked up and said, "Father, I thank You that You have heard Me. I knew that You always hear Me, but I said this for the benefit of the people standing here, that they may believe that You sent Me." When He had said this, Jesus called in a loud voice, "**Lazarus, come out!**" The dead man came out, his hands and feet wrapped with strips of linen, and a cloth around his face. Jesus said to them, "Take off the grave clothes and let him go"* (John 11:38-44).

The Bible says that the Words of Jesus are spirit and life (see John 6:63). The Bible also says that life and death are in the power of the tongue (see Prov. 18:21). When we speak negative, argumentative, hateful, condemning things, it literally creates death in the spirits of all who hear. When we speak the Words of God, words of life full of peace, encouragement, and love, we are literally reviving people's spirits and bringing life to their souls. Furthermore, these words can even restore their physical bodies: *"A heart at peace gives life to the body..."* (Prov. 14:30).

The key to reviving someone's spirit, soul, and body lies in speaking the words of God, the words of life into any situation, person, or circumstance that we may come across, including any situation where the dead can be raised for the glory of God. Revival is released upon the earth through the Church's words and actions.

TESTIMONIES

The works of God have no expiration date. Raising the dead wasn't reserved for only a certain period of time. God is the same yesterday, today, and forever (see Heb. 13:8), and His works, which come from His character, are as real today as they have ever been. Today, around the world, Christian martyrs are dying for their faith. At the same time, dead people are being raised daily around the world. You may question this irony, but God's ways are certainly not our ways. The blood of the martyrs propels the message of the Gospel to permeate a resistant nation.

The life of the dead being raised is a testimony to God's continued miracle-working power. Both bring glory to God. I will share now a few testimonies of the dead being raised to encourage your faith in this soon-to-be normal Christian practice.

A pastor here in Tucson, Arizona, was ministering to a group of evangelists one Saturday afternoon and was teaching us about faith. He told us the story of when he found out his mother had died. She apparently had died in such a way that her face muscles froze in an awkward and crooked way that was not pretty to the eyes. When he heard the news, he said a mantle of faith came over him, and he had total boldness to resurrect her. He said it was like he just knew it was going to happen.

> To raise the dead you don't need "more faith," and you don't need to be a believer for many years first.

He boldly charged into the hospital full of faith and the Spirit. His family sent him to the back room where she was. Almost immediately, he commanded life back into her body and she awoke! She awoke, however, just long enough to look him in the eyes and say, "Son, you've got to let me go." She quietly and calmly closed her eyes again, and went back to be with her Savior.

The nurses came in, totally shocked and confused when they saw her, and asked him, "What did you do?" They said it was impossible that her face had become calm and peaceful, with what looked like a smile softly frozen in place. The pastor said that the mantle of faith immediately left him when she passed away the second time, and he began to weep as the pain of her loss began to set in.

IN OTHER NEWS

My wife and I had dinner once with a young brother we met from Guatemala who actually raised the dead shortly after giving his life to the Lord. Talk about solidifying your relationship with God's ability to do the impossible! To raise the dead you don't need "more faith," and you don't need to be a believer for many years first. You just need to be at the right place at the right time (divine appointment) and be listening to God and willing to usher in His will.

Revivalist David Herzog prophesied to an evangelist that he would shortly raise the dead. A week later, he had the opportunity in a hospital room. He promptly commanded life into a dead body, and God answered that cry for a miracle![2] Over 20 years ago, Mahesh Chavda called a man forward in a revival meeting in Africa whose son had died earlier that morning. God gave him a word that his son would live, and at the moment of that declaration, the son came back to life![3]

You may have heard other stories from David Hogan or Heidi Baker of many dead being raised in the countries they minister in. The Bakers have created such a culture of Heaven manifesting on earth that pastors and leaders associated with their ministry in Mozambique claim that dozens have been raised from the dead through this ministry. She tells of a couple of these occurrences in her book, *Always Enough*.[4]

A man named Caspar McCloud recounts of the time that he, himself, was supernaturally restored back to life in his book *Nothing is Impossible*.[5]

In 2010, at a Jesus Culture conference in Cleveland, Ohio, a young lady testified that she prayed and commanded life into a toddler who had just drowned. He did not respond to CPR but he did respond to the name of Jesus Christ, Glory to God![6]

At a Reinhard Bonnke evangelistic crusade in Africa, a man was raised from the dead as he was being prayed for in a basement beneath the stage of the crusade. This was caught on video and is amazing to see![7]

Through a move of God's revivalists in America and throughout the world, we are hearing reports of the dead being raised as something that is becoming much more common. When miracle-working opportunities presented themselves, like when Lazarus was in his tomb, Jesus recognized them as opportunities for the glory of God (see John 11:40).

These are simply modern-day examples for us to see and know that this is possible for us today.

THE ONLY FAILURE IS NOT TRYING

Praying for the sick, dying, broken, and beaten-down is not always an easy thing to do. I've had my share of spiritual breakthroughs by praying the prayer of faith, but I've also had some disappointments. I've prayed for four or five people on their deathbeds, and they all died. In addition, I prayed for a man in a wheelchair who had cancer, and I even dumped anointing oil all down his head. A couple weeks later, he died.

Do any of these experiences persuade me to no longer pray for the sick, dead, or dying? Of course not. The point is that *we must continue to act on the commandments of God regardless of perceived external, immediate results*. Revivalists' mindsets are never shaped by their natural circumstances. *My experiences cannot shape my view of who God is to the point of overriding what the Scriptures say about Him!* That is an illegal spiritual response. Besides, I have seen God heal brain tumors, cancer, and other manners of sickness and disease; certainly, raising the dead is not that big of a deal for Him if we pray the prayers of faith in the power of His Spirit.

It's important to remember that my faith is limited and is just an opening for God to release His faith into the situation. I know that when I lay hands on the sick they will recover because Jesus said so. I know the dead will be raised by the name of Jesus, through my prayers, soon enough, so I simply must respond to what I know and let the rest work itself out. I just must respond in faith when the situation presents itself.

We must stay encouraged and stay responsive. It's OK to feel a little fear and nervousness in situations that need the impossible; that's natural. But we must not be paralyzed by fear. Rather, if we persevere in prayer, God will show up! Think about it this way: When we act on something that is impossible to achieve without God, we are acting on our faith, something that in itself can be commended. When we do this, regardless of external results, at the very least we are pleasing

God—and that's what we should be living for. *"But without faith it is impossible to please Him, for he who comes to God must believe that He is, and that He is a rewarder of those who diligently seek Him"* (Heb. 11:6 NKJV).

ANY LAST WORDS?

When we do raise people from the dead and disciple them, we will want to explain to them that eternal life is still our goal, our prize, and where our treasure is. Jesus, Himself, encouraged His disciples with this:

> *Behold, I give you the authority to trample on serpents and scorpions, and over all the power of the enemy, and nothing shall by any means hurt you. Nevertheless do not rejoice in this, that the spirits are subject to you, but rather rejoice because your names are written in heaven* (Luke 10:19-20 NKJV).

Furthermore, the Bible says:

> *For the Father loves the Son, and shows Him all things that He Himself does; and He will show Him greater works than these, that you may marvel. For as the Father raises the dead and gives life to them, even so the Son gives life to whom He will* (John 5:20-21 NKJV).

Jesus healed *all* who came to Him, but He gives life to whom He will, meaning not all will continually be raised forever and ever. Remember, Lazarus still died again after he was raised in the natural.

God wants us to remember that our eternal life should be our focus. If God wants to take us without seeing death, like Enoch or Elijah, that's great, but most of us have a better chance of getting hit by lightning on a sunny day.

Death is just a part of life and nothing to be feared. We should worry much more about not living the life God has planned for us than about when we may pass through this life to enter our eternal abode in heaven. As Paul said, *"For to me, to live is Christ, and to die is gain"* (Phil. 1:21 NKJV).

QUESTIONS

1. Have you prayed for somebody dead or dying? Did they get better? I encourage you to log God's answers to your prayers so that you can keep track of His answers.

———————————————————————

———————————————————————

———————————————————————

———————————————————————

2. Have you been afraid to pray for somebody or respond in faith to an impossible situation? What can you do to get over this fear?

———————————————————————

———————————————————————

———————————————————————

———————————————————————

3. Will you be God's answer to prayer if a crazy situation presents itself? Come up with a scenario or two and start thinking now about your emotions and response.

———————————————————————

———————————————————————

———————————————————————

———————————————————————

PRAYER (YOU TO GOD)

God, I pray that You would give me the opportunity and the mantle of faith when the time comes to raise the dead. Thank You, Jesus.

PRAYER (ME TO GOD, FOR YOU)

In Jesus' name, I cast out all fear and doubt regarding believing the Scriptures for the impossible! God, mantle this saint with Your faith, break away any false and limiting mindsets regarding raising the dead, and provide the opportunity one day to see the dead raised to bring glory to You! Amen.

Endnotes

1. Charles Price, *The Real Faith for Healing* (Alachua, FL: Bridge-Logos Publishers, 1998).

2. Read about this testimony in David Herzog's book, *Mysteries of the Glory Unveiled* (Hagerstown, MD: McDougal Publishing Company, 2000).

3. Read about this testimony in Mahesh Chavda, *Only Love Can Make a Miracle* (Mahesh Chavda, 2002).

4. Heidi and Roland Baker, *Always Enough: God's Miraculous Provision among the Poorest Children on Earth* (Grand Rapids, MI: Chosen Books, a division of Baker Book House company, 2003); Caspar McCloud, *Nothing Is Impossible* (Gainesville, GA: Praxi Press, 2006).

5. Jesus Culture, Cleveland, May 22, 2010, http://www.youtube.com/watch?v=z4HwXwqgf1s. Accessed September 8, 2010.

6. This is the remarkable story of a Nigerian pastor, Daniel Ekechukwu, who was fatally injured in a car accident near the town of Onitsha, Nigeria, Africa on November 30, 2001. Order the video from Amazon.com, http://www.amazon.com/Raised-Dead-Evangelist-Reinhard-Bonnke/dp/1933106085. Released January 1, 2001.

"The Anthem"

I am royalty
I have destiny
I have been set free
I'm gonna shake history
I'm gonna change the world!

—Jake Hamilton[1]

Chapter 22

Passport to Greatness

In Him we were also chosen, having been predestined according to the plan of Him who works out everything in conformity with the purpose of His will (Ephesians 1:11)

*God's in charge of your **destiny** but first you must agree with your **identity.***

Your significance is tied to who God says you are not what others may or may not think about you.

GREATER THAN JOHN

The Bible said of John the Baptist that there was no greater prophet born of a woman than this man (see Matt. 11:11). Yet the Bible also says that the least born into the Kingdom is greater than he (see Luke 7:28). That's a pretty bold statement! The truth is that John was a bridge between the Old and New, between the law unfulfilled and the law fulfilled, between the law written on tablets to the law written on hearts (see Heb. 10:15-17), between the spirit coming *upon* men and women of old (see Jude 15:14, 2 Chon. 15:1, 2 Chron. 20:14, to name a few) to the Spirit dwelling *within* those who believe in Jesus in faith (see Rom. 8:23, 2 Cor. 6:6). John's very name means "grace" because he was a voice crying in the wilderness proclaiming a new season of God's grace through the Messiah born to take away the sins of the world!

Do you feel like you're *greater* than John the Baptist, than Elijah, Elisha, than Isaiah, than Samson, than David? Your identity in Christ has little to do with how you feel and everything to do with what the Word says. The Bible says God numbered every hair on your head (see Luke 12:7)! To me, that means He thinks you're pretty important. He does not love any one person over another. We all can have equal access to the throne of God and all have an equal opportunity to find favor with the King.

For a couple years, I was a licensed Realtor. What I learned in buying and selling houses with clients is that something is only worth market value—and market value is what somebody is willing to pay for something given equal exposure in a market with other similar items. It doesn't take a business major to figure out that something is worth the price somebody is willing to pay for it. God gave His only begotten Son, to lay aside His deity to be mocked, ridiculed, and rejected by man and crucified for our sakes so that we may live forever. You cannot put a price on that! It is a priceless price that has been paid for you—meaning you are priceless! God cares about you as much as anyone else and has a deep yearning desire to have a love relationship with you. He wants to pour out His Father's love on us and stir our bridal love affections through His Spirit to His Church toward His Son, Jesus. Through this love relationship we begin to believe more in ourselves and who God says we are.

Like many Christians, I struggled greatly with unworthiness. Although a seemingly more humble sin than pride, unworthiness is still a sin and will hinder you from God's best. Shortly after rededicating my life to Jesus, I called up an old minister friend of mine and shared with him my struggle. He said he went through the same thing and encouraged me by saying that "on our best day we are not worthy. But because of what Jesus did, you are worthy. God now sees Jesus when He looks at you." These words resonated in my spirit and I realized that, like salvation, our identity as Kingdom people is a free gift of God. We will still have to come into agreement with this truth if we want to fully submit to the perfect plans God architected for our lives since before the foundations of the earth.

GOD'S NOT MAD

Some people never fully understand God's love for them or God's purpose for them because they think He is just a bitter, angry, disciplinarian. Consciously or subconsciously, many Christians have been taught to believe that God is up in Heaven just waiting for you to make a mistake so you can be punished, monitoring you like a shopping mall security guard with a camera pointed at every area of your life. Unfortunately, a religious upbringing like this does much more harm than good. While the concept may be based on some truth, it lacks the understanding of God's heart and His full opinions of man.

If God was so mad at you for your sins, why would He have given the greatest sacrifice in history, and sent His own Son to die in your place? While we were yet His enemies, Christ died for us (see Rom. 5:8-10). Wow, God even loves His enemies! God loves sinners and wants them to kick their sin out so they can spend eternity with Him! He doesn't hate sinners. His heart is broken for them. His thoughts of goodness abound toward them. God is not mad at you.

To have an awareness of God's ridiculous (*amazing*) love toward us, no matter what kind of evil we have done in the past, is to have a revelation of His kindness. The Bible says that His kindness will lead us to repentance (see Rom. 2:4), not His anger. When we preach God's anger, people run and hide! When we preach God's abounding love for people in spite of His hatred of their sin, people come running to Him! God certainly disciplines those whom He loves, and Christians who should know better regarding living in disobedience sometimes get a taste of God's anger and wrath, but overall, He *always wants the best for you!* All of you! If you still don't believe me, just read the Holy Word of God. All throughout Scripture, God's great desires for His people are expressed.

Here are some Scripture references for you to start believing in what God believes about you:

You are chosen before the creation of the world to be holy and blameless in His sight (see Ephesians 1:4).

You have been born again (see I Peter 1:23).

You are a new creation (see 2 Corinthians 5:17).

You are God's child (see John 1:12).

You are a citizen of Heaven (see Philippians 3:20).

You are rescued from the dominion of darkness and brought into the Kingdom of the Son He loves (see Colossians 1:13).

You are from God and have overcome them, because the one who is in you is greater than the one who is in the world (see I John 4:4).

You have the victory through our Lord Jesus Christ (see 1 Corinthians 15:57).

You are the light of the world (see Matthew 5:14).

You are more than conquerors through Him who loved us (see Romans 8:37).

You are the righteousness of God (see 2 Corinthians 5:21).

Your body is a temple of the Holy Spirit, who is in you (see 1 Corinthians 6:19).

You too are being built together to become a dwelling in which God lives by His Spirit (see Ephesians 2:22).

You are raised up with Christ (see Ephesians 2:6).

You are a saint (see Ephesians 1:18).

You have been saved and called to a holy life (see 2 Timothy 1:9).

You were created to bring glory to God (see Ephesians 3:21).

TO BE GREAT IN THE KINGDOM MEANS TO GO LOWER

Greatness is an attitude and a mindset. It's knowing you're great because that's what God thinks about you. To *demean, discredit,* and *discourage* your value is to *dishonor* what Jesus did for you on the cross and disappoint God, who created you to be great. True humility is knowing and acting like a child of the most High God in spite of knowing your past faults and failures. Such an attitude requires a dependency on God and will allow God to get all of the Glory from anything good that comes from your life. Once you believe in God, He will lead you to believe in yourself. Once you really start believing in yourself, you will not be afraid of the greatness that God can birth from inside you, and eventually you will just start to do bigger and bigger things knowing that your God is a *big* God, a God of the *possible,* not *impossible.* What's impossible with us is quite simple for Him.

In my early years, I would often pray, "God, less of me, more of You." A great prayer in its intentions, however, it lacks one vital point. God keeps us on earth for a reason, so that His glory can shine brightly through His Church as a testimony of His goodness. God doesn't want less of us and more of Him; He wants more of Him to shine through more of us! The more He teaches us, grows us, and guides us, the more we can carry a greater capacity of the knowledge of the Glory of the Lord, and be a brighter light for the world to see! God doesn't want us to try to pull Him down to our level of despair, humanness, and struggle. He meets us at that place so He can pull us up to a place of His heavenly *glory, victory,* and *joy!*

Greatness isn't always what you think it is. Greatness in regards to doing *bigger* and *better* things in the Americanized interpretation of things is not how we should look at God's Kingdom. Doing bigger and better things for God without God is a sure way to propagate powerless Churchianity, not powerful Christianity.

Greatness in God's Kingdom starts small, like a mustard seed (see Luke 13:18-19), but can grow into something quite impressive over time. Greatness comes with consistency and discipline, passing God's character tests and embracing the process that comes with every prophecy that may have been spoken over your life. Salvation is a free gift of God, but much of the promises of God and greater honor in His Kingdom can come only from selfless, responsible stewardship birthed from obedience to God's Spirit and God's Word.

Jesus often teaches about stewardship. He asks, how can we steward true spiritual riches if we cannot even manage our own finances? (See Luke 16:11.) Furthermore the Bible says that to even be a deacon, a man must be able to manage his own life and his own family well (see 1 Tim. 3:12). Proverbs says that a man with no discipline is like a city with no walls (see Prov. 25:28).

When we steward our life, and every little step of obedience that God puts in front of our paths, then greater opportunities for being a vessel of honor will surely come our way. There have been so many occasions where God has had me pick up a small piece of trash somewhere, clean up after myself, or others, in a public restroom, or perform some other small act of kindness or consideration for those around me. These are things that may seem trivial, mundane, unimportant. However, these kinds of test are of the *utmost* importance to God! He is testing us! Yes, I said it, God tests us. He tests us with small acts of obedience when we pray for Him to use us for BIG acts of obedience. He longs to answer our prayers but wants to make sure that we can handle the lion and the bear before He throws us up against a Goliath, like David. He wants to make sure we are going to be true Sons and Daughters who will sacrifice ourselves to take care of Daddy's business rather than spoiled kids wanting our way or the highway. This is part of God's pruning and refining process.

We pray to go up another level in knowledge of Christ, in Kingdom responsibility, in visible authority, and God takes us down a few levels to see if we will honor Him with obedience in the small things. The Kingdom is about pastoring your family before you pastor a church. It's about evangelizing the neighborhoods before the nations!

Jesus says that the *least* of you will be the *greatest* in God's Kingdom (see Luke 9:48). For a Kingdom Revivalist, oftentimes greatness the way we would define it comes after death. It comes with getting our approval and rewards in heaven and laying our crowns at the feet of Jesus. It was not until after His death that Jesus' name was made famous throughout the world. The same goes for many past saints whose names cannot compare to Jesus, nor would they want them to, but who God greatly exalted after they passed away—Brother Lawrence, St. Francis of Avila, Thomas Kempis, the Apostle Paul, to name a few. As long as your eyes are set steadfastly on the giver of Life, the Author and Finisher of your faith, Jesus Christ, and you desire to serve and not be served, you will attain greatness in God's Kingdom. That is, if you don't limit yourself with stinkin'thinkin', unworthiness, prideful humility, self-degradation, lack of faith

INTIMACY LEADS TO IDENTITY

Your identity is understood and made clearer the more time you spend with the Lord. As God is worshiped and magnified, His thoughts and His ways are revealed. The more intimate we are with Him, the more Oneness with Him becomes a reality. This Oneness leads to us feeling what He feels and seeing things the way He sees things. By no means does this put us as equals with God, but it does make us One with Him. When we abide in this place of true worship, what God thinks of us begins to permeate our souls. In a practical sense, I tell people that if they want to find their purpose in life, they must do what everything else that has been created must do—go to their Creator and ask! They must read the manual. The manual in our case is the Bible. Intimacy with God goes beyond just reading His Word, but it also is not prayer alone. I believe a combination of prayer and reading the Bible will help us to know God and know ourselves better than any combination of methods out there. We all have a place and a purpose, and most of us have looked or are looking for answers regarding that age-old question, "Who Am I?" If you answer that question the way God would answer it on your behalf, if you answer that question the way that the Word of God says you should, you may be surprised at how great God already sees you, and what kind of greatness He expects from one of His greatest creations of all time, *us!*

How can you hear God if you have not learned to recognize His voice? When a good friend who calls you up, even after many years, you don't need caller ID to determine who he is. You instantly know his voice. God says, *"My sheep listen to my voice..."* (John 10:27).

If the Lord's voice in your life has grown faint, if you're confused by the clutter of your mind, if the tares of the cares of this world are choking out the Kingdom seeds from sprouting and bearing much fruit in your life, I implore you to please, reestablish a place of intimate fellowship with our Lord and Savior, Jesus Christ. The concept of talking to God, hearing from Him, and interacting with Him as a person may be foreign to some. However, it is necessary to walk this Christian walk with any spiritual success. Man's discipline and religion's rules only last so long without the empowerment that comes from knowing God's Spirit and having Him write the law on our hearts and give us the ability to follow the Lord's will and please God in all that we do.

Our love affair with the Creator of the universe is what opens up the keys to His heart to better understand and feel how He feels about us. This same intimacy also leads to greater authority in God's Kingdom. Those who love Him and obey Him can be trusted, like any good children (see John 14:21). Our Kingdom privileges are also cultivated from the place of our knees and the study of the Word. The privileges become a reality when we are faced with a situation that needs Kingdom intervention and we promptly act in faith.

No matter what spiritual tools you have been equipped with, the key to activate them for use is given by God in the throne room of His presence. The power behind these tools is the Spirit of God. You must become familiar with the presence and power of God before you can impart these fruits of God's Anointing to others. Without love, no prophetic word or great sermon will be of use in God's Kingdom. Without love, to God these things are just noise (see 1 Cor. 13:1). With love, your words carry the power of life (see Prov. 18:21)! Spending time with God, soaking in His love, will soften the hard places of your heart, purify your motives, and give you a burden to want to minister to people for all the right reasons.

PROFILES OF REVIVAL

Your significance is not tied to what you do in God's Kingdom. It rests in who you are, in who Jesus is, and who we all are together. You can be a doctor, lawyer, fireman, computer analyst, NASA scientist, paleontologist, professional athlete, real estate agent, post office clerk, "In and Out" burger boy or girl, or Starbucks barista—it doesn't really matter. Being a Kingdom person and somebody used greatly of the Lord is not dependent on your profession, years of experience as a Christian, or title before your name. It has no limitations. You may have been born with a debilitating condition or have suffered from a great loss of some kind. These things do not limit your effectiveness in God's Kingdom; in many times, they strengthen your testimony and your resolve!

My wife and I recently attended a prayer meeting with a group of adults who met together specifically to pray for a woman who recently had a stroke and could not walk without assistance. We prayed for her, and God's glory really came down. She basked in His glory and later was able to stand up on her own! She was talking normally and coherently! She then began to freely give what she had just received from the Lord and began praying for others in the room and imparting God's love and power! What a testimony!

Here are some other everyday revivalists that I know who are changing their world, one testimony at a time:

- *Rifqa Bary.* A young woman of God whose testimony is captivating millions, Rifqa Bary is an Islamic convert to Christianity. Her fire and passion for the Lord are evident in her online video posts and interviews.[2] She had to run away from home because her crime is punishable by death according to Islamic law.[3] Regardless of the consequences, she is taking a bold stand for Jesus, dedicated to living for Him at all costs! What an example!

- *Brandon Smith.* Some people would say Brandon is undersized for a starting point guard for one of the best college basketball programs in the Nation, The University of California–Berkley. However, this guy has the fundamentals of a Champion and is *huge* in stature in the Kingdom of God with a love and humility not found in many. When not on the court, he is often found praying and ministering at large youth and young adult events.

- *Brian Porzio.* A Christian motivational speaker and revivalist, openly rejected a beautiful girl on ABC's, *Dating in the Dark* because he didn't want to compromise his values. Go Brian!

- *Matt Merrill.* An everyday revivalist who prays for anybody, anywhere, who has any sign of need! This guy really took the "preach the Gospel to every nation" part of the Great Commission seriously. Anytime I run errands with Matt, we need to plan for an extra hour or so for prayer time at the Walmart or grocery store. He sees people healed wherever he goes.

- *Todd Perroud.* With no official titles or budgets, Todd led home worship and Bible study meetings for many years, seeing God perform many signs and wonders. He has seen dozens grow in spiritual maturity and godliness. He has recently written a book that exposes the spirit of religion and ungodly influences in churches across America while encouraging others to depend on hearing and knowing Jesus Christ for themselves.

- *Dr. Dean Landis.* At 75 years young, Dr. Landis is constantly meeting and connecting with anointed individuals to see them partner in building the Kingdom. Worldwide crusades and the rapid growth of a university have all come together because of the relentless efforts of his behind-the-scenes godly networking.

- *Dominick Cruz.* The son of Pima County National Day of Prayer Coordinator Suzette Howe, Dominick was taught to be great at a young age. At the time of the writing of the book, he is the WEC MMA World Champion in the Bantamweight division and considered one of the best pound-for-pound fighters in the world! Dominick publicly gave God all the glory for his victory for millions to see when he first won the belt.

- *Mike Jones, aka microphonejones.* Enormously talented musician, artist, and producer since he was a teenager! He demonstrates his musical talents for the world to see on YouTube as he gives all the glory to Jesus.[4] He is the Christian Kanye West (famous musician and producer)...but, in my opinion, better!

- *Jesse Kelley.* A Christian man with strong convictions, he decided he should help change the U.S. government by running for Congress against an extremely popular Arizona Democrat.[5] He believes in God and thus

believes that he can make a difference in this nation. I
believe he has a bright future in politics.

- *Claudaniel and Melody Fabien.* These friends of mine
  didn't just save their "first time" for their wedding night,
  they also saved their first kiss! Many young couples talk
  about doing this, but they actually did it! This is so rare
  that it made the news in Chicago; both television and
  newspaper. This God-fearing couple proved to God,
  themselves, and the world that purity is possible in the
  midst of a culture of compromise.[6]

These men and women are truly sons and daughters of God.
All are just being who they were created to be, and letting God use
their lives to be a witness to the world and give Him glory. How
many more stories could I share here of everyday greatness? How
many people do you know that are laying down their lives for Jesus,
and letting Him develop greatness in and through their lives? There
are countless others dying to live in the fullness of who they were
created to be. To those people, I, like Ezekiel, say, "Dry bones, live"
(see Ezekiel 37:9-10)! Stand to your feet and come alive, you vast
army of the Lord!

GO CHANGE THE WORLD

Paul mentions in Second Timothy 2:20 that in God's Kingdom
there are vessels of honor and dishonor. God may need me as a mop
bucket one day (dishonored) and a golden vase (honored) another day.
These metaphors relate to how God may pour through us in ministry. All metaphors aside, practically speaking, I just want to be teach-
able and available to God at any time to accomplish anything that He
desires. The Apostle Paul said it very well in 1 Corinthians 9:22: *"To
the weak I became weak, to win the weak. I have become all things to all
people so that by all possible means I might save some."*

The Bible also says the following:

But who are you, a human being, to talk back to God? Shall what is formed say to the one who formed it, "Why did you make me like this?" Does not the potter have the right to make out of the same lump of clay some pottery for special purposes and some for common use? (Romans 9:20-21)

Regardless of what God needs me for, I want to allow God to work through me in whatever way He sees fit, whenever He wants to pour through me or use me for some special assignment. We all have a place and a purpose. We do not need to be perfect, only willing. Our willingness to be all we can be for God, to assist in some way of representing His Kingdom on earth and helping to lead others to Christ, is all we need. God will partner with us to do the rest, providing that which we lack, and guiding us every step of the way.

May the God of peace, who through the blood of the eternal covenant brought back from the dead our Lord Jesus, that great Shepherd of the sheep, equip you with everything good for doing his will, and may he work in us what is pleasing to him, through Jesus Christ, to whom be glory for ever and ever (Hebrews 13:20-21).

The stuff in this book is not out of reach for you—quite the contrary! Jesus was not only tempted in every way as a man to prove that He is the Ultimate Overcomer (see Heb. 4:15), but also He laid aside His divinity to prove that a man in human flesh, with human limitations, can still be filled with God's Spirit and see supernatural manifestations. If you do the stuff that Jesus did, you can do the stuff that Jesus did! It's as simple as that.

We like to think about the great works of healing and teaching that Jesus did, but what about the great works of *all-night prayer sessions with the Father* (see Luke 6:12)? What about the great work of not losing His temper and completely walking away when the disciples would say dumb things? What about the great work of being a humble and obedient carpenter for at least 18 years when He knew the entire time that He was the Son of God and the one true Messiah (see Luke 2:42-49)? The relentless obedience of Jesus Christ, empowered by God's Spirit within, allowed Him to complete the greatest task in all of history—the cross (see Mark 15). Now we must take up our crosses and follow in His footsteps (see Matt. 10:38). Our crosses are different and they're not as heavy, but necessary, just the same, if we are to be good disciples and follow in the footsteps of Jesus and carry on with the mission He commissioned.

Jesus did the little things so He could succeed in the greater things. God has great plans for this generation and great thoughts for you to prosper and not to harm you:

> *"For I know the plans I have for you," declares the LORD, "plans to prosper you and not to harm you, plans to give you hope and a future"* (Jeremiah 29:11).

God desires for a people to rise up in true holiness and humility to carry the power of the Gospel and the knowledge of Christ in obedience to the Holy Spirit with them wherever they go! Whether that's going to work on Monday morning to labor with ungodly coworkers or dealing with rebellious teenage children, God does not want to be separated from your life. We will not all be traveling itinerant ministers or pastors of megachurches, but we can all be revivalists.

As the Lord leads your life, you'll live with no regrets. Your spirit comes alive by faith, and your soul is refreshed as you are filled with God's Spirit. The rest of the journey is up to you. You must take personal responsibility to press into God's Kingdom and seek first God's ways. You must be open and willing to be revived, and you must be desperate to see God move in your generation. I pray that you are encouraged and equipped and that you feel released to live at a whole new level in your Christian spiritual walk. From this day forward, you have no reason to not live a remarkable life! You are a son or daughter of God.

*You **are** revival!*

Endnotes

1. Jake Hamilton, "The Anthem," *Marked by Heaven* (Jesus Culture Music, produced by Banning Liebscher 2009), track 3.

2. http://www.youtube.com/watch?v=ne0MdUyJ1GU, last accessed September 7, 2010.

3. See http://rifqabary.com.

4. http://www.youtube.com/user/microphonejones

5. http://www.votejessekelly.com/http://www.votejessekelly.com/

6. http://www.youtube.com/watch?v=pjxYph_F8VE.

Continue to read through the Appendixes; you will be encouraged. If you go to our Web site, http://www.youarerevival.com, and order a new book, I will be happy to sign it for you as a personal copy so you can give this copy away to a friend. Let's spread the message of this book around to ignite a generation of revivalists whom we can help train, equip, and send around the world for the work of the ministry! We will see revival spread throughout America and the world!

Also check out our Facebook site and blog sites, updated often with revival teachings and news from the move of God around the world, http://youarerevival.typepad.com.

We love you, and thank you for your kind support!

Matthew and Elizabeth Skamser

PRACTICAL TIPS FOR DAILY REVIVAL

Hang out with God as much as humanly possible.

Pray with people at any and every opportunity.

Avoid arguments and useless or vain conversations.

Journal as God speaks to your heart.

Hang around anointed people (if you see it, you can be it).

Volunteer for 24/7 prayer shifts at your local house of prayer. If there is no house of prayer, start one!

Raise money and go on a mission trip.

Read the Gospels as often as possible.

Show love, joy, and patience wherever you go; put others' interests always above your own.

Schedule solemn assemblies and prayer or revival conferences.

Talk to the Holy Spirit as a person all through the day.

Read books on historic revival.

When you go places like the hospital, Walmart, the mall, or wherever, give yourself some extra time for possible divine appointments (God putting people in your path for His purposes).

Prophesy encouraging words over your waiter or waitress whenever you go out to eat, and then tip well.

Steward your family relationships above ministry at all times. Revivalists are first revivalists at home.

Organize Holy Spirit parties at your home or volunteer to have a "Home Blessing" meeting at someone else's home who is not yet a believer. Ask them if you can just pray and bless their home and their family, and then watch God win their hearts!

Volunteer for an altar team at your church or be properly trained in the principles of healing and prophetic prayer, knowing that the only formula is faith and the only method is flowing with the Holy Spirit.

Fast one or two days a week like the early church, or fast three to seven days at a time once every month or two. Practice fasting as a lifestyle.

Make sure you have someplace where you can consistently have alone time with God. Then set the atmosphere for the anointing at that location.

Take a needy person who can't pay you back out to eat, and don't tell anyone about it.

Make reconciliation with anyone from the past whom you may have sinned against.

Implement accountability measures for any struggle or weak points, such as downloading software like X3Watch (www.x3watch.com) to your home PC or laptop to guard against pornography.

Write the occasional song or poem to your Savior, our precious Jesus.

Show poise, character, leadership, and righteousness at your workplace; dress well, get there early, volunteer for the hard stuff, respect others, and do not compromise your speech or any other moral standard.

Don't stress over anything; have eternal perspective.

Smile and tell a total stranger that Jesus loves them at least once a week.

If anyone says he or she is sick, hurting, desperate, or in need, pray for them right on the spot.

Take a new believer out for coffee and just talk about Jesus.

Preach a sermon for the first time, if only for a room full of friends.

If someone somewhere seems close to giving his or her life to the Lord, stay with the person and challenge him or her to commit. Help the person seal the deal and truly be converted.

Baptize any new believers who get saved through your everyday evangelistic efforts in your pool, a friend's pool, a community pool, a lake, or the ocean.

Make a habit of praying in the Spirit always.

Write down your dreams and visions.

Smile and bless someone who is rude to you; then think about and do something nice for that person the next time you get a chance.

If you are burdened for a need, be the ministry for that need.

Pray for your boss, pastor, and local and national politicians.

Intercede for God to move powerfully in and through people in your city.

Schedule a date with God.

Identify a gift of the Spirit you have not moved in yet and pray that God would show you how to receive and use that gift.

Post social networking messages on your Web page about how much you love the Lord and wish all your friends knew Him in the same way.

If you face some bad situation or circumstance, just verbally bless, thank, and worship God. When you do, He will take your burden and give you His perspective in the matter.

Cut out any repetitious prayers.

Stop saying stuff like "God can" and say *"God will!"*

Encourage others to press in for their miracles.

Take on a prodigal son or daughter as a prayer project. Pray for their salvation until God floods your soul with peace and assurance that they will be rescued from the grasp of satan.

Grab a guitar or some other random instrument and start singing to God outside some bars or shopping malls.

Visit the nearest ER or urgent care center just to hang out and pray for miracles as the Spirit leads.

Volunteer to be an online missionary at www.globalmediaout-reach.com.

Pray about any and all other possible daily expressions of faith that the Lord would have you do and act on them.

The Revival Manifesto

We are a network of thousands of believers from around this nation.

You may have seen us before, casting out demons downtown or praying for the person in the wheelchair in Walmart.

We contend for the promises of God through prayer and fasting.

We bring renewal to churches. We dance when we worship.

We can preach, teach, prophesy, or heal. Why not? If it's in the Good Book, we'll do it.

We're an army armed with only intimacy with Christ. It's a weapon no evil can stand against.

We don't blame the devil for our problems.

We don't wait on God to grace us with His presence; we act as carriers of His presence.

When there is injustice or pain in this world, we don't blame God. The problem is never with God, the source of our redemption; the problem is with the channels the source has to flow through—us.

We embrace uncomfortability; we live on purpose; we press into the Kingdom.

We reject status quo Christianity, powerless traditions, and any doctrine that doesn't support the person and the power of the Holy Spirit. He is our best friend. Without Him, truth would be incomprehensible and our words of faith would merely fall to the ground.

Every thought and action is focused on one person; His name is Jesus.

We are consumed by God's Word and compelled by His Spirit.

We will not wait around for Jesus to come or sit around, hoping and praying that God do something in our lives and in this nation. Instead, we will be an answer to prayer.

You may find us demonstrating for the rights of the unborn, volunteering to raise funds for noble ministries, or handing out burritos to the poor in the park.

Twenty-four/seven prayer rooms at 2 A.M.—we're there. Open-air preaching outside of the bars and strip clubs, you bet!

We are all professional ministers, yet almost none of us get paid to do so. This is our life.

We're hungry and thirsty for holiness in our own lives and righteousness in the land—and we will be filled!

You won't necessarily know our names, but you'll take notice when we enter a room.

Our first love remains strong; our fires burn brightly.

If sin comes our way, it cannot stay. If sickness or disease crosses our paths, it must go.

We want more of Jesus every day, and we won't be denied. No distraction of the world can compare.

We are known in Heaven and hell; we speak with authority!

We are committed to breaking shackles of religious bondage in the Church.

We walk in freedom as sons and daughters of God, yet are completely slaves to Him.

When He speaks, we listen. What He says, we do.

We are no longer praying for a Great Awakening; we are living as those who are already awake.

We value being over doing. We are because He is. We live to bring Him glory.

We are God's silent army who are silent no more!

We burn with a passion for what God hates and what God loves.

We know that God has not changed. He desires revival more than we do.

Jesus is interceding on our behalf right now so that we will do greater things on earth than He did, and we will honor those prayers.

We give and live radically. We surrender to His will.

We want to get back to the power of Pentecost in our churches—the power of the Holy Spirit and living the message of a Jesus who is alive and well and can be experienced now.

We can't change who we were created to be, and wouldn't want to anyway.

We don't need anyone's permission or credentials to live as anointed ones.

God's opinion of us makes people's opinions of us irrelevant. We fear Him above all else. We love Him by loving others. A priceless price has been paid that we may live forever, a message we are committed to spreading.

Jesus is life and truth. His heavenly treasures are our desire.

We will not stop and hang out at the door of salvation, but will be led by the Spirit into a life of the Kingdom.

As long as there is evil in this world, we are not satisfied. As long as there is one who has not heard the Gospel, we will not stop. We will not quit!

We serve the greatest of these to the least of these; we are no respecter of persons. We give greatest honor to the least honorable parts in the body of Christ.

We desire enemies so we can learn to love them. We fight for the truth of the simplicity of the Gospel.

We are filled with the Holy Spirit. The Word of the Lord propels us. The wind of His Spirit pushes our sails where He wills.

We believe God is moving powerfully in this city and in this nation through His people. We are those people.

We *are* revival in America and around the world!

This is what revival looks like. It's not about a meeting, ministry, or denomination. Revival is a movement—and it starts with you!

Believe with us for a massive harvest of souls and the next great awakening that will rock the world!

Check out my blog at youarerevival.typepad.com to forward this manifesto to all of your friends. Visit www.youarerevival.com to order revival materials and to get news and announcements about God's move around this nation and any of our upcoming books.

COMING SOON

Another world-changing book from revivalist, Matt Skamser, *"Glorious Uprising—The New Reformation"*

In the right hands, This Book will Change Lives!

Most of the people who need this message will not be looking for this book. To change their lives, you need to put a copy of this book in their hands.

> *But others (seeds) fell into good ground, and brought forth fruit, some a hundred-fold, some sixty-fold, some thirty-fold* (Matthew 13:8).

Our ministry is constantly seeking methods to find the good ground, the people who need this anointed message to change their lives. Will you help us reach these people?

> *Remember this—a farmer who plants only a few seeds will get a small crop. But the one who plants generously will get a generous crop* (2 Corinthians 9:6).

EXTEND THIS MINISTRY BY SOWING
3 BOOKS, 5 BOOKS, 10 BOOKS, **OR MORE TODAY,**
AND BECOME A LIFE CHANGER!

Thank you,

Don Nori Sr., Publisher
Destiny Image
Since 1982